Lecture Notes in Computer Scie

Commenced Publication in 1973
Founding and Former Series Editors:
Gerhard Goos, Juris Hartmanis, and Jan van Leeuwen

Patricia M. Hill (Ed.)

Logic Based Program Synthesis and Transformation

15th International Symposium, LOPSTR 2005
London, UK, September 7-9, 2005
Revised Selected Papers

 Springer

Volume Editor

Patricia M. Hill
University of Leeds, School of Computing
Leeds LS2 9JT, UK
E-mail: hill@comp.leeds.ac.uk

Library of Congress Control Number: 2006921342

CR Subject Classification (1998): F.3.1, D.1.1, D.1.6, D.2.4, I.2.2, F.4.1

LNCS Sublibrary: SL 1 – Theoretical Computer Science and General Issues

ISSN   0302-9743
ISBN-10   3-540-32654-5 Springer Berlin Heidelberg New York
ISBN-13   978-3-540-32654-0 Springer Berlin Heidelberg New York

Springer is a part of Springer Science+Business Media

springer.com

© Springer-Verlag Berlin Heidelberg 2006
Printed in Germany

Typesetting: Camera-ready by author, data conversion by Scientific Publishing Services, Chennai, India
Printed on acid-free paper   SPIN: 11680093   06/3142   5 4 3 2 1 0

Preface

This volume contains a selection of papers presented at LOPSTR 2005, the 15th International Symposium on Logic-Based Program Synthesis and Transformation, held September 7–9, 2005.

The aim of the LOPSTR series is to stimulate and promote international research and collaboration on logic-based program development. Previous LOPSTR events have been held in Manchester, UK (1991, 1992, 1998), Louvain-la-Neuve, Belgium (1993), Pisa, Italy (1994), Arnhem, The Netherlands (1995), Stockholm, Sweden (1996), Leuven, Belgium (1997), Venice, Italy (1999), London, UK (2000), Paphos, Cyprus (2001), Madrid, Spain (2002), Uppsala, Sweden (2003), Verona, Italy (2004). Since 1994 the proceedings have been published in the LNCS series of Springer.

We would like to thank all those who submitted papers to LOPSTR. Overall, we received 33 submissions (full papers and extended abstracts). Each submission was reviewed by at least three people. The committee decided to accept 17 of these papers for presentation and for inclusion in the pre-conference proceedings. This volume contains a selection of revised full versions of ten of these papers. Thanks to all the authors of the accepted papers for the versions printed here and their presentations of these papers at LOPSTR 2005. We would like to thank François Fages for agreeing to give an invited talk and his contribution of a short paper included in these proceedings.

I am very grateful to the Program Committee as well as all the external reviewers for the reviewing of the submitted papers and invaluable help in the selection of these papers for presentation.

The submission, reviewing, electronic Program Committee meeting and preparation of the pre-conference proceedings and these proceedings were greatly simplified by the use of EasyChair (see http://www.easychair.org/). Special thanks are therefore due to Andrei Voronkov, who developed and supports this system.

LOPSTR 2005 was held concurrently with SAS 2005, the Symposium on Static Analysis in Imperial College, University of London. I would like to thank the SAS 2005 organizers, and, particularly, Chris Hankin, who took on all the hard work of the overall planning of the events.

LOPSTR 2005 was sponsored by ALP, the Association for Logic Programming.

December 2005   Patricia M. Hill

Conference Organization

Program Chair

Patricia M. Hill

Program Committee

Maria Alpuente
Roberto Bagnara
Gilles Barthe
Annalisa Bossi
Giorgio Delzanno
John Gallagher
Lindsay Groves
Gopal Gupta
Michael Hanus
Michael Leuschel
Fabio Martinelli
Fred Mesnard
Andreas Podelski
Maurizio Proietti
German Puebla
C.R. Ramakrishnan
Abhik Roychoudhury
Wim Vanhoof

External Reviewers

Christel Baier
Stephen-John Craig
Julien Forest
Frank Huch
Andy King
Jim Lipton
Sun Meng
Tamara Rezk
Josep Silva

Jesús Correas
Vicent Estruch-Gregori
Angel Herranz
Siau-Cheng Khoo
Gabriele Lenzini
Salvador Lucas
Alberto Pettorossi
Jaime Sánchez-Hernández
Fausto Spoto

Table of Contents

Temporal Logic Constraints in the Biochemical Abstract Machine BIOCHAM

François Fages

INRIA Rocquencourt, France
`Francois.Fages@inria.fr`

Abstract. Recent progress in Biology and data-production technologies push research toward a new interdisciplinary field, named Systems Biology, where the challenge is to break the complexity walls for reasoning about large biomolecular interaction systems. Pioneered by Regev, Silverman and Shapiro, the application of process calculi to the description of biological processes has been a source of inspiration for many researchers coming from the programming language community.

In this presentation, we give an overview of the Biochemical Abstract Machine (BIOCHAM), in which biochemical systems are modeled using a simple language of reaction rules, and the biological properties of the system, known from experiments, are formalized in temporal logic. In this setting, the biological validation of a model can be done by model-checking, both qualitatively and quantitatively. Moreover, the temporal properties can be turned into specifications for learning modifications or refinements of the model, when incorporating new biological knowledge.

1 Introduction

Systems biology is a cross-disciplinary domain involving biology, computer science, mathematics, and physics, aiming at elucidating the high-level functions of the cell from their biochemical bases at the molecular level. At the end of the Nineties, research in Bioinformatics evolved, passing from the analysis of the genomic sequence to the analysis of post-genomic data and interaction networks (expression of RNA and proteins, protein-protein interactions, etc). The complexity of these networks requires a large research effort to develop symbolic notations and analysis tools applicable to biological processes and data.

Our objective with the design of the Biochemical Abstract Machine BIOCHAM [1, 2] is to offer a software environment for modeling complex cell processes, making simulations (i.e. *"In silico* experiments"), formalizing the biological properties of the system known from real experiments, checking them and using them as specification when refining a model. The most original aspect of our approach can be summarized by the following identifications:

$$biological\ model = transition\ system,$$
$$biological\ property = temporal\ logic\ formula,$$
$$biological\ validation = model\text{-}checking.$$

P.M. Hill (Ed.): LOPSTR 2005, LNCS 3901, pp. 1–5, 2006.

2   Syntax of Biomolecular Interaction Rules

The objects manipulated in BIOCHAM represent molecular compounds, ranging from small molecules to proteins and genes. The syntax of objects and reaction rules is given by the following grammar:

object   = molecule | molecule : : location
molecule = name | molecule–molecule |molecule~{name,...,name}
reaction = solution => solution | kinetics for solution => solution
solution = _ | object | number*object | solution+solution

The objects can be localized in space with the operator ":::" followed by a location name, such as the membrane, the cytoplasm, the nucleus, etc. The binding operator – is used to represent the binding of a molecule on a gene, the complexation of two proteins, and any form of intermolecular bindings. The alteration operator "~" is used to attach a set of modifications to a protein, like for instance the set of its phosphorylated sites (as long as they impact its activity).

Reaction rules express elementary biochemical interactions. There are essentially seven main rule schemas :

- G => G + A for the synthesis of A by gene G,
- A => _ for the degradation of A,
- A + B => A–B for the complexation of two proteins A and B,
- A–B => A + B for the reversed decomplexation,
- A + B => A~{p} + B for the phosphorylation of protein A at site p catalyzed by B,
- A~{p} + B => A + B for the reversed dephosphorylation,
- A::L => A::L' for the transport of A from location L to L'.

The reaction rules can also be given with a kinetic expression, like for instance 0.1*[A][B] for A + B => A–B where a mass action law kinetics with constant rate 0.1 is specified for the formation of the complex.

This rule-based language is used to model biochemical systems at three abstraction levels which correspond to three formal semantics: boolean, concentration (continuous dynamics) and population (stochastic dynamics).

A second language based on Temporal Logic [3] is used in BIOCHAM to formalize the biological properties of the system, and validate a model by model-checking [4, 5]. More precisely, symbolic and numerical model-checking tools are used respectively for CTL in the boolean semantics, for LTL with constraints over real numbers in the concentration semantics, and for PCTL with constraints over integers in the stochastic semantics.

3   Boolean Semantics

The most abstract semantics is the boolean semantics which ignores kinetic expressions. In that semantics, a boolean variable is associated to each BIOCHAM object, representing simply its presence or absence in the system. Reaction rules are then interpreted as an *asynchronous transition system* over states defined by the vector of boolean variables (similarly to the term rewriting formalism used in [6]). A rule such as A + B => C + D defines four possible state transitions corresponding to the possible consumption of the reactants: $A \wedge B \rightarrow A \wedge B \wedge C \wedge D$, $A \wedge B \rightarrow \neg A \wedge B \wedge C \wedge D$, $A \wedge B \rightarrow A \wedge \neg B \wedge C \wedge D$, $A \wedge B \rightarrow \neg A \wedge \neg B \wedge C \wedge D$. In that semantics, the choice of asynchrony and non-determinism is important to represent basic biological phenomena such as competitive inhibition, where a reaction "hides" another one because it consumes the reactants before the other reaction can occur. Formally, the boolean semantics of a set of BIOCHAM rules is defined by a *Kripke structure* $K = (S, R)$ where S is the set of states defined by the vector of boolean variables, and $R \subseteq S \times S$ is the transition relation between states.

In that boolean semantics, Computation Tree Logic (CTL) formulae are used to formalize the known biological properties of the system, and to query such properties in a model. Given an initial state specifying the biological conditions of the property, typical CTL formulae used in this context are :

- $EF(P)$, abbreviated as `reachable(P)`, stating that the organism is able to produce molecule P;
- $\neg E(\neg Q \ U \ P)$, abbreviated as `checkpoint(Q,P)`, stating that Q is a checkpoint for producing P;
- $EG(P)$, abbreviated as `steady(P)`, stating that the system can remain infinitely in a set of states described by formula P;
- $AG(P)$, abbreviated as `stable(P)`, stating that the system remains infinitely in P and cannot escape;
- $AG((P \Rightarrow EF \ \neg P) \wedge (\neg P \Rightarrow EF \ P))$, abbreviated as `oscil(P)`, a necessary (yet not sufficient without strong fairness assumption) consition for oscillations w.r.t. the presence of molecule P;
- $AG((P \Rightarrow EF \ Q) \wedge (Q \Rightarrow EF \ P))$, abbreviated as `loop(P,Q)`, a necessary condition for the alternance between states P and Q.

BIOCHAM evaluates CTL properties through an interface to the OBDD-based symbolic model checker NuSMV [7]. This technology makes it possible to check or query large models, like the model of the cell cycle control involving 165 proteins and genes, 500 variables and 800 reaction rules reported in [5].

4   Concentration Semantics

Basically the same scheme is applied to quantitative models, where each rule is given with a kinetic expression. The concentration semantics associates to each BIOCHAM object a real number representing its concentration. A set of BIOCHAM reaction rules $E = \{e_i \text{ for } S_i \Rightarrow S'_i\}_{i=1,...,n}$ with variables $\{x_1, ..., x_m\}$, is then interpreted by the following set of (non-linear) ordinary differential equations (ODE) :

$$dx_k/dt = \sum_{i=1}^{n} r_i(x_k) * e_i - \sum_{j=1}^{n} l_j(x_k) * e_j$$

where $r_i(x_k)$ (resp. l_i) is the stoichiometric coefficient of x_k in the right (resp. left) member of rule i. Given an initial state, i.e. initial concentrations for each of the objects, the evolution of the system is deterministic and numerical integration methods compute discrete time series (i.e. linear Kripke structures) describing the evolution of the concentrations over time.

The concentration semantics being deterministic, Linear Time Logic (LTL) is used here to formalize the temporal properties. A first-order fragment of LTL is used to express numerical constraints on the concentrations of the molecules, or on their derivatives. For instance, F([A]>10) expresses that the concentration of A eventually gets above the threshold value 10. Oscillation properties, abbreviated as oscil(M,K), are defined here as a change of sign of the derivative of M at least K times. These LTL formulae with constraints are checked with an ad-hoc model-checker implemented in Prolog, using the trace of the numerical integration of the ODEs associated to the rules.

5   Population Semantics

The population semantics is the most realistic semantics. It associates to each BIOCHAM object an integer representing the number of molecules in the system, and interprets reaction rules as a continuous time Markov chain. The kinetic expression e_i for the reaction i is converted into a transition rate τ_i (giving a transition probability after normalization) as follows [8]:

$$\tau_i = e_i \times (V_i \times K)^{(1-\sum_{k=1}^{m} l_i(x_k))} \times \prod_{k=1}^{m} (!l_i(x_k))$$

where l_i is the stoichiometric coefficient of the reactant x_k in the reaction rule i. Stochastic simulation techniques [9] compute realizations of the process. They are generally noisy versions of those obtained with the concentration semantics, however qualitatively different behaviors may also appear when small number of molecules are considered, which justifies the use of a stochastic dynamics.

In this setting, LTL formulae can be evaluated with their probability using a Monte Carlo method, which has proved to be more efficient than existing model-checkers for the probabilistic temporal logic PCTL. However, both the stochastic simulation and the model-checking are computationally more expensive than in the concentration semantics.

6   Learning Reaction Rules from Temporal Properties

Beyond making simulations, and checking properties of the models, the temporal properties can also be turned into specifications and temporal logic constraints for automatically searching and learning modifications or refinements of the model, when incorporating new biological knowledge. This is implemented in BIOCHAM by a combination of model-checking and search in the three abstraction levels.

This methodology is currently investigated with models of the cell cycle control (which regulates cell division) for the learning of kinetic parameter values from LTL properties in the concentration semantics [10], and for the learning of reaction rules from CTL properties in the boolean semantics [11]. A coupled model of the cell cycle and the circadian cycle is under development along these lines in BIOCHAM with applications to cancer chronotherapies.

Acknowledgements. This is a joint work with Nathalie Chabrier-Rivier, Sylvain Soliman and Laurence Calzone, with contributions from Sakina Ayata, Loïc Fosse, Lucie Gentils, Shrivaths Rajagopalan and Nathalie Sznajder. Support and fruitful discussions with our partners of the EU STREP project April-II are warmly acknowledged.

References

1. Fages, F., Soliman, S., Chabrier-Rivier, N.: Modelling and querying interaction networks in the biochemical abstract machine BIOCHAM. Journal of Biological Physics and Chemistry **4** (2004) 64–73
2. Chabrier, N., Fages, F., Soliman, S.: BIOCHAM's user manual. INRIA. (2003–2005)
3. Clarke, E.M., Grumberg, O., Peled, D.A.: Model Checking. MIT Press (1999)
4. Chabrier, N., Fages, F.: Symbolic model cheking of biochemical networks. In Priami, C., ed.: CMSB'03: Proceedings of the first Workshop on Computational Methods in Systems Biology. Volume 2602 of Lecture Notes in Computer Science., Rovereto, Italy, Springer-Verlag (2003) 149–162
5. Chabrier-Rivier, N., Chiaverini, M., Danos, V., Fages, F., Schächter, V.: Modeling and querying biochemical interaction networks. Theoretical Computer Science **325** (2004) 25–44
6. Eker, S., Knapp, M., Laderoute, K., Lincoln, P., Meseguer, J., Sönmez, M.K.: Pathway logic: Symbolic analysis of biological signaling. In: Proceedings of the seventh Pacific Symposium on Biocomputing. (2002) 400–412
7. Cimatti, A., Clarke, E., Enrico Giunchiglia, F.G., Pistore, M., Roveri, M., Sebastiani, R., Tacchella, A.: Nusmv 2: An opensource tool for symbolic model checking. In: Proceedings of the International Conference on Computer-Aided Verification, CAV'02, Copenhagen, Danmark (2002)
8. Gibson, M.A., Bruck, J.: A probabilistic model of a prokaryotic gene and its regulation. In Bolouri, H., Bower, J., eds.: Computational Methods in Molecular Biology: From Genotype to Phenotype. MIT press (2000)
9. Gillespie, D.T.: General method for numerically simulating stochastic time evolution of coupled chemical-reactions. Journal of Computational Physics **22** (1976) 403–434
10. Calzone, L., Chabrier-Rivier, N., Fages, F., Soliman, S.: A machine learning approach to biochemical reaction rules discovery. In III, F.J.D., ed.: Proceedings of Foundations of Systems Biology and Engineering FOSBE'05, Santa Barbara (2005) 375–379
11. Calzone, L., Chabrier-Rivier, N., Fages, F., Gentils, L., Soliman, S.: Machine learning bio-molecular interactions from temporal logic properties. In Plotkin, G., ed.: CMSB'05: Proceedings of the third Workshop on Computational Methods in Systems Biology. (2005)

Declarative Programming with Function Patterns[*]

Sergio Antoy[1] and Michael Hanus[2]

[1] Computer Science Dept., Portland State University, Oregon, USA
antoy@cs.pdx.edu
[2] Institut für Informatik, CAU Kiel, D-24098 Kiel, Germany
mh@informatik.uni-kiel.de

Abstract. We propose an extension of functional logic languages that allows the definition of operations with patterns containing other defined operation symbols. Such "function patterns" have many advantages over traditional constructor patterns. They allow a direct representation of specifications as declarative programs, provide better abstractions of patterns as first-class objects, and support the high-level programming of queries and transformation of complex structures. Moreover, they avoid known problems that occur in traditional programs using strict equality. We define their semantics via a transformation into standard functional logic programs. Since this transformation might introduce an infinite number of rules, we suggest an implementation that can be easily integrated with existing functional logic programming systems.

1 Motivation

Functional logic languages (see [16] for a survey) integrate the most important features of functional and logic languages to provide a variety of programming concepts to the programmer. For instance, the concepts of demand-driven evaluation, higher-order functions, and polymorphic typing from functional programming are combined with logic programming features like computing with partial information (logic variables), constraint solving, and non-deterministic search for solutions. This combination, supported by optimal evaluation strategies [6] and new design patterns [8], leads to better abstractions in application programs such as implementing graphical user interfaces [18] or programming dynamic web pages [19].

A functional logic program consists of a set of datatype definitions and a set of functions or operations, defined by equations or rules, that operate on these types. For instance, the concatenation operation "++" on lists can be defined by the following two rules, where "[]" denotes the empty list and "x:xs" the non-empty list with first element x and tail xs:

```
[]     ++ ys = ys
(x:xs) ++ ys = x : xs++ys
```

Expressions are evaluated by rewriting with rules of this kind. For instance, [1,2] ++[3] evaluates to [1,2,3], where $[x_1, x_2, \ldots, x_n]$ denotes $x_1:x_2:\ldots:x_n:[]$, in three rewrite steps:

---

[*] This work was partially supported by the German Research Council (DFG) under grant Ha 2457/5-1 and the NSF under grant CCR-0218224.

P.M. Hill (Ed.): LOPSTR 2005, LNCS 3901, pp. 6–22, 2006.

$$[1,2]{+}{+}[3] \rightarrow 1{:}([2]{+}{+}[3]) \rightarrow 1{:}(2{:}([]{+}{+}[3])) \rightarrow [1,2,3]$$

Beyond such functional-like evaluations, functional logic languages also compute with unknowns (logic variables). For instance, a functional logic language is able to *solve* an equation like xs++[x] =:= [1,2,3] (where xs and x are logic variables) by guessing the bindings [1,2] and 3 for xs and x, respectively.

This constraint solving capability can be exploited to define new operations using already defined functions. For instance, the operation last, which yields the last element of a list, can be defined as follows (the "where...free" clause declares logic variables in rules):

last l | xs++[x] =:= l = x   where xs,x free   (*last1*)

In general, a *conditional equation* has the form $l \mid c = r$ and is applicable for rewriting if its condition c has been solved. A subtle point is the meaning of the symbol "=:=" used to denote equational constraints. Since modern functional logic languages, like Curry [17, 22] or Toy [25], are based on a non-strict semantics [6, 14] that supports lazy evaluation and infinite structures, it is challenging to compare arbitrary, in particular infinite, objects. Thus, the equality symbol "=:=" in a condition is usually interpreted as *strict equality*—the equation t_1 =:= t_2 is satisfied iff t_1 and t_2 are reducible to the same *constructor term* (see [13] for a more detailed discussion on this topic). A constructor term is a fully evaluated expression; a formal definition appears in Section 3.

Strict equality evaluates both its operands to a constructor term to prove the validity of the condition. For this reason, the strict equation "x =:= head []" does not hold for any x. The operation head is defined by the single rule head (x:xs) = x. Therefore, the evaluation of head [] fails to obtain a constructor term. While the behavior of "=:=" is natural and intuitive in this example, it is less so in the following example.

A consequence of the strict equality in the definition of last in Display (*last1*) is that the list argument of last is fully evaluated. In particular, last [failed,2], where failed is an operation whose evaluation fails, has no result. This outcome is unnatural and counterintuitive. In fact, the usual functional recursive definition of last would produce the expected result, 2, for the same argument. Thus, strict equality is harmful in this example (further examples will be shown later) since it evaluates more than one intuitively requires and, thus, reduces the inherent laziness of the computation.

There are good reasons for the usual definition of strict equality [13]; we will see that just dropping the strictness requirements in equational conditions leads to a non-intuitive behavior. Therefore, we propose in this paper an extension of functional logic languages with a new concept that solves all these problems: *function patterns*. Traditional patterns (i.e., the arguments of the left-hand sides of rules) are required to be constructor terms. Function patterns can also contain defined operation symbols so that the operation last is simply defined as

last (xs++[x]) = x

This definition leads not only to concise specifications, but also to a "lazier" behavior. Since the pattern variables xs and x are matched against the actual (possibly unevaluated) parameters, with this new definition of last, the expression last [failed,2] evaluates to 2.

The next section defines the notations used in this paper. Section 3 defines the concept of function patterns, and Section 4 shows examples of its use. Section 5 proposes an implementation of function patterns and shows its performance on some benchmarks. We compare our approach with related work in Section 6 and conclude in Section 7.

2   Preliminaries

In this section we review some notations for term rewriting [9, 10] and functional logic programming [16] concepts used in the remaining of this paper.

Since polymorphic types are not important for our proposal, we ignore them and consider a many-sorted *signature* Σ partitioned into a set $\mathcal{C}$ of *constructors* and a set $\mathcal{F}$ of (defined) *functions* or *operations*. We write $c/n \in \mathcal{C}$ and $f/n \in \mathcal{F}$ for n-ary constructor and operation symbols, respectively. Given a set of variables $\mathcal{X}$, the set of *terms* and *constructor terms* are denoted by $\mathcal{T}(\mathcal{C} \cup \mathcal{F}, \mathcal{X})$ and $\mathcal{T}(\mathcal{C}, \mathcal{X})$, respectively. As in the concrete syntax of Curry, we indicate the application of a function to arguments by juxtaposition, e.g., $f\ t_1 \ldots t_n$. A term is *linear* if it does not contain multiple occurrences of a variable. A term is *operation-rooted* (*constructor-rooted*) if its root symbol is an operation (constructor). A *head normal form* is a term that is not operation-rooted, i.e., it is a variable or a constructor-rooted term.

Given a signature $\Sigma = (\mathcal{C}, \mathcal{F})$, a *functional logic program* is set of rules of the form

$$f\ d_1 \ldots d_n \mid c\ =\ e$$

where $f/n \in \mathcal{F}$ is the function defined by this rule, $d_1, \ldots, d_n$ are constructor terms (also called *patterns*) such that the *left-hand side* $f\ d_1 \ldots d_n$ is linear, the *condition* c (which can be omitted) is a constraint, and the *right-hand side* is an expression.[1] A *constraint* is any expression of type `Success`, e.g., the trivial constraint `success` which is always satisfied, the equational constraint $t_1 =:= t_2$ which is satisfied if both sides are reducible to the same constructor term, or the conjunction $c_1\ \&\ c_2$ which is satisfied if both arguments are satisfied (operationally, "`&`" is the basic concurrency combinator since both arguments are evaluated concurrently). To provide a simple operational meaning of conditional rules, we consider the rule "$l \mid c\ =\ r$" as equivalent to the unconditional rule "$l\ =\ \texttt{cond}\ c\ r$" where the auxiliary operation `cond` is defined by

```
cond success x = x
```

Note that rules can overlap so that operations can be *non-deterministic*. For instance, the rules

```
x ? y = x
x ? y = y
```

define a non-deterministic operation "?" that returns one of its arguments, and

```
insert x []     = [x]
insert x (y:ys) = x : y : ys  ?  y : insert x ys
```

define a non-deterministic insertion of an element into a list.

---

[1] In the concrete syntax, the variables $x_1, \ldots, x_k$ occurring in c or e but not in the left-hand side must be explicitly declared by a where-clause (`where` $x_1, \ldots, x_k$ `free`) to enable some consistency checks.

We need a few additional notions to formally define computations w.r.t. a given program. A *position* p in a term t is represented by a sequence of natural numbers. Positions are used to identify specific subterms. Thus, $t|_p$ denotes the *subterm* of t at position p, and $t[s]_p$ denotes the result of *replacing the subterm* $t|_p$ by the term s (see [10] for details). A *substitution* is an idempotent mapping $\sigma : \mathcal{X} \to \mathcal{T}(\mathcal{C} \cup \mathcal{F}, \mathcal{X})$. Substitutions are extended to morphisms on terms in the obvious way. A *rewrite step* $t \to t'$ is defined w.r.t. a given program P if there are a position p in t, a rule $l = r \in P$ with fresh variables, and a substitution σ with $t|_p = \sigma(l)$ and $t' = t[\sigma(r)]_p$. A term t is called *irreducible* or in *normal form* if there is no term s such that $t \to s$.

Functional logic languages also compute solutions of free variables occurring in expressions by instantiating them to constructor terms so that a rewrite step becomes applicable. The combination of variable instantiation and rewriting is called *narrowing*. Formally, $t \leadsto_\sigma t'$ is a *narrowing step* if $\sigma(t) \to t'$ and $t|_p$ is not a variable for the position p used in this rewrite step. Although the latter condition is a substantial restriction on the possible narrowing steps, there are still too many possibilities to apply this definition of narrowing in practice. Therefore, older narrowing strategies (see [16] for a detailed account), influenced by the resolution principle, require that the substitution used in a narrowing step is a most general unifier of $t|_p$ and the left-hand side of the applied rule. As shown in [6], this condition prevents the development of optimal evaluation strategies. Therefore, many recent narrowing strategies relax this requirement but provide other constructive methods to compute a small set of unifiers and positions used in narrowing steps [5]. In particular, *needed* or *demand-driven* strategies perform narrowing steps only if they are necessary to compute a result. For instance, consider the following program containing a declaration of natural numbers in Peano's notation and operations for addition and a "less than or equal" test (the pattern "_" denotes an unnamed *anonymous variable*):

```
data Nat = 0 | S Nat

                             leq 0       _     = True
add 0     y = y              leq (S _) 0       = False
add (S x) y = S (add x y)    leq (S x) (S y) = leq x y
```

Then the subterm t in the expression "leq 0 t" need not be evaluated since the first rule for leq is directly applicable. On the other hand, the first argument of "leq (add v w) 0" must be evaluated to rewrite this expression. Furthermore, the expression "leq v (S 0)" becomes reducible after the instantiation of v to either 0 or S z.

This strategy, called *needed narrowing* [6], is optimal for the class of inductively sequential programs that do not allow overlapping left-hand sides. Its extension to more general programs with possibly overlapping left-hand sides can be found in [3,4]. A precise description of this strategy with the inclusion of sharing, concurrency, and external functions is provided in [1]. In the following, we denote by $t \overset{*}{\leadsto}_\sigma t'$ a sequence of needed narrowing steps evaluating t to t', where σ is the composition of all the substitutions applied in the sequence's steps.

3   Function Patterns

As already mentioned, strict equality is the usual interpretation of equational conditions in functional logic languages based on a non-strict semantics. Since this looks like a contradiction, first we explain the reasons for using strict equality, then we explain our proposal.

Strict equality holds between two expressions if both can be reduced to a same constructor term. Consequently, strict equality is not reflexive; e.g., "head [] =:= head []" does not hold. One motivation for this restriction is the difficulty of solving equations with a reflexive meaning in the presence of non-terminating computations. For instance, consider the following functions:

```
from x = x : from (x+1)
rtail (x:xs) = rtail xs
```

Demanding reflexivity in equational conditions implies that the condition

```
rtail (from 0) =:= rtail (from 5)
```

should hold since both sides are reducible to `rtail (from` n`)` for every $n \geq 5$. However, this is not a normal form, so it is unclear how far some side of the equation should be reduced. Although this problem could be solved by an exhaustive search of the infinite reduction space (clearly not a practical approach), there are also problems with reflexivity in the presence of infinite data structures. For instance, the condition

```
from 0 =:= from 0
```

should hold if "=:=" is reflexive. Since both sides describe the infinite list of natural numbers, the condition

```
from 0 =:= from2 0
```

should also hold w.r.t. the definition

```
from2 x = x : x+1 : from2 (x+2)
```

Obviously, the equality of infinite structures defined by syntactically different functions is undecidable in general (since this requires solving the halting problem). Therefore, one needs to restrict the meaning of equational conditions to a non-reflexive interpretation. Note that this condition is not specific to functional logic languages: Haskell [27] also defines the equality symbol "==" as strict equality by default (this could be changed by the use of type classes).

Although the previous examples have shown that there are good reasons to avoid reflexivity of equality, one might think that the evaluation of some parts of an expression in an equational condition is unnecessary or even unintended, as discussed with the function `last` defined in Section 1. For instance, one could propose to relax strict equality as follows: to solve the equation $x =:= t$, bind x to t (instead of binding x to the evaluation of t). Although in some cases, such as the operation `last`, this policy seems to produce the desired behavior, in other cases it would lead to a non-intuitive behavior. For instance, consider the function:

```
f x | x =:= from 0 = 99
```

The expression "let x free in f x" would evaluate to 99 since x would be bound to from 0 which would not be further evaluated. Similarly, "let x free in (f x,99)" would evaluate to (99,99). However, the evaluation of "let x free in (f x,f x)" would not terminate, since the evaluation of the equational condition "from 0 =:= from 0" would not terminate. In fact, "f x" should be evaluated twice, the first time with x unbound and the second time with x bound to "from 0".

This example shows that a simple binding of logic variables to unevaluated expressions is also problematic. Therefore, non-strict functional logic languages usually bind logic variables only to constructor terms. However, *pattern variables*, i.e., variables occurring in patterns, can be bound to unevaluated expressions. Thus, in order to relax the strictness conditions in equational conditions, one needs a finer control over the kind of involved variables, i.e., one needs to distinguish between logic variables that are bound to constructor terms and pattern variables that can be bound to unevaluated expressions. For this purpose, we propose to use function patterns as an intuitive and simple solution to the problems discussed above. We explain the details below.

A *function pattern* is a pattern that contains, in addition to pattern variables and constructor symbols, defined operation symbols. For instance, if "++" is the list concatenation operation defined in Section 1, (xs++[x]) is a function pattern. Using function patterns, we can define the function last as

last (xs++[x]) = x   (*last2*)

This definition not only is concise but also introduces xs and x as pattern variables rather than logic variables as in definition (*last1*) above. Since pattern variables can be bound to unevaluated expressions, last returns the last element of the list without evaluating any element of the list. For instance, last [failed,2] evaluates to 2, as intended.

To extend functional logic languages with function patterns, we have to clarify two issues: what is the precise meaning of function patterns, and how are operations defined using function patterns executed? We prefer to avoid the development of a new theory of such extended functional logic programs and to reuse existing results about semantics and models of traditional functional logic programs (e.g., [14]). Therefore, we define the meaning of such programs by a transformation into standard programs. The basic idea is to transform a rule containing a function pattern into a set of rules where the function pattern is replaced by its evaluation(s) to a constructor term.

Consider the definition (*last2*) above. The evaluations of xs++[x] to a constructor term are

$$xs++[x] \overset{*}{\leadsto}_{xs \mapsto []} \quad [x]$$
$$xs++[x] \overset{*}{\leadsto}_{xs \mapsto [x1]} \quad [x1,x]$$
$$xs++[x] \overset{*}{\leadsto}_{xs \mapsto [x1,x2]} \quad [x1,x2,x]$$
...

Thus, the single rule (*last2*) is an abbreviation of the set of rules

    last [x] = x
    last [x1,x] = x
    last [x1,x2,x] = x
    ...

These rules exactly describe the intended meaning of the operation `last`. Obviously, this transformation cannot be done at compile time since it may lead to an infinite set of program rules. Therefore, in Section 5 we discuss techniques to perform this transformation at run time. The basic idea is, for an invocation of `last` with argument l, to compute the single ordinary (constructor) pattern p of the rule that would be fired by that invocation and to match, or more precisely to unify since we narrow, l and p.

This idea has two potential problems. First, we have to avoid its potential underlying circularity. Evaluating a function pattern must not involve executing the operation being defined since its definition is not available before the function pattern has been evaluated. For instance, a rule like

```
(xs ++ ys) ++ zs = xs ++ (ys ++ zs)
```

is not allowed since the meaning of the function pattern (`xs++ys`) depends on the definition of "`++`". In order to formalize such dependencies, we introduce level mappings.

Definition 1. A *level mapping* l for a functional logic program P is a mapping from functions defined in P to natural numbers such that, for all rules $f\ t_1 \ldots t_n \mid c = e$, if g is a function occurring in c or e, then $l(g) \leq l(f)$. □

For instance, consider the program P consisting of the rule *(last1)* and the rules defining "`++`". Then $l(\text{++}) = 0$ and $l(\text{last}) = 1$ is a possible level mapping for P. Using level mappings, we can define the class of acceptable programs.

Definition 2. A functional logic program P with function patterns is *stratified* if there exists a level mapping l for P such that, for all rules $f\ t_1 \ldots t_n \mid c = e$, if g is a defined function occurring in some t_i ($i \in \{1, \ldots, n\}$), then $l(g) < l(f)$. □

The restriction to stratified programs ensures that, if an operation f is defined using a function pattern p, the evaluation of p to a constructor term does not depend, directly or indirectly, on f.

The second potential problem of our intended transformation of rules containing function patterns is nonlinearity. For instance, consider the operation `idpair` defined by

```
idpair x = (x,x)
```

and the rule

```
f (idpair x) = 0
```
                                                                                    (f1)

After evaluating the function pattern (`idpair x`), the rule *(f1)* would be transformed into

```
f (x,x) = 0
```
                                                                                    (f2)

However, this rule is not left-linear and therefore is not allowed in traditional functional logic programs. Relaxing the left-linearity condition on rules is not viable since it causes difficulties similar to those we discussed for relaxing strict equality. Usually, the intended meaning of multiple occurrences of a variable in the left-hand side is that the actual arguments at these variables' positions should be equal in the sense of an equational condition [4]. This can be expressed by introducing new pattern variables and equational conditions. Thus, the rule (f2) is finally transformed into the valid rule

```
f (x,y) | x=:=y = 0
```

The above considerations motivate the following interpretation of functional logic programs with function patterns.

Definition 3. Let P be a stratified functional logic program with function patterns. The meaning of P is the program P^* defined by:

$$P^* = \{lin(f\ t_1 \ldots t_n \mid \sigma(c) = \sigma(e))\ \text{ s.t. } f\ e_1 \ldots e_n \mid c = e \in P,$$
$$(e_1, \ldots, e_n) \overset{*}{\leadsto}_\sigma (t_1, \ldots, t_n),\ \text{and}$$
$$t_1, \ldots, t_n \text{ are constructor terms}\}$$

where lin denotes the linearization of a rule defined by

$$lin(l \mid c = r) = \begin{cases} l \mid c = r & \text{if } l \text{ is linear;} \\ lin(l[y]_q \mid (x\,\text{=:=}\,y\ \&\ c) = r) & \text{if } l|_p = x = l|_q, p \neq q, \\ & x \text{ is a variable and } y \text{ is fresh.} \quad \square \end{cases}$$

The associated program P^* is well defined (since P is stratified) and a valid functional logic program, since the patterns in the left-hand sides are linear constructor terms. Since function patterns are transformed into ordinary patterns, the variables occurring in function patterns become ordinary pattern variables that can be bound to unevaluated expressions. Thus, function patterns relax the strict evaluation conditions of strict equality without any difficulties. The only potential problem is the generation of an infinite number of rules for P^* in case of function patterns involving recursive functions. Therefore, we show in Section 5 a transformation, executed at run time, that generates only the rules that are required for a specific application of an operation defined by a function pattern.

4 Examples

In this section we present a few more examples of programs that use function patterns. The following example makes essential use of function patterns. The proposed design would not work with strict equality.

Example 1. This example is a problem of the 1993 East-Central Regionals of the ACM International Collegiate Programming Contest. Given a number n, we form the chain of n by:

(1) arranging the digits of n in descending order,
(2) arranging the digits of n in ascending order,
(3) subtracting the number obtained in (2) from the number obtained in (1) to form a new number, and
(4) repeating these steps for the new number.

E.g., the chain of 123 is 198, 792, 693, 594, 495, 495... The problem is to compute the length of the chain up to the first repeated number—seven for 123.

The implementation is simpler if one separates the task of constructing the chain of a number from the task of finding the first repeated element in the chain. The solution of the problem is obtained by ("." denotes function composition):

```
lengthUpToRepeat . chain
```

where the function `chain` constructs the chain of a number and the function `lengthUpToRepeat` measures the length of the chain up to the first repeated element. The latter function, coded below, uses a function pattern.

```
lengthUpToRepeat (p++[r]++q)
   | nub p == p && elem r p
   = length p + 1
```

The pattern breaks the infinite chain of a number into a prefix p, the first repeated element r, and the rest of the chain q. The symbols nub and elem denote library functions. nub removes repeated elements from a list. Hence, the condition nub p == p ensures that there are no repeated elements in p. elem tells whether an element is a member of list. The conjunction of the two conditions ensures that r is the first repeated element in the chain.

By contrast, an implementation that uses strict equality, i.e., that attempts to solve p++[r]++q =:= chain n, would be flawed. By design, chain n is an infinite list, and therefore strict equality would not terminate.   □

The second example shows the use of function patterns to specify transformations in tree-like structures.

Example 2. This example addresses the simplification of symbolic arithmetic expressions. E.g., $1 * (x + 0)$ simplifies to x. We define expressions as

```
data Exp = Lit Int | Var [Char] | Add Exp Exp | Mul Exp Exp
```

The following non-deterministic function, evalTo, defines a handful of expressions that for every expression e evaluate to e itself. Obviously, many more are possible, but the following ones suffice to make our point.

```
evalTo e = Add (Lit 0) e
         ? Add e (Lit 0)
         ? Mul (Lit 1) e
         ? Mul e (Lit 1)
```

The following function replaces in an expression a subexpression identified by a position with another subexpression.

```
replace _ [] x = x
replace (Add l r) (1:p) x = Add (replace l p x) r
replace (Add l r) (2:p) x = Add l (replace r p x)
replace (Mul l r) (1:p) x = Mul (replace l p x) r
replace (Mul l r) (2:p) x = Mul l (replace r p x)
```

Observe that `replace` c p e, where c is a "context", p is a position and e is an expression, is the term replacement operation denoted by $c[e]_p$ in Section 2. Finally, the simplification operation, `simplify`, replaces in a context c an expression that evaluates to x with x itself. p is the position of the replacement in the context.

```
simplify (replace c p (evalTo x)) = replace c p x
```

E.g., if t_1 = `Mul (Lit 1) (Add (Var "x") (Lit 0))`, then `simplify` t_1 evaluates to t_2 = `Add (Var "x") (Lit 0)` and `simplify` t_2 evaluates to `Var "x"`. If an expression t cannot be simplified, `simplify` t fails; otherwise, it non-deterministically executes a single simplification step. The application of repeated simplification steps to an expression until no more simplification steps are available can be controlled by Curry's search primitives [21]. Note that this example shows two useful applications of function patterns: the possibility to define abstractions for complex collections of patterns (via operation `evalTo`) and the ability to specify transformations at arbitrary positions inside an argument (via operation `replace`). The latter technique can be also exploited to formulate queries on expressions. For instance, the operation

```
varInExp (replace c p (Var v)) = v
```

non-deterministically returns a variable occurring in an expression. One can easily extract all variables occurring in an expression, by wrapping this operation with search primitives like `findall` [21]. □

Thus, function patterns are handy to provide executable high-level definitions of complex transformation tasks and queries on tree-like structures. Further examples of this kind (which we omit due to space limitations) are transformations and queries of XML terms.

5   Implementation

The transformational definition of the meaning of function patterns (Definition 3) does not lead to a constructive implementation since it might generate an infinite set of program rules. Any execution of a program, though, would make use of only a finite subset of these rules. In this section, we show a specialization of this transformation that, under suitable assumptions discussed later, enumerates the results of all the program rules that would be used in a specific execution of a program. These rules can be determined only at run time. This approach is easily integrated into existing implementations of functional logic languages, e.g., the Curry programming environment PAKCS [20]. We present some benchmarks of our implementation of this approach.

To integrate function patterns into existing implementations of functional logic languages, we eliminate the function patterns from the left-hand sides and move their functionality into the conditional part by means of a new *function pattern unification operator* "`=:<=`". The following transformation formalizes this process:

Definition 4. Let P be a stratified functional logic program with function patterns. The *function pattern elimination* function $elim$ maps each rule into a rule without function patterns as follows:

$$elim(f\ t_1 \ldots t_n \mid c = r) =$$

$$\begin{cases} elim(f\ t_1 \ldots t_{i-1}\ x\ t_{i+1} \ldots t_n \mid t_i \texttt{=:<=} x \mathbin{\&} c = r) & \text{if } t_1, \ldots, t_{i-1} \in \mathcal{T}(\mathcal{C}, \mathcal{X}), \\ & t_i \text{ contains functions,} \\ & x \text{ fresh variable;} \\ f\ t_1 \ldots t_n \mid c = r & \text{otherwise} \end{cases} \qquad \square$$

For instance, $elim$ maps rule ($last2$) to

```
last ys | xs++[x] =:<= ys = x   where xs,x free                 (last3)
```

i.e., the pattern variables `xs` and `x` become logic variables in the transformed program. Their specific status will be used in the implementation of "`=:<=`".

It remains to implement the operator "`=:<=`". Its semantics is determined by Definition 3, i.e., the left argument must be evaluated to a constructor term that is finally matched against the right argument. This must be done with some care since the computation space of the left argument may be infinite. For instance, this situation occurs with the rule ($last3$). Consider again the computation of `last [failed,2]`. There are infinitely many evaluations of `xs++[x]` to a constructor term. However, among these evaluations every list with more or less than two elements cannot match `[failed,2]`.

To handle this situation, the evaluation of the function pattern by "`=:<=`" is demand-driven. This means that the function pattern is evaluated to a head normal form that is compared with the structure of the right argument and is further evaluated only if necessary. The details of function pattern unification follow.

To evaluate $e_1 \texttt{=:<=} e_2$:
1. Evaluate e_1 to a head normal form h_1
2. If h_1 is a variable: bind it to e_2
3. If $h_1 = c\ t_1 \ldots t_n$ (where c is a constructor):
   (a) Evaluate e_2 to a head normal form h_2
   (b) If h_2 is a variable: instantiate h_2 to $c\ x_1 \ldots x_n$ ($x_1, \ldots, x_n$ are fresh variables) and evaluate $t_1 \texttt{=:<=} x_1 \mathbin{\&} \ldots \mathbin{\&} t_n \texttt{=:<=} x_n$
   (c) If $h_2 = c\ s_1 \ldots s_n$: evaluate $t_1 \texttt{=:<=} s_1 \mathbin{\&} \ldots \mathbin{\&} t_n \texttt{=:<=} s_n$
   (d) Otherwise: fail

Obviously, this implements the evaluation of the left argument of "`=:<=`" to a constructor term that is matched against the right argument. Since the evaluation of the left argument is interleaved with the matching, the search space of the evaluation of `xs++[x] =:<= [failed,2]` using the rule ($last3$) is finite (due to the failure in case 3d).

So far, we have only described the evaluation and binding of function patterns. However, the semantics of Definition 3 requires also the linearization of the evaluated function pattern combined with the addition of a strict equality constraint. One could consider integrating the linearization with the evaluation of "`=:<=`" in step 3: if the left argument is evaluated to the constructor-rooted term $c\ t_1 \ldots t_n$, we could replace multiple occurrences of a variable by new variables and generate strict equality constraints that are solved after the variables have been bound. Unfortunately, this method would be incorrect according to the semantics of Definition 3, since some repeated occurrences of a variable could be erased before the end of the evaluation. For instance, consider the following program:

```
k0 x = 0
pair x y = (x,y)
f (pair (k0 x) x) = 0
```

The meaning of f is equivalent to

```
f (0,x) = 0
```

by Definition 3. Consequently, f (0,failed) should evaluate to 0. In the evaluation of pair (k0 x) x =:<= (0,failed), the left argument is reduced to the constructor-rooted term (k0 x,x) where the variable x occurs twice. If we replace the first occurrence by y and generate the strict equality y=:=x, eventually we have to solve the strict equality y=:=failed which causes the failure of the complete evaluation. Thus, the generation of strict equalities for the linearization of function patterns is a dynamic property. We have to keep track of the variables in function patterns that occur in the evaluated term. We can do this by marking the pattern variables that appear in the evaluated function pattern (i.e., in step 2). In this case the generated strict equality constraints are only executed when both involved variables have been marked during the evaluation of "=:<=". Thus, we obtain an incremental implementation of matching with function patterns conforming to the semantics specified by Definition 3.

Since the checking for multiple variable occurrences and the demand-driven generation of strict equality constraints for the involved variables might consume a considerable amount of time during function pattern unification, it is reasonable to optimize this part. Therefore, we have also implemented a second function pattern unification operator "=:<<=", which behaves like "=:<=" but does not check for multiple occurrences of variables in evaluated function patterns. It is safe to replace "=:<=" by the more efficient operation "=:<<=" if all the evaluations of the function pattern are linear. For instance, if a function pattern is linear and all the involved operations (i.e., also the ones that might be indirectly called) have rules with right-linear sides, then one can safely replace "=:<=" by "=:<<=". This is the case for our definition of last with rule (*last2*).

We formalize the correctness of our implementation as follows. For the sake of simplicity, we consider only unary functions, which typically are the only functions defined by a function pattern. *Let R be a TRS, $m = f\,p \to r$ a rule defined by a function pattern and $m' = f\,x \mid p$=<:=$x \to r$ the transformed rule, where x is a fresh variable. For all terms t and u, $f\,t \to u$ in $R \cup \{m\}$ iff $f\,t \to u$ in $R \cup \{m'\}$.* The proof is simple except for the following claim: *In R, for all terms p and t, p=<:=t iff there exists a constructor term l and a substitution σ such that $p \overset{*}{\leadsto} l$ and $\sigma(l) = \sigma(t)$.* A rigorous proof of this result hinges on a formalization of our pattern unification algorithm that goes beyond the scope of this paper. In particular, the implementation requires a complete strategy to ensure that any constructor term l such that $p \overset{*}{\leadsto} l$ is computed.

We have implemented function patterns in the Curry programming environment PAKCS [20]. This environment includes a compiler from Curry into Prolog [7], which we used for our benchmarks. The implementation is based on the ideas sketched above. Rules with function patterns are transformed into standard rules by putting the calls to "=:<=" in the condition part. Although function patterns aim at expressiveness rather than efficiency, we also show a few benchmarks where execution differences between function patterns and traditional strict equality are substantial. The benchmarks refer to the examples in this paper and are executed with strict equality ("=:="), general function patterns ("=:<="), and linear function patterns ("=:<<="). The following table shows the execution results on a Pentium-M (1.6GHz) (all the times, in milliseconds, are the average of ten executions):[2]

Expression:	"=:="	"=:<="	"=:<<="
`last (take 10000 (repeat failed) ++ [1])`	no solution	380	250
`last (map (inc 0) [1..2000])`	20900	90	60
`lengthUpToRepeat ([1..50]++[1]++[51..])`	∞	200	200
`simplify*`	1200	1080	690
`varsInExp`	2240	1040	100

As one can see, the specialization of matching linear function patterns with "=:<<=" can improve the efficiency considerably. Further improvements can be obtained by specializing the function patterns at compile time. For this purpose, we define an auxiliary operation

```
evalFP fp x e | fp =:<= x = e
```

Now, consider again the definition of `last`. Using `evalFP`, we can transform rule (*last3*) into (here, we omit the declaration of logic variables by where-clauses):

```
last zs = evalFP (xs++[x]) zs x                              (last4)
```

According to Definition 3, the argument (`xs++[x]`) must be evaluated by narrowing before it is matched against `zs`. Since there are two possible narrowing steps for (`xs++[x]`), we can replace the latter rule by:

```
last zs = last1 zs ? last2 zs
last1 zs = evalFP [x] zs x             ⟹    last1 [x] = x
last2 zs = evalFP (y:(ys++[x])) zs x
              ⟹    last2 (y:zs) = evalFP (ys++[x]) zs x
```

Since "`evalFP (ys++[x]) zs x`" is a variant of the right-hand side of rule (*last4*), with a folding step, we replace it by `last zs` and obtain the final definition

```
last zs = last1 zs ? last2 zs
last1 [x] = x
last2 (y:zs) = last zs
```

This is a functional logic program without function patterns. If we execute our previous benchmarks with this transformed program, we obtain the following results:

Expression:	Transformed `last`
`last (take 10000 (repeat failed) ++ [1])`	120
`last (map (inc 0) [1..2000])`	30

---

[2] The operation `inc x n` increments n times x by 1. All the other operations are defined either in the standard prelude or in this paper. `simplify*` is the repeated application of the operation `simplify` to a large term with many opportunities for simplification, and `varsInExp` extracts all variables from a large term based on the operation `varInExp`.

The speedup by a factor of 2 shows the advantages of this transformation. The specialization of a program rule with function patterns is similar to the partial evaluation of functional logic programs [2]. As such, it is difficult to predict whether a rule will yield a finite set of specialized rules and/or these rules will execute more efficiently then the transformation. The setting of function patterns differs from partial evaluation so that existing results and techniques cannot be directly applied. This demands for the development of new techniques — an interesting topic for future work.

6 Related Work

Although the idea to allow arbitrary user-defined functions in patterns is new in the context of functional logic languages, there exist many approaches to improve pattern matching in declarative languages. Here we discuss the ones which have a closer relation to our work.

In functional logic languages, the considered kinds of patterns are usually constructor terms. Exceptions are languages like SLOG [12] or ALF [15], which allow functions in patterns that are useful to simplify terms before narrowing them. However, these languages are based on strict evaluation strategies and require the termination of the underlying rewrite system. Most other work in functional logic programming related to pattern matching considers only constructor patterns and concentrates mainly on sophisticated matching strategies in order to reduce the search space of narrowing computations (see [5, 16] for surveys).

Also in purely logic languages, patterns are constructor terms, and pattern matching is generalized to unification. An exception is constraint logic programming [23], where evaluable functions over constraint domains are allowed in patterns. However, they do not play any role in the pattern matching process since they are usually compiled into the right-hand side and passed to a separate constraint solver. Thus, most of the related work has been done for purely functional languages, as we will discuss next.

Context patterns [26], proposed for the functional language Haskell, are most closely related to our approach. The motivation for context patterns is somehow similar to the introduction of function patterns, since context patterns support the definition of functions based on the matching of subterms at an arbitrary depth. For instance, our last example can be defined with context patterns as

```
last (c [x]) = x
```

Here, c denotes a *context*, i.e., a term with a hole that is filled with the argument [x]. Similarly to function patterns, context patterns are useful to define queries and transformations over complex structures with a relatively small effort. However, due to the underlying functional base language, context patterns are more restricted. The holes in a context pattern are matched in a top-down left-to-right traversal against the actual argument and only the first match is taken. The author argues that this behavior, although incomplete, fits well into the framework of functional programming. Actually, he writes that a "non-deterministic approach would fit better in a integrated functional-logic language like Curry." It is interesting to note that the functional logic setting allows also to omit some other restrictions of context patterns, like the strict order of the traversal.

First-class patterns [28] are an approach to treat patterns as first-class objects (by considering patterns as functions of type "a -> Maybe b") in order to build abstractions for patterns and support user-defined strategies for pattern matching. This covers one aspect of function patterns in a purely functional setting, but the definition of operations with first-class patterns is rather clumsy even after introducing a specific language extension to support syntactic sugar for first-class patterns.

Transformational patterns [11] are another extension that supports the inclusion of user-defined functions in patterns. These functions are applied to the actual arguments before pattern matching in order to support a different view of the actual data (whose structure might be hidden in an abstract data type). This is orthogonal to our approach, in which functions are formal parameters that are evaluated and matched against the actual parameters.

Other related works include approaches to simplify writing code for term traversals. For instance, [24] shows a technique to support generic term traversals by defining small code pieces for each data type (comparable to the operation `replace` of Example 2) from which general functions to transform and query data structures can be derived. Although this technique leads to generic and efficient programs for manipulating trees, it does not have the generality of function patterns that can be also used to specify complex conditions on data structures (compare definition of `last` and Example 1).

7   Conclusions

We have proposed extending functional logic languages with function patterns. We have defined their semantics by transformation into traditional programs and shown that their implementation can be obtained by a specific unification procedure. Function patterns are advantageous because they evaluate conditions on actual arguments more lazily and thus avoid some known problems of strict equality. Moreover, they allow the high-level programming of queries and transformations of complex structures and support new abstractions of patterns.

This extension is specific to integrated functional logic languages since purely logic languages do not support evaluable functions and purely functional languages do not support nondeterminism and function inversion. The versatility and ease of implementation of function patterns show that an integrated functional logic language is an excellent environment for building high-level abstractions.

In future work, we plan to develop techniques to partially evaluate programs with function patterns at compile time to improve their efficiency. It might be interesting to develop specific calculi to support reasoning directly about programs with function patterns instead of using the transformational approach defined in this paper.

References

1. E. Albert, M. Hanus, F. Huch, J. Oliver, and G. Vidal. Operational Semantics for Declarative Multi-Paradigm Languages. *Journal of Symbolic Computation*, Vol. 40, No. 1, pp. 795–829, 2005.

2. M. Alpuente, M. Falaschi, and G. Vidal. Partial Evaluation of Functional Logic Programs. *ACM Transactions on Programming Languages and Systems*, Vol. 20, No. 4, pp. 768–844, 1998.

3. S. Antoy. Optimal Non-Deterministic Functional Logic Computations. In *Proc. International Conference on Algebraic and Logic Programming (ALP'97)*, pp. 16–30. Springer LNCS 1298, 1997.

4. S. Antoy. Constructor-based Conditional Narrowing. In *Proc. of the 3rd International ACM SIGPLAN Conference on Principles and Practice of Declarative Programming (PPDP 2001)*, pp. 199–206. ACM Press, 2001.

5. S. Antoy. Evaluation Strategies for Functional Logic Programming. *Journal of Symbolic Computation*, Vol. 40, No. 1, pp. 875–903, 2005.

6. S. Antoy, R. Echahed, and M. Hanus. A Needed Narrowing Strategy. *Journal of the ACM*, Vol. 47, No. 4, pp. 776–822, 2000.

7. S. Antoy and M. Hanus. Compiling Multi-Paradigm Declarative Programs into Prolog. In *Proc. International Workshop on Frontiers of Combining Systems (FroCoS'2000)*, pp. 171–185. Springer LNCS 1794, 2000.

8. S. Antoy and M. Hanus. Functional Logic Design Patterns. In *Proc. of the 6th International Symposium on Functional and Logic Programming (FLOPS 2002)*, pp. 67–87. Springer LNCS 2441, 2002.

9. F. Baader and T. Nipkow. *Term Rewriting and All That*. Cambridge University Press, 1998.

10. N. Dershowitz and J.-P. Jouannaud. Rewrite Systems. In J. van Leeuwen, editor, *Handbook of Theoretical Computer Science, Vol. B*, pp. 243–320. Elsevier, 1990.

11. M. Erwig and S. Peyton Jones. Pattern Guards and Transformational Patterns. *Electronic Notes in Theoretical Computer Science*, Vol. 41, No. 1, 2000.

12. L. Fribourg. SLOG: A Logic Programming Language Interpreter Based on Clausal Superposition and Rewriting. In *Proc. IEEE Internat. Symposium on Logic Programming*, pp. 172–184, Boston, 1985.

13. E. Giovannetti, G. Levi, C. Moiso, and C. Palamidessi. Kernel LEAF: A Logic plus Functional Language. *Journal of Computer and System Sciences*, Vol. 42, No. 2, pp. 139–185, 1991.

14. J.C. González-Moreno, M.T. Hortalá-González, F.J. López-Fraguas, and M. Rodríguez-Artalejo. An approach to declarative programming based on a rewriting logic. *Journal of Logic Programming*, Vol. 40, pp. 47–87, 1999.

15. M. Hanus. Compiling Logic Programs with Equality. In *Proc. of the 2nd Int. Workshop on Programming Language Implementation and Logic Programming*, pp. 387–401. Springer LNCS 456, 1990.

16. M. Hanus. The Integration of Functions into Logic Programming: From Theory to Practice. *Journal of Logic Programming*, Vol. 19&20, pp. 583–628, 1994.

17. M. Hanus. A Unified Computation Model for Functional and Logic Programming. In *Proc. of the 24th ACM Symposium on Principles of Programming Languages (Paris)*, pp. 80–93, 1997.

18. M. Hanus. A Functional Logic Programming Approach to Graphical User Interfaces. In *International Workshop on Practical Aspects of Declarative Languages (PADL'00)*, pp. 47–62. Springer LNCS 1753, 2000.

19. M. Hanus. High-Level Server Side Web Scripting in Curry. In *Proc. of the Third International Symposium on Practical Aspects of Declarative Languages (PADL'01)*, pp. 76–92. Springer LNCS 1990, 2001.

20. M. Hanus, S. Antoy, M. Engelke, K. Höppner, J. Koj, P. Niederau, R. Sadre, and F. Steiner. PAKCS: The Portland Aachen Kiel Curry System. Available at `http://www.informatik.uni-kiel.de/~pakcs/`, 2004.

21. M. Hanus and F. Steiner. Controlling Search in Declarative Programs. In *Principles of Declarative Programming (Proc. Joint International Symposium PLILP/ALP'98)*, pp. 374–390. Springer LNCS 1490, 1998.
22. M. Hanus (ed.). Curry: An Integrated Functional Logic Language (Vers. 0.8). Available at `http://www.informatik.uni-kiel.de/~curry`, 2003.
23. J. Jaffar and J.-L. Lassez. Constraint Logic Programming. In *Proc. of the 14th ACM Symposium on Principles of Programming Languages*, pp. 111–119, Munich, 1987.
24. R. Lämmel and S.L. Peyton Jones. Scrap your boilerplate: a practical design pattern for generic programming. In *Proceedings of the 2003 ACM SIGPLAN International Workshop on Types in Languages Design and Implementation (TLDI'03)*, pp. 26–37. ACM Press, 2003.
25. F. López-Fraguas and J. Sánchez-Hernández. TOY: A Multiparadigm Declarative System. In *Proc. of RTA'99*, pp. 244–247. Springer LNCS 1631, 1999.
26. M. Mohnen. Context Patterns in Haskell. In *Implementation of Functional Languages*, pp. 41–57. Springer LNCS 1268, 1997.
27. S. Peyton Jones, editor. *Haskell 98 Language and Libraries—The Revised Report*. Cambridge University Press, 2003.
28. M. Tullsen. First class patterns. In *2nd International Workshop on Practical Aspects of Declarative Languages (PADL'00)*, pp. 1–15. Springer LNCS 1753, 2000.

Transformational Verification of Parameterized Protocols Using Array Formulas

Alberto Pettorossi[1], Maurizio Proietti[2], and Valerio Senni[1]

[1] DISP, University of Roma Tor Vergata, Via del Politecnico 1, I-00133 Roma, Italy
pettorossi@info.uniroma2.it, senni@disp.uniroma2.it
[2] IASI-CNR, Viale Manzoni 30, I-00185 Roma, Italy
proietti@iasi.rm.cnr.it

Abstract. We propose a method for the specification and the automated verification of temporal properties of parameterized protocols. Our method is based on logic programming and program transformation. We specify the properties of parameterized protocols by using an extension of stratified logic programs. This extension allows premises of clauses to contain first order formulas over arrays of parameterized length. A property of a given protocol is proved by applying suitable unfold/fold transformations to the specification of that protocol. We demonstrate our method by proving that the parameterized Peterson's protocol among N processes, for any $N \geq 2$, ensures the mutual exclusion property.

1 Introduction

Protocols are rules that govern the interactions among concurrent processes. In order to guarantee that these interactions enjoy some desirable properties, many sophisticated protocols have been designed and proposed in the literature. These protocols are, in general, difficult to verify because of their complexity and ingenuity. This difficulty has motivated the development of methods for the formal specification and the automated verification of properties of protocols. One of the most successful methods is *model checking* [5]. It can be applied to any protocol that can be formalized as a *finite state system*, that is, a finite set of transitions over a finite set of states.

Usually, the number of interacting concurrent processes is not known in advance. Thus, people have designed protocols that can work properly for any number of interacting processes. These protocols are said to be *parameterized* with respect to the number of processes. Several extensions of the model checking technique based upon *abstraction* and *induction* have been proposed in the literature for the verification of parameterized protocols (see, for instance, [3, 18, 27, 29]). However, since the general problem of verifying temporal properties of parameterized protocols is undecidable [2], these extensions cannot be fully mechanical.

In this paper we propose an alternative verification method based on *program transformation* [4]. Our main objective is to establish a correspondence between protocol verification and program transformation, so that the large number of semi-automatic techniques developed in the field of program transformation can be applied to the verification of properties of parameterized protocols.

P.M. Hill (Ed.): LOPSTR 2005, LNCS 3901, pp. 23–43, 2006.

Since arrays are often used in the design of parameterized protocols, we will consider a specification language that allows us to write *array formulas*, that is, first order formulas over arrays. We will specify a parameterized protocol and a property of interest by means of a logic program whose clause bodies may contain array formulas. Our verification method works by transforming this logic program, in which we assume that the head of the clause specifying the property has predicate *prop*, into a new logic program where the clause *prop* ← occurs. Our verification method is an extension of many other techniques based on logic programming which have been proposed in the literature [7, 9, 11, 15, 19, 22, 23].

We will demonstrate our method by considering the parameterized Peterson's protocol [20]. This protocol ensures mutually exclusive use of a given resource which is shared among N processes. The number N is the parameter of the parameterized protocol. In order to formally show that Peterson's protocol ensures mutual exclusion, we cannot use the model checking technique directly. Indeed, since the parameter N is unbounded, the parameterized Peterson's protocol, as it stands, cannot be viewed as a finite state system. Now, one can reduce it to a finite state system, thereby enabling the application of model checking, by using the above mentioned techniques based on abstraction [3]. However, it is not easy to find a powerful abstraction function which works for the many protocols and concurrent systems one encounters in practice.

In contrast, our verification method based on program transformation does not rely on an abstraction function which is applied once at the beginning of the verification process, but it relies, instead, on a *generalization strategy* which is applied *on demand* during the construction of the proof, possibly many times, depending on the structure of the portion of proof constructed so far. This technique provides a more flexible approach to the problem of proving properties of protocols with an infinite state space.

The paper is structured as follows. In Section 2 we recall the parameterized Peterson's protocol for mutual exclusion which will be used throughout the paper as a working example. In Section 3 we present our specification method which makes use of an extension of stratified logic programs where bodies of clauses may contain first order formulas over arrays of parameterized length. We consider properties of parameterized protocols that can be expressed by using formulas of the branching time temporal logic CTL [5] and we show how these properties can be encoded by stratified logic programs with array formulas. Then, in Section 4, we show how CTL properties can be proved by applying unfold/fold transformation rules to a given specification. In Section 5 we discuss some issues regarding the automation of our transformation method. Finally, in Section 6 we briefly discuss the related work in the area of the verification of parameterized protocols.

2   Peterson's Mutual Exclusion Protocol

In this section we provide a detailed description of the parameterized Peterson's protocol [20]. The goal of this protocol is to ensure the mutually exclusive access to a resource that is shared among N (≥ 2) processes. Let assume that for any i, with $1 \leq i \leq N$, process i consists of an infinite loop whose body is made out of two portions of code: (i) a portion called *critical section*, denoted *cs*, in which the process uses the resource, and (ii) a portion called *non-critical section*, denoted *ncs*, in which the process does not use the resource. We also assume that every process is initially in its non-critical section.

We want to establish the following *Mutual Exclusion* property of the computation of the given system of N processes: *for all i and j in $\{1, \ldots, N\}$, while process i executes a statement of its critical section, process j, with $j \neq i$, does not execute any statement of its critical section.*

The parameterized Peterson's protocol consists in adding two portions of code to every process: (i) a first portion to be executed before entering the critical section, and (ii) a second portion to be executed after exiting the critical section (see in Figure 1 the code relative to process i).

Peterson's protocol makes use of two arrays $Q[1, \ldots, N]$ and $S[1, \ldots, N]$ of natural numbers, which are shared among the N processes. The N elements of the array Q may get values from 0 to $N-1$ and are initially set to 0. The N elements of the array S may get values from 1 to N and their initial values are not significant (in [20] it is assumed that they are all 1's). Notice that in [20] the array S is assumed to have $N-1$ elements, not N as we do. Indeed, the last element $S[N]$ is never used by Peterson's protocol. Its introduction, however, allows us to write formulas which are much simpler.

In Peterson's protocol we also have the array $J[1, \ldots, N]$ whose i-th element, for $i = 1, \ldots, N$, is a local variable of process i and may get values from 1 to N. Notice that the array J is *not* shared and indeed, for $i = 1, \ldots, N$, process i reads and/or writes $J[i]$ only.

In Figure 2 process i is represented by a finite state diagram. In that diagram a transition from state a to state b is denoted by an arrow from a to b labelled by a test t and a statement s. We have omitted from the label of a transition the test t when it is *true*. Likewise, we have omitted the statement s when it is *skip*. A transition is said to be *enabled* iff its test t evaluates to *true*. An enabled transition takes place by executing its statement s.

For $i = 1, \ldots, N$, process i is deterministic in the sense that in any of its states at most one transition is enabled. However, in the given system of N processes, it may be the case that more than one transition is enabled (obviously, no two enabled transitions belong to the same process). In that case we assume that exactly one of the enabled transitions takes place. Note that we do not make any fairness assumption so that, for instance, if the same configuration of enabled transitions occurs again in the future, nothing can be said about the transition which will actually take place in that repeated configuration.

The N processes execute their code in a concurrent way according to the following four atomicity assumptions. Here and in what follows, we denote by φ the formula $\forall k \, (k \neq i \;\rightarrow\; Q[k] < J[i]) \vee (S[J[i]] \neq i)$.

(1) The assignments '$Q[i] := 0$' and '$J[i] := 1$' are atomic,

(2) the tests '$\neg J[i] < N$' and '$\neg \varphi$' are atomic,

while *true* **do**
  ncs : non-critical section of process i;
      $J[i] := 1$;
  w: **while** $J[i] < N$ **do**
      $Q[i] := J[i];\ \ S[J[i]] := i$;
  λ: **if** $\forall k\,(k \neq i \rightarrow Q[k] < J[i]) \vee (S[J[i]] \neq i)$ **then** $J[i] := J[i]+1$ **else** *goto* λ
      od;
  cs : critical section of process i;
      $Q[i] := 0$
od

Fig. 1. Process i of a system of N processes using Peterson's protocol

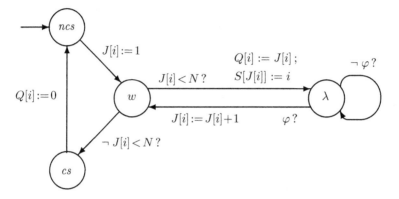

Fig. 2. Finite state diagram corresponding to process i of a system of N processes using Peterson's protocol. *ncs* is the initial state. The formula φ stands for $\forall k\,(k \neq i \rightarrow Q[k] < J[i]) \vee (S[J[i]] \neq i)$.

(3) the sequence of the test '$J[i] < N$' followed by the two assignments '$Q[i] := J[i];\ S[J[i]] := i$' is atomic, and

(4) the sequence of the test 'φ' followed by the assignment '$J[i] := J[i]+1$' is atomic.

We have made these atomicity assumptions (which correspond to the labels of the transitions of the diagram of Figure 2) for keeping the presentation of our proof of the mutual exclusion property as simple as possible. However, this property has also been proved by using our method which we will present in Section 4, under weaker assumptions, in which one only assumes that every single assignment and test is atomic [26]. (In particular, in [26] it is assumed that each test $k \neq i$ and '$Q[k] < J[i]$' in the formula φ, and *not* the entire formula φ, is atomic. Likewise, it is assumed that in the transition from state w to state λ, each assignment '$Q[i] := J[i]$' and '$S[J[i]] := i$', and *not* the sequence '$Q[i] := J[i]; S[J[i]] := i$' of assignments, is atomic.)

We assume that the number N of processes does *not* change over time, in the sense that while the computation progresses, neither a new process is constructed nor an existing process is destroyed.

In the original paper [20], the proof of the mutual exclusion property of the parameterized Peterson's protocol is left to the reader. The author of [20] simply says that it can be derived from the proof provided for the case of two processes (and, actually, that proof is an informal one) by observing that, for each value of $J[i] = 1, \ldots, N-1$, at least one process is discarded from the set of those which may enter their critical section. Thus, at the end of the for-loop, at most one process may enter its critical section.

In Peterson's protocol, the value of the variable $J[i]$ of process i indicates, as we will now explain, the 'level' that process i has reached since it first requested to enter its critical section (and this request was done by starting the execution of the while-loop with label w, see Figure 1). When process i completes its non-critical section and requests to enter its critical section, it goes to state w where its level $J[i]$ is 1. When process i completes one execution of the body of the while-loop with label w (that is, it goes from state w to state λ and back to state w), it increases its level by one unit. For each level $J[i] = 1, \ldots, N-1$, process i tests whether or not property φ holds, and for $J[i] = 1, \ldots, N-2$, if φ holds at level $J[i]$, then process i goes to the next level up, that is, $J[i]$ is increased by one unit. If φ holds at the final level $N-1$, then process i enters its critical section.

3   Specification of Parameterized Protocols Using Array Formulas

In this section we present our method for the specification of parameterized protocols and their temporal properties. The main novelty of our method with respect to other methods based on logic programming is that in the specification of protocols we use the first order theory of arrays introduced below.

Similarly to the model checking approach, we represent a protocol as a set of transitions between states. Notice, however, that in the case of parameterized protocols the number of states may be infinite. For the formal specification of the transition relation we consider a *typed first order language* [16] with the following two types: (i) $\mathbb{N}$, denoting natural numbers, and (ii) $\mathbb{A}$, denoting arrays of natural numbers. A *state* is represented by a term of the form $s(X_1, \ldots, X_n)$, where $X_1, \ldots, X_n$ are variables of type $\mathbb{N}$ or $\mathbb{A}$. The *transition relation* is specified by a set of statements of the form:

$t(a, a') \leftarrow \tau$

where t is a fixed binary predicate symbol, a and a' are terms representing states, and τ is an *array formula* defined as we now describe.

An array formula is a typed first order formula constructed by using a language consisting of: (i) *variables* of type $\mathbb{N}$, (ii) *variables* of type $\mathbb{A}$ (called *array variables*), (iii) the constant 0 of type $\mathbb{N}$ and the successor function *succ* of type $\mathbb{N} \rightarrow \mathbb{N}$, and (iv) the following predicates, whose informal meaning is given between parentheses (the names *rd* and *wr* stand for *read* and *write*, respectively):

ln of type $\mathbb{A} \times \mathbb{N}$ ($ln(A, l)$ means 'the array A has length l')
rd of type $\mathbb{A} \times \mathbb{N} \times \mathbb{N}$ ($rd(A, i, n)$ means 'in the array A the i-th element is n')

wr of type $\mathbb{A} \times \mathbb{N} \times \mathbb{N} \times \mathbb{A}$ ($wr(A, i, n, B)$ means 'the array B is equal to the
array A except that the i-th element of B is n')
$=_{\mathbb{N}}, <, \leq$, all of type $\mathbb{N} \times \mathbb{N}$ (equality and inequalities between natural numbers)
$=_{\mathbb{A}}$ of type $\mathbb{A} \times \mathbb{A}$ (equality between arrays)

Given a term n of type $\mathbb{N}$, the term $succ(n)$ will also be written as $n + 1$. For
reasons of simplicity, we will write $=$, instead of $=_{\mathbb{N}}$ and $=_{\mathbb{A}}$, when the type of
the equality is clear from the context.

Array formulas are constructed as usual in typed first order logic by using
the connectives $\wedge$, $\vee$, $\neg$, $\rightarrow$, and $\leftrightarrow$, and the quantifiers $\forall$ and $\exists$. However, for
every statement of the form $t(a, a') \leftarrow \tau$ which specifies a transition relation, we
assume that every array variable occurring in τ is not quantified within τ itself.

The semantics of a statement of the form $t(a, a') \leftarrow \tau$ is defined in a transformational way by transforming this statement into a stratified set of clauses. This
set of clauses is obtained by applying the variant of the Lloyd-Topor transformation for typed first order formulas described in [10], called the *typed Lloyd-Topor
transformation*. This transformation works like the Lloyd-Topor transformation
for untyped first order formulas [16], except that it adds *type atoms* to the bodies
of the transformed clauses so that each variable ranges over the domain specified
by the corresponding type atom. In our case, the transformation adds the type
atoms $nat(N)$ and $array(A)$ for each occurrence of a variable N of type $\mathbb{N}$ and a
variable A of type $\mathbb{A}$, respectively. The definition of the predicates nat and $array$
is provided by the following definite clauses:

$$nat(0) \leftarrow \qquad\qquad array([\,]) \leftarrow$$
$$nat(N+1) \leftarrow nat(N) \qquad array([A|As]) \leftarrow nat(A) \wedge array(As)$$

Note that in these clauses arrays are represented as lists. These four clauses
are included in a set, called *Arrays*, of definite clauses that also provide the
definitions of the predicates ln, rd, wr, $=_{\mathbb{N}}$, $<$, $\leq$, and $=_{\mathbb{A}}$ of our first order
language of arrays. In particular, *Arrays* contains the clauses:

$$ln([\,], 0) \leftarrow$$
$$ln([A|As], L) \leftarrow L = N+1 \wedge ln(As, N)$$
$$rd([A|As], 1, D) \leftarrow A = D$$
$$rd([A|As], L, D) \leftarrow L = K+1 \wedge rd(As, K, D)$$
$$wr([A|As], 1, D, [B|Bs]) \leftarrow B = D \wedge As = Bs$$
$$wr([A|As], L, D, [B|Bs]) \leftarrow A = B \wedge L = K+1 \wedge wr(As, K, D, Bs)$$

We omit to list here the usual clauses defining the predicates $=_{\mathbb{N}}$, $<$, $\leq$, and $=_{\mathbb{A}}$.
As an example of application of the typed Lloyd-Topor transformation, let us
consider the following statement:

$$t(s(A), s(B)) \leftarrow \exists n \, \forall i \; wr(A, i, n, B)$$

where: (i) A and B are array variables, and (ii) $s(A)$ and $s(B)$ are terms representing states. By applying the typed Lloyd-Topor transformation to this statement, we get the following two clauses:

$$t(s(A), s(B)) \leftarrow array(A) \wedge array(B) \wedge nat(N) \wedge \neg newp(A, N, B)$$
$$newp(A, N, B) \leftarrow array(A) \wedge nat(I) \wedge nat(N) \wedge array(B) \wedge \neg wr(A, I, N, B)$$

Given a statement of the form $H \leftarrow \tau$, where H is an atom and τ is an array formula, we denote by $LT_t(H \leftarrow \tau)$ the set of clauses which are derived by applying the typed Lloyd-Topor transformation to $H \leftarrow \tau$. For reasons of conciseness, in what follows we will feel free to write statements with array formulas, instead of the corresponding set of clauses, and by abuse of language, statements with array formulas will also be called 'clauses'.

Let us now specify the parameterized Peterson's protocol for N processes by using statements with array formulas. In this specification a *state* is represented by a term of the form $s(P, J, Q, S)$, where:

- P is an array of the form $[p_1, \ldots, p_N]$ such that, for $i = 1, \ldots, N$, p_i is a constant in the set $\{ncs, cs, w, \lambda\}$ representing the state of process i (see Figure 2). In order to comply with the syntax of array formulas, the constants $ncs, cs, w,$ and λ should be replaced by distinct natural numbers, but, for reasons of readability, in the formulas below we will use the more expressive identifiers $ncs, cs, w,$ and λ.
- J is an array of the form $[j_1, \ldots, j_N]$, where, for $i = 1, \ldots, N$, j_i belongs to the set $\{1, \ldots, N\}$ and is a local value in the sense that it can be read and written by process i only.
- Q and S are arrays of the form $[q_1, \ldots, q_N]$ and $[s_1, \ldots, s_N]$, respectively, where, for $i = 1, \ldots, N$, q_i belongs to the set $\{0, \ldots, N-1\}$ and s_i belongs to the set $\{1, \ldots, N\}$. These two arrays Q and S are shared in the sense that they can be read and written by any of the N processes.

The transition relation of the parameterized Peterson's protocol is defined by the seven statements $T_1, \ldots, T_7$ which we now introduce. For $r = 1, \ldots, 7$, statement T_r is of the form:

$$t(s(P, J, Q, S), s(P', J', Q', S')) \leftarrow \tau_r(s(P, J, Q, S), s(P', J', Q', S'))$$

where $\tau_r(s(P, J, Q, S), s(P', J', Q', S'))$ is an array formula defined as follows (see also Figure 2).

1. For the transition from ncs to w:
$\tau_1(s(P, J, Q, S), s(P', J', Q', S')) \equiv_{def}$
$\quad \exists i \ (rd(P, i, ncs) \ \wedge \ wr(P, i, w, P') \ \wedge \ wr(J, i, 1, J')) \ \wedge$
$\quad Q' = Q \ \wedge \ S' = S$

2. For the transition from w to λ:
$\tau_2(s(P, J, Q, S), s(P', J', Q', S')) \equiv_{def}$
$\quad \exists i, k, l \ (rd(P, i, w) \ \wedge \ wr(P, i, \lambda, P') \ \wedge \ rd(J, i, k) \ \wedge$
$\quad\quad wr(Q, i, k, Q') \ \wedge \ wr(S, k, i, S') \ \wedge \ ln(P, l) \ \wedge \ k < l) \ \wedge$
$\quad J' = J$

3. For the transition from λ to λ:
$\tau_3(s(P, J, Q, S), s(P', J', Q', S')) \equiv_{def}$
$\quad \exists i, k, m, n \ (rd(P, i, \lambda) \ \wedge \ rd(J, i, m) \ \wedge \neg (k = i) \ \wedge \ rd(Q, k, n) \ \wedge$
$\quad\quad n \geq m \ \wedge \ rd(S, m, i)) \ \wedge$
$\quad P' = P \ \wedge \ J' = J \ \wedge \ Q' = Q \ \wedge \ S' = S$

4. For the transition from λ to w when $\forall k \, (k \neq i \rightarrow Q[k] < J[i])$ holds:
$$\tau_4(s(P, J, Q, S), s(P', J', Q', S')) \equiv_{def}$$
$$\exists i, l, m \, (rd(P, i, \lambda) \wedge wr(P, i, w, P') \wedge rd(J, i, m) \wedge ln(P, l) \wedge$$
$$\forall k, n((1 \leq k \leq l \wedge rd(Q, k, n) \wedge \neg(k=i)) \rightarrow n<m) \wedge$$
$$wr(J, i, m+1, J')) \wedge$$
$$Q'=Q \wedge S'=S$$

5. For the transition from λ to w when $S[J[i]] \neq i$ holds:
$$\tau_5(s(P, J, Q, S), s(P', J', Q', S')) \equiv_{def}$$
$$\exists i, m \, (rd(P, i, \lambda) \wedge wr(P, i, w, P') \wedge$$
$$rd(J, i, m) \wedge \neg rd(S, m, i) \wedge wr(J, i, m+1, J')) \wedge$$
$$Q'=Q \wedge S'=S$$

6. For the transition from w to cs:
$$\tau_6(s(P, J, Q, S), s(P', J', Q', S')) \equiv_{def}$$
$$\exists i, m \, (rd(P, i, w) \wedge wr(P, i, cs, P') \wedge$$
$$rd(J, i, m) \wedge ln(P, l) \wedge m \geq l) \wedge$$
$$J'=J \wedge Q'=Q \wedge S'=S$$

7. For the transition from cs to ncs:
$$\tau_7(s(P, J, Q, S), s(P', J', Q', S')) \equiv_{def}$$
$$\exists i \, (rd(P, i, cs) \wedge wr(P, i, ncs, P') \wedge wr(Q, i, 0, Q')) \wedge$$
$$J'=J \wedge S'=S$$

We will express the properties of parameterized protocols by using the branching time temporal logic CTL [5]. In particular, the mutual exclusion property of Peterson's protocol will be expressed by the following temporal formula:

$$initial \rightarrow \neg \, EF \; unsafe$$

where $initial$ and $unsafe$ are atomic properties of states which we will specify below. This temporal formula holds at a state a whenever the following is true: if a is an $initial$ state then there exists no $unsafe$ state in the future of a.

The truth of a CTL formula is defined by the following locally stratified logic program, called $Holds$, where the predicate $holds(X, F)$ means that a temporal formula F holds at a state X:

$holds(X, F) \leftarrow atomic(X, F)$
$holds(X, \neg F) \leftarrow \neg holds(X, F)$
$holds(X, F \wedge G) \leftarrow holds(X, F) \wedge holds(X, G)$
$holds(X, ef(F)) \leftarrow holds(X, F)$
$holds(X, ef(F)) \leftarrow t(X, X') \wedge holds(X', ef(F))$

Other connectives, such as $\vee$, $\rightarrow$ and $\leftrightarrow$, defined as usual in terms of $\wedge$ and $\neg$, can be used in CTL formulas. The unary constructor ef encodes the temporal operator EF. Other temporal operators, such as the operator AF which is needed for expressing $liveness$ properties, can be defined by using locally stratified logic programs [9, 15]. Here, for reasons of simplicity, we have restricted ourselves to the operator EF which is the only operator needed for specifying the mutual exclusion property (which is a $safety$ property).

The atomic properties of the states are specified by a set of statements of the form:

$$atomic(a, p) \leftarrow \alpha$$

where a is a term representing a state, p is a constant representing an atomic property, and α is an array formula stating that p holds at state a. We assume that the array variables occurring in α are not quantified within α itself. In particular, the *initial* and *unsafe* atomic properties are defined by the following two statements A_1 and A_2.

$A_1:$ $atomic(s(P, J, Q, S), initial) \leftarrow$
$$\exists l\,(\forall k\,(1 \leq k \leq l \rightarrow (rd(P, k, ncs) \wedge rd(Q, k, 0))) \wedge$$
$$ln(P, l) \wedge ln(J, l) \wedge ln(Q, l) \wedge ln(S, l))$$

$A_2:$ $atomic(s(P, J, Q, S), unsafe) \leftarrow \exists i, j\,(rd(P, i, cs) \wedge rd(P, j, cs) \wedge \neg (j = i))$

The premise of A_1, which will also be denoted by $init\_state(s(P, J, Q, S))$, expresses the fact that in an initial state every process is in its non-critical section, Q is an array whose elements are all 0's, and the arrays P, J, Q, and S have the same length. The premise of A_2, which will also be denoted by $unsafe\_state(s(P, J, Q, S))$, expresses the fact that in an unsafe state at least two distinct processes are in their critical section.

Now we formally define when a CTL formula holds for a specification of a parameterized protocol. Let us consider a protocol specification *Spec* consisting of the following set of statements:

$$Spec: \{T_1, \ldots, T_m, A_1, \ldots, A_n\}$$

where: (i) $T_1, \ldots, T_m$ are statements that specify a transition relation, and (ii) $A_1, \ldots, A_n$ are statements that specify atomic properties. We denote by P_{Spec} the following set of clauses:

$$P_{Spec}: LT_t(T_1) \cup \ldots \cup LT_t(T_m) \cup LT_t(A_1) \cup \ldots \cup LT_t(A_n) \cup Arrays \cup Holds$$

Given a specification *Spec* of a parameterized protocol and a CTL formula φ, we say that

φ *holds for Spec*   iff $M(P_{Spec}) \models \forall X\ holds(X, \varphi)$

where $M(P_{Spec})$ denotes the perfect model of P_{Spec}. Note that the existence of $M(P_{Spec})$ is guaranteed by the fact that P_{Spec} is locally stratified [1]. In the next section we will prove the mutual exclusion property for the parameterized Peterson's protocol by proving that

$$M(P_{Peterson}) \models \forall X\ holds(X, initial \rightarrow \neg\,ef(unsafe)) \qquad \text{(ME)}$$

where *Peterson* is the specification of the parameterized Peterson's protocol consisting of the set $\{T_1, \ldots, T_7, A_1, A_2\}$ of statements we have listed above.

Note that the above formula (ME) guarantees the mutual exclusion property of the parameterized Peterson's protocol for any number N (≥ 2) of processes. Indeed, in (ME) the variable X ranges over terms of the form $s(P, J, Q, S)$ and the parameter N of Peterson's protocol is the length of the arrays P, J, Q, and S.

4   Transformational Verification of Parameterized Protocols

In this section we describe our method for the verification of CTL properties of parameterized protocols. This method follows the approach based on program transformation which has been proposed in [21]. As an example of application of our method, we prove that the mutual exclusion property holds for the parameterized Peterson's protocol.

Suppose that, given a specification $Spec$ of a parameterized protocol and a CTL property φ, we want to prove that φ holds for $Spec$, that is, $M(P_{Spec}) \models \forall X\ holds(X, \varphi)$. We start off by introducing the statement:

$prop \leftarrow \forall X\ holds(X, \varphi)$

where $prop$ is a new predicate symbol. By applying the Lloyd-Topor transformation (for untyped formulas) to this statement and by using the equivalence:

$M(P_{Spec}) \models \forall X, F\ (\neg holds(X, F) \leftrightarrow holds(X, \neg F))$

we get the following two clauses:

1. $prop \leftarrow \neg new1$
2. $new1 \leftarrow holds(X, \neg \varphi)$

Our verification method consists in showing $M(P_{Spec}) \models \forall X\ holds(X, \varphi)$ by applying unfold/fold transformation rules that preserve the perfect model [9, 25] and deriving from the program $P_{Spec} \cup \{1, 2\}$ a new program T which contains the clause $prop \leftarrow$.

The soundness of our method is a straightforward consequence of the fact that both the Lloyd-Topor transformation and the unfold/fold transformation rules preserve the perfect model, that is, the following holds:

$$M(P_{Spec}) \models \forall X\ holds(X, \varphi) \quad \text{iff} \quad M(P_{Spec} \cup \{1, 2\}) \models prop \quad \text{iff} \quad M(T) \models prop$$

Notice that in the case where T contains no clause for $prop$, we conclude that $M(P_{Spec} \cup \{1, 2\}) \not\models prop$ and, thus, $M(P_{Spec}) \models \exists X\ holds(X, \neg \varphi)$. Unfortunately, our method is necessarily incomplete due to the undecidability of CTL for parameterized protocols. Indeed, the unfold/fold transformation may not terminate or it may terminate by deriving a program T that contains one or more clauses of the form $prop \leftarrow Body$, where $Body$ is not the empty conjunction.

The application of the unfold/fold transformation rules is guided by a transformation strategy which extends the ones presented in [9, 21] to the case of logic programs with array formulas. Now we outline this strategy and then we will see it in action in the verification of the mutual exclusion property of the parameterized Peterson's protocol.

Our transformation strategy is divided into two phases, called Phase A and Phase B, respectively.

In Phase A we compute a specialized definition of $holds(X, \neg \varphi)$ as we now describe. Starting from clause 2 above, we perform the following transformation steps: (i) we unfold clause 2, thereby deriving a new set, say Cls, of clauses, (ii) we manipulate the array formulas occurring in the clauses of Cls, by replacing these formulas by equivalent ones and by removing each clause whose body contains an unsatisfiable formula, (iii) we introduce definitions of new predicates and we fold every instance of $holds(X, F)$. Starting from each definition of a new predicate, we repeatedly perform the above three transformation steps (i), (ii), and (iii). We stop when we are able to fold all instances of $holds(X, F)$ by using predicate definitions already introduced at previous transformation steps.

In Phase B we derive a new program T where as many predicates as possible are defined either by a single fact or by an empty set of clauses, in the hope that *prop* is among such predicates. In order to derive program T we use the unfolding rule and the *clause removal* rule. In particular, we remove all clauses that define *useless* predicates [9]. Recall that: (i) the set U of all useless predicates of a program P is defined as the largest set such that for every predicate p in U and for every clause C that defines p in P, there exists a predicate q in U which occurs positively in the body of C, and (ii) the removal of the clauses that define useless predicates preserves the perfect model of the program at hand [9].

This two-phase transformation technique has been fruitfully used for proving properties of infinite state systems in [9].

Let us now show how the mutual exclusion property of the parameterized Peterson's protocol can be verified by using our method based on program transformation. The property φ to be verified is $initial \rightarrow \neg\, ef(unsafe)$. Thus, we start from the statement:

$$mutex \leftarrow \forall X \; holds(X, initial \rightarrow \neg\, ef(unsafe))$$

and by applying the Lloyd-Topor transformation, we get the following two clauses:

1. $mutex \leftarrow \neg\, new1$
2. $new1 \leftarrow holds(X, initial \wedge ef(unsafe))$

Now we apply our transformation strategy starting from $P_{Peterson} \cup \{1, 2\}$, where $P_{Peterson}$ is the program which encodes the specification of the parameterized Peterson's protocol as described in Section 3. Let us now show some of the transformation steps performed during Phase A of this strategy. By unfolding clause 2 we get:

3. $new1 \leftarrow init\_state(s(P, J, Q, S)) \wedge unsafe\_state(s(P, J, Q, S))$
4. $new1 \leftarrow init\_state(s(P, J, Q, S)) \wedge t(s(P, J, Q, S), s(P', J', Q', S')) \wedge$
$\quad\quad holds(s(P', J', Q', S'), ef(unsafe))$

Clause 3 is removed because the array formula

$$init\_state(s(P, J, Q, S)) \wedge unsafe\_state(s(P, J, Q, S))$$

occurring in its body is unsatisfiable (indeed, every process is initially in its non-critical section and, thus, the initial state is not unsafe). In the next section we will discuss the issue of how to mechanize satisfiability tests.

We unfold clause 4 with respect to the atom with predicate t and we get seven new clauses, one for each statement $T_1, \ldots, T_7$ defining the transition relation (see Section 3). The clauses derived from $T_2, \ldots, T_7$ are removed because their bodies contain unsatisfiable array formulas. Thus, after these unfolding steps and removal steps, from clause 2 we get the following clause only:

5. $new1 \leftarrow init\_state(s(P, J, Q, S)) \wedge \tau_1(s(P, J, Q, S), s(P', J', Q', S')) \wedge$
   $\qquad holds(s(P', J', Q', S'), ef(unsafe))$

where $\tau_1(s(P, J, Q, S), s(P', J', Q', S'))$ is the array formula defined in Section 3. Now let us consider the formula $c_1(s(P', J', Q', S'))$ defined as follows:

$c_1(s(P', J', Q', S')) \equiv_{def}$
$\qquad \exists P, J, Q, S \ (init\_state(s(P, J, Q, S)) \wedge \tau_1(s(P, J, Q, S), s(P', J', Q', S')))$

By eliminating from it the existentially quantified variables P, J, Q and S, we obtain the following equivalence:

$$c_1(s(P', J', Q', S')) \leftrightarrow \qquad\qquad\qquad\qquad\qquad\qquad\qquad (C)$$
$$\exists l, i \ (\forall k((1 \le k \le l \ \wedge \neg (k=i)) \rightarrow (rd(P', k, ncs) \ \wedge \ rd(Q', k, 0))) \wedge$$
$$rd(P', i, w) \ \wedge \ rd(J', i, 1) \ \wedge \ rd(Q', i, 0)$$
$$ln(P', l) \ \wedge \ ln(J', l) \ \wedge \ ln(Q', l) \ \wedge \ ln(S', l))$$

Now, in order to fold clause 5 w.r.t. the atom $holds(s(P', J', Q', S'), ef(unsafe))$, a suitable condition has to be fulfilled (see the folding rule for constraint logic programs described in [9]). Let us present this condition in the case of programs with array formulas that we consider in this paper.

Suppose that we are given a clause of the form $H \leftarrow \alpha \wedge holds(X, \psi) \wedge G$ and we want to fold it by using a (suitably renamed) clause of the form $newp(X) \leftarrow \beta \wedge holds(X, \psi)$. This folding step is allowed only if we have that $M(Arrays) \models \forall(\alpha \rightarrow \beta)$ holds, that is, $\alpha \wedge \neg\beta$ is unsatisfiable in $M(Arrays)$. If this condition is fulfilled, then by folding we obtain the new clause $H \leftarrow \alpha \wedge newp(X) \wedge G$.

Now, in order to fold clause 5, we introduce a new predicate definition of the form:

6. $new2(s(P, J, Q, S)) \leftarrow genc_1(s(P, J, Q, S)) \ \wedge \ holds(s(P, J, Q, S), ef(unsafe))$

The formula $genc_1(s(P, J, Q, S))$ is a *generalization* of $c_1(s(P, J, Q, S))$, in the sense that the following holds:

$$M(Arrays) \models \forall P, J, Q, S \ (c_1(s(P, J, Q, S)) \rightarrow genc_1(s(P, J, Q, S)))$$

This ensures that the condition for folding is fulfilled.

As usual in program transformation techniques, this generalization step from c_1 to $genc_1$ requires ingenuity. We will not address here the problem of how to mechanize this generalization step and the other generalization steps required in the remaining part of our program derivation. However, some aspects of this crucial generalization issue will be discussed in Section 5.

In our verification of the parameterized Peterson's protocol we introduce the following array formula $genc_1(s(P, J, Q, S))$ which holds iff zero or more processes are in state w and the remaining processes are in state ncs:

$$genc_1(s(P, J, Q, S)) \equiv_{def} \qquad\qquad\qquad\qquad\qquad\qquad\qquad (G)$$
$$\exists l \ (\forall k \ (1 \le k \le l \ \rightarrow ((rd(P, k, ncs) \ \wedge \ rd(Q, k, 0)) \vee$$
$$(rd(P, k, w) \ \wedge \ rd(J, k, 1) \ \wedge \ rd(Q, k, 0)))) \wedge$$
$$ln(P, l) \ \wedge \ ln(J, l) \ \wedge \ ln(Q, l) \ \wedge \ ln(S, l))$$

This formula defining $genc_1(s(P, J, Q, S))$ is indeed a generalization of the formula $c_1(s(P, J, Q, S))$, as the reader may check by looking at the above equivalence (C). By folding clause 5 using the newly introduced clause 6 we get:

5.f $new1 \leftarrow init\_state(s(P, J, Q, S)) \wedge \tau_1(s(P, J, Q, S), s(P', J', Q', S')) \wedge$
$\qquad new2(s(P', J', Q', S'))$

Now, starting from clause 6, we repeat the transformation steps (i), (ii), and (iii) described above, until we are able to fold every instance of $holds(X, F)$ by using a predicate definition introduced at a previous transformation step. By doing so we terminate Phase A and we derive the following program R where:

- $genc_1$ is defined as indicated in (G),
- $genc_2, \ldots, genc_8$ are defined as indicated in the Appendix,
- $\tau_1, \ldots, \tau_7$ are the array formulas that define the transition relation as indicated in Section 3, and
- the arguments a and a' stand for the states $s(P, J, Q, S)$ and $s(P', J', Q', S')$, respectively.

---

1. $mutex \leftarrow \neg new1$ $\hfill$ Program R

5.f $new1 \leftarrow initial(a) \wedge \tau_1(a, a') \wedge new2(a')$

7. $new2(a) \leftarrow genc_1(a) \wedge \tau_1(a, a') \wedge new2(a')$
8. $new2(a) \leftarrow genc_1(a) \wedge \tau_2(a, a') \wedge new3(a')$
9. $new2(a) \leftarrow genc_1(a) \wedge \tau_6(a, a') \wedge new7(a')$

10. $new3(a) \leftarrow genc_2(a) \wedge \tau_1(a, a') \wedge new3(a')$
11. $new3(a) \leftarrow genc_2(a) \wedge \tau_2(a, a') \wedge new3(a')$
12. $new3(a) \leftarrow genc_2(a) \wedge \tau_3(a, a') \wedge new3(a')$
13. $new3(a) \leftarrow genc_2(a) \wedge \tau_4(a, a') \wedge new4(a')$
14. $new3(a) \leftarrow genc_2(a) \wedge \tau_5(a, a') \wedge new5(a')$

15. $new4(a) \leftarrow genc_3(a) \wedge \tau_1(a, a') \wedge new4(a')$
16. $new4(a) \leftarrow genc_3(a) \wedge \tau_2(a, a') \wedge new4(a')$
17. $new4(a) \leftarrow genc_3(a) \wedge \tau_2(a, a') \wedge new6(a')$
18. $new4(a) \leftarrow genc_3(a) \wedge \tau_4(a, a') \wedge new4(a')$
19. $new4(a) \leftarrow genc_3(a) \wedge \tau_6(a, a') \wedge new7(a')$

20. $new5(a) \leftarrow genc_4(a) \wedge \tau_1(a, a') \wedge new5(a')$
21. $new5(a) \leftarrow genc_4(a) \wedge \tau_2(a, a') \wedge new5(a')$
22. $new5(a) \leftarrow genc_4(a) \wedge \tau_3(a, a') \wedge new5(a')$
23. $new5(a) \leftarrow genc_4(a) \wedge \tau_4(a, a') \wedge new5(a')$
24. $new5(a) \leftarrow genc_4(a) \wedge \tau_5(a, a') \wedge new5(a')$
25. $new5(a) \leftarrow genc_4(a) \wedge \tau_6(a, a') \wedge new8(a')$

26. $new6(a) \leftarrow genc_5(a) \wedge \tau_1(a, a') \wedge new6(a')$
27. $new6(a) \leftarrow genc_5(a) \wedge \tau_2(a, a') \wedge new6(a')$
28. $new6(a) \leftarrow genc_5(a) \wedge \tau_3(a, a') \wedge new6(a')$
29. $new6(a) \leftarrow genc_5(a) \wedge \tau_4(a, a') \wedge new6(a')$
30. $new6(a) \leftarrow genc_5(a) \wedge \tau_5(a, a') \wedge new6(a')$
31. $new6(a) \leftarrow genc_5(a) \wedge \tau_6(a, a') \wedge new9(a')$

32. $new7(a) \leftarrow genc_6(a) \wedge \tau_1(a, a') \wedge new7(a')$
33. $new7(a) \leftarrow genc_6(a) \wedge \tau_2(a, a') \wedge new9(a')$
34. $new7(a) \leftarrow genc_6(a) \wedge \tau_7(a, a') \wedge new2(a')$

35. $new8(a) \leftarrow genc_7(a) \wedge \tau_3(a, a') \wedge new8(a')$
36. $new8(a) \leftarrow genc_7(a) \wedge \tau_7(a, a') \wedge new5(a')$

37. $new9(a) \leftarrow genc_8(a) \wedge \tau_1(a, a') \wedge new9(a')$
38. $new9(a) \leftarrow genc_8(a) \wedge \tau_2(a, a') \wedge new9(a')$
39. $new9(a) \leftarrow genc_8(a) \wedge \tau_3(a, a') \wedge new9(a')$
40. $new9(a) \leftarrow genc_8(a) \wedge \tau_5(a, a') \wedge new9(a')$
41. $new9(a) \leftarrow genc_8(a) \wedge \tau_7(a, a') \wedge new6(a')$

Now we proceed to Phase B of our strategy. Since in program R the predicates $new1$ through $new9$ are useless, we remove clause 5.f, and clauses 7 through 41, and by doing so, we derive a program consisting of clause 1 only. By unfolding clause 1 we get the final program T, which consists of the clause $mutex \leftarrow$ only. Thus, $M(T) \models mutex$ and we have proved that:

$$M(P_{Peterson}) \models \forall X \ holds(X, initial \rightarrow \neg ef(unsafe))$$

As a consequence, we have that for any initial state and for any number $N(\geq 2)$ of processes, the mutual exclusion property holds for the parameterized Peterson's protocol.

5   Mechanization of the Verification Method

In order to achieve a full mechanization of our verification method, two main issues have to be addressed: (i) how to test the satisfiability of array formulas, and (ii) how to perform suitable generalization steps.

Satisfiability tests for array formulas are required at the following two points of Phase A of the transformation strategy described in Section 4: (1) at Step (ii), when we remove each clause whose body contains an unsatisfiable array formula, and (2) at Step (iii), when we fold each clause whose body contains a *holds* literal.

In order to clarify Point (2), we recall that, before applying the folding rule [9], we need to test that in $M(Arrays)$ the array formula occurring in the body of the clause to be folded implies the array formula occurring in the body of the clause that we use for folding. For instance, in Section 4 before folding clause 5 using clause 6, we need to prove that:

$$M(Arrays) \models \forall P, J, Q, S \ (c_1(s(P, J, Q, S)) \rightarrow genc_1(s(P, J, Q, S)))$$

which holds iff the following formula:

$$c_1(s(P, J, Q, S)) \wedge \neg genc_1(s(P, J, Q, S)) \tag{CG}$$

is unsatisfiable in $M(Arrays)$.

Now the problem of testing the satisfiability of array formulas is in general undecidable. (The reader may refer to [28] for a short survey on this subject.)

However, some decidable fragments of the theory of arrays, such as the *quantifier-free extensional theory of arrays*, have been identified [28]. Unfortunately, the array formulas occurring in our formalization of the parameterized Peterson's protocol cannot be reduced to formulas in those decidable fragments. Indeed, due to the assumptions made in Section 3 on the array formulas which are used in the specifications of protocols, we need to test the satisfiability of array formulas where the variables of type $\mathbb{A}$ are not quantified, while the variables of type $\mathbb{N}$ can be quantified in an unrestricted way.

In order to perform the satisfiability tests required by our verification of the parameterized Peterson's protocol, we have followed the approach based on program transformation which has been proposed in [21]. Some of these satisfiability tests have been done in a fully automatic way by using the MAP transformation system [17], which implements the unfold/fold proof strategy described in [21]. Examples of array formulas whose unsatisfiability we have proved in an automatic way include: (i) the formula occurring in the body of clause 3 shown in Section 4, and (ii) the formula (CG) shown above in this section. Some other satisfiability tests have been done in a semi-automatic way, by interleaving fully automatic applications of the unfold/fold proof strategy and some manual applications of the unfold/fold transformation rules.

Generalization steps are needed when, during Step (iii) of Phase A of our transformation strategy, a new predicate definition is introduced to fold the instances of the atom $holds(X, F)$. The introduction of suitable new definitions by generalization is a crucial issue of the program transformation methodology [4]. The invention of these definitions corresponds to the discovery of suitable invariants of the protocol to be verified. Due to the undecidability of CTL for parameterized protocols, it is impossible to provide a general, fully automatic technique which performs the suitable generalization steps in all cases. However, we have followed an approach that, in the case of the parameterized Peterson's protocol, works in a systematic way. This approach extends to the case of logic programs with array formulas some generalization techniques which are used for the specialization of (constraint) logic programs [8, 14] and it can be briefly described as follows.

The new predicate definitions introduced during Step (iii) of Phase A of the transformation strategy are arranged as a tree *DefsTree* of clauses. The root of *DefsTree* is clause 2. Given a clause N, the children of N are the predicate definitions which are introduced to fold the instances of $holds(X, F)$ in the bodies of the clauses obtained by unfolding N at Step (i) and not removed at Step (ii).

If the new predicate definitions are introduced without any guidance, then we may construct a tree *DefsTree* with infinite paths, and the transformation strategy may not terminate. In order to avoid the construction of infinite paths and achieve the termination of the transformation strategy, before adding a new predicate definition D to *DefsTree* as a child of a clause N, we match D against every clause A occurring in the path from the root of *DefsTree* to N. Suppose that A is of the form $newp(X) \leftarrow \alpha \land holds(X, \psi)$ and D is of the form $newq(X) \leftarrow \delta \land holds(X, \psi)$. If the array formula α is *embedded* (with respect to a suitable ordering) into the array formula δ, then instead of introducing D, we introduce a clause of the form $gen(X) \leftarrow \gamma \wedge holds(X, \psi)$, where γ is a generalization of both α and δ, that is, both $M(Arrays) \models \forall (\alpha \rightarrow \gamma)$ and $M(Arrays) \models \forall (\delta \rightarrow \gamma)$ holds.

Thus, in order to fully mechanize our generalization technique we need to address the following two problems: (i) the introduction of a formal definition of the *embedding* relation between array formulas, and (ii) the computation of the array formula γ from α and δ. Providing solutions to these two problems is beyond the scope of the present paper. However, a possible approach to follow for solving these problems consists in extending to logic programs with array formulas the notions that have been introduced in the area of specialization of (constraint) logic programs (see, for instance, [8, 14]).

6   Related Work and Conclusions

The method for protocol verification presented in this paper is based on the program transformation approach which has been proposed in [21] for the verification of properties of locally stratified logic programs. We consider concurrent systems of *finite state* processes. We assume that systems are *parameterized*, in the sense that they consist of an *arbitrary* number of processes. We also assume that parameterized systems may use arrays of parameterized length. The properties of the systems we want to verify, are the temporal logic properties which can be expressed in CTL (Computational Tree Logic) [5]. Our method consists in: (i) encoding a parameterized system and the property to be verified as a locally stratified logic program extended with array formulas, and then (ii) applying suitable unfold/fold transformations to this program so to derive a new program where it is immediate to check whether or not the property holds.

In general, the problem of verifying CTL properties of parameterized systems is undecidable [2] and thus, in order to find decision procedures, one has to consider subclasses of systems where the problem is decidable. Some of these decidable subclasses in the presence of arrays have been studied in [13], but unfortunately, our formalization of the parameterized Peterson's protocol does not belong to any of those classes, because it requires more than two arrays of natural numbers, and also requires assignments and reset operations.

As yet, our method is *not* fully mechanical and human intervention is needed for: (i) the test of satisfiability for array formulas, and (ii) the introduction of new definitions by generalization. We have discussed these two issues in Section 5.

Other verification methods for concurrent systems based on the transformational approach are those presented in [9, 10, 15, 23, 24].

In [9] it is presented a method for verifying CTL properties of systems consisting of a *fixed number* of infinite state processes. That method makes use of locally stratified constraint logic programs, where the constraints are linear equations and disequations on real numbers. In this paper we have followed an approach similar to constraint logic programming, but in our setting we have array formulas, instead of constraints. The method presented here can easily be extended to deal with parameterized infinite state systems by considering, for instance, arrays of infinite state processes.

The paper [10] describes the verification of the mutual exclusion property for the parameterized Bakery protocol which was introduced in [12]. In [10] the authors use locally stratified logic programs extended with formulas of the Weak Monadic Second Order Theory of k-Successors (WSkS) which expresses monadic properties of strings. The array formulas considered in this paper are more expressive than WSkS formulas, because array formulas can express polyadic properties. However, there is price to pay, because in general the theory of array formulas is undecidable, while the theory WSkS is decidable.

The method described in [15] uses partial deduction and abstract interpretation of logic programs for verifying safety properties of infinite state systems. Partial deduction is strictly less powerful than unfold/fold program transformation, which, on the other hand, is more difficult to mechanize when unrestricted transformations are considered. One of the main objectives of our future research is the design of suitably restricted unfold/fold transformations which are easily mechanizable and yet powerful enough for the verification of program properties.

The work presented in [23, 24] is the most similar to ours. The authors of these two papers use unfold/fold rules for transforming programs and proving properties of parameterized concurrent systems. Our paper differs from [23, 24] in that, instead of using definite logic programs, we use logic programs with locally stratified negation and array formulas for the specification of concurrent systems and their properties. As a consequence, also the transformation rules we consider are different and more general than those used in [23, 24].

Besides the above mentioned transformational methods, some more verification methods based on (constraint) logic programming have been proposed in the literature [7, 11, 19, 22].

The methods proposed in [19, 22] deal with finite state systems only. In particular, the method presented in [19] uses constraint logic programming with finite domains, extended with constructive negation and tabled resolution, for finite state local model checking, and the method described in [22] uses tabled logic programming to efficiently verify μ-calculus properties of finite state systems expressed in the CCS calculus.

The methods presented in [7, 11] deal with infinite state systems. In particular, [7] describes a method which is based on constraint logic programming and can be applied for verifying CTL properties of infinite state systems by computing approximations of least and greatest fixpoints via abstract interpretation. An extension of this method has also been used for the verification of parameterized cache coherence protocols [6]. The method described in [11] uses logic programs with linear arithmetic constraints and Presburger arithmetic for the verification of safety properties of Petri nets. Unfortunately, however, parameterized systems that use arrays, like Peterson's protocol, cannot be directly specified and verified using the methods considered in [7, 11] because, in general, array formulas cannot be encoded as constraints over real numbers or Presburger formulas.

Several other verification techniques for parameterized systems have been proposed in the literature outside the area of logic programming (see [29] for a survey of some of these techniques). These techniques extend finite state model checking with various forms of *abstraction* (for reducing the verification of a parameterized system to the verification of a finite state system) or *induction* (for proving properties for every value of the parameter).

We do not have space here to discuss the relationships of our work with the many techniques for proving properties based on abstraction. We only want to mention the technique proposed in [3], which has also been applied for the verification of the parameterized Peterson's protocol. That technique can be applied for verifying in an automatic way safety properties of all systems that satisfy a so-called *stratification* condition. Indeed, when this condition holds for a given parameterized system, then the verification task can be reduced to the verification of a finite number of finite state systems that are instances of the given parameterized system for suitable values of the parameter. However, Peterson's protocol does *not* satisfy the stratification condition and its treatment with the technique proposed in [3] requires a significant amount of ingenuity.

Our verification method is also related to the verification techniques based on induction (see, for instance, [18]). These techniques use interactive theorem proving tools where many tasks are mechanized, but the construction of a whole proof requires substantial human guidance. Our method has advantages and disadvantages with respect to these techniques based on induction. On one hand, in our approach we need neither explicit induction on the parameter of the system nor the introduction of suitable induction hypotheses. On the other hand, as already mentioned, our method needs suitable generalization steps which cannot be fully mechanized.

References

1. K. R. Apt and R. N. Bol. Logic programming and negation: A survey. *Journal of Logic Programming*, 19, 20:9–71, 1994.
2. K. R. Apt and D. C. Kozen. Limits for automatic verification of finite-state concurrent systems. *Information Processing Letters*, 22(6):307–309, 1986.
3. T. Arons, A. Pnueli, S. Ruah, J. Xu, and L. D. Zuck. Parameterized verification with automatically computed inductive assertions. In *Proceedings of CAV 2001*, Lecture Notes in Computer Science 2102, pages 221–234. Springer, July 2001.
4. R. M. Burstall and J. Darlington. A transformation system for developing recursive programs. *Journal of the ACM*, 24(1):44–67, January 1977.
5. E. M. Clarke, O. Grumberg, and D. Peled. *Model Checking*. MIT Press, 2000.
6. G. Delzanno. Constraint-based verification of parameterized cache coherence protocols. *Formal Methods in System Design*, 23(3):257–301, 2003.
7. G. Delzanno and A. Podelski. Constraint-based deductive model checking. *International Journal on Software Tools for Technology Transfer*, 3(3):250–270, 2001.
8. F. Fioravanti, A. Pettorossi, and M. Proietti. Automated strategies for specializing constraint logic programs. In K.-K. Lau, editor, *Proceedings of LOPSTR 2000, London, UK, 24-28 July, 2000*, LLNCS 2042, pages 125–146. Springer, 2001.

9. F. Fioravanti, A. Pettorossi, and M. Proietti. Verifying CTL properties of infinite state systems by specializing constraint logic programs. In *Proceedings of VCL '01, Florence, Italy*, DSSE-TR-2001-3, pages 85–96. Univ. of Southampton, UK, 2001.

10. F. Fioravanti, A. Pettorossi, and M. Proietti. Verification of sets of infinite state systems using program transformation. In *Proceedings of LOPSTR '01*, Lecture Notes in Computer Science 2372, pages 111–128. Springer, 2002.

11. L. Fribourg and H. Olsén. A decompositional approach for computing least fixedpoints of Datalog programs with Z-counters. *Constraints*, 2(3/4):305–335, 1997.

12. L. Lamport. A new solution of Dijkstra's concurrent programming problem. *Communications of the ACM*, 17(8):453–455, 1974.

13. R. Lazic, T. C. Newcomb, and A. W. Roscoe. On model checking data-independent systems with arrays with whole-array operations. In *Communicating Sequential Processes: The First 25 Years*, LNCS 3525, pages 275–291. Springer, 2004.

14. M. Leuschel and M. Bruynooghe. Logic program specialisation through partial deduction: Control issues. *Theory and Practice of Logic Programming*, 2(4&5): 461–515, 2002.

15. M. Leuschel and T. Massart. Infinite state model checking by abstract interpretation and program specialization. In A. Bossi, editor, *Proceedings of LOPSTR '99, Venice, Italy*, LNCS 1817, pages 63–82. Springer, 1999.

16. J. W. Lloyd. *Foundations of Logic Programming*. Springer-Verlag, Berlin, 1987. Second Edition.

17. MAP group. The MAP transformation system. Available from: http://www.iasi.rm.cnr.it/~proietti/system.html, 1995–2005.

18. K. L. McMillan, S. Qadeer, and J. B. Saxe. Induction in compositional model checking. In *Proceedings of CAV '00*, LNCS 1855, pages 312–327. Springer, 2000.

19. U. Nilsson and J. Lübcke. Constraint logic programming for local and symbolic model-checking. In *Proceedings of CL '00*, LNAI 1861, pp. 384–398. Springer, 2000.

20. G. L. Peterson. Myths about the mutual exclusion problem. *Information Processing Letters*, 12(3):115–116, 1981.

21. A. Pettorossi and M. Proietti. Perfect model checking via unfold/fold transformations. In J. W. Lloyd, editor, *First International Conference on Computational Logic, CL 2000*, LNAI 1861, pages 613–628. Springer, 2000.

22. Y. S. Ramakrishna, C. R. Ramakrishnan, I. V. Ramakrishnan, S. A. Smolka, T. Swift, and D. S. Warren. Efficient model checking using tabled resolution. In *Proceedings of CAV '97*, LNCS 1254, pages 143–154. Springer-Verlag, 1997.

23. A. Roychoudhury and I. V. Ramakrishnan. Automated inductive verification of parameterized protocols. In *Proceedings of CAV '01*, pages 25–37, 2001.

24. A. Roychoudhury and C. R. Ramakrishnan. Unfold/fold transformations for automated verification. In M. Bruynooghe and K.-K. Lau, editors, *Program Development in Computational Logic*, LNCS 3049, pages 261–290. Springer, 2004.

25. H. Seki. Unfold/fold transformation of stratified programs. *Theoretical Computer Science*, 86:107–139, 1991.

26. V. Senni. Transformational verification of the parameterized Peterson's protocol. Unpublished note, July 2005.

27. N. Shankar. Combining theorem proving and model checking through symbolic analysis. In *CONCUR 2000*, LNCS 1877, pages 1–16, Springer, 2000.

28. A. Stump, C. W. Barrett, D. L. Dill, and J. R. Levitt. A decision procedure for an extensional theory of arrays. In *LICS '01*, pages 29–37. IEEE Press, 2001.

29. L. D. Zuck and A. Pnueli. Model checking and abstraction to the aid of parameterized systems (a survey). *Computer Languages, Systems & Structures*, 30(3-4): 139–169, 2004.

Appendix

Below we give the definitions of the array formulas $genc_2$ through $genc_8$ occurring in the program R of Section 4.

$genc_2(s(P,J,Q,S)) \equiv_{def}$
$\quad \exists i,l(rd(P,i,\lambda) \wedge l>1 \wedge rd(J,i,1) \wedge rd(Q,i,1) \wedge rd(S,1,i) \wedge$
$\qquad \forall k(1 \leq k \leq l \rightarrow ((rd(P,k,ncs) \wedge rd(Q,k,0)) \vee$
$\qquad\qquad\qquad\qquad\quad (rd(P,k,w) \wedge rd(J,k,1) \wedge rd(Q,k,0)) \vee$
$\qquad\qquad\qquad\qquad\quad (rd(P,k,\lambda) \wedge rd(J,k,1) \wedge rd(Q,k,1)))) \wedge$
$\quad ln(P,l) \wedge ln(J,l) \wedge ln(Q,l) \wedge ln(S,l))$

$genc_3(s(P,J,Q,S)) \equiv_{def}$
$\quad \exists i,k,l(2 \leq k < l \wedge ((rd(P,i,w) \wedge rd(J,i,k+1) \wedge rd(Q,i,k) \wedge rd(S,k,i)) \vee$
$\qquad\qquad\qquad\qquad (rd(P,i,\lambda) \wedge rd(J,i,k) \wedge rd(Q,i,k) \wedge rd(S,k,i))) \wedge$
$\qquad \forall j((1 \leq j \leq l \wedge \neg(j=i)) \rightarrow ((rd(P,j,ncs) \wedge rd(Q,j,0)) \vee$
$\qquad\qquad\qquad\qquad\qquad\qquad\qquad (rd(P,j,w) \wedge rd(J,j,1) \wedge rd(Q,j,0)))) \wedge$
$\quad ln(P,l) \wedge ln(J,l) \wedge ln(Q,l) \wedge ln(S,l))$

$genc_4(s(P,J,Q,S)) \equiv_{def}$
$\quad \exists m,l(1 \leq m \leq l \wedge \forall k(1 \leq k < m \rightarrow$
$\qquad\qquad\qquad\qquad\qquad \exists i(rd(P,i,\lambda) \wedge rd(J,i,k) \wedge rd(Q,i,k) \wedge rd(S,k,i))) \wedge$
$\qquad \forall j(1 \leq j \leq l \rightarrow ((rd(P,j,ncs) \wedge rd(Q,j,0)) \vee$
$\qquad\qquad\qquad\qquad \exists k(1 \leq k < m \wedge ((rd(P,j,w) \wedge rd(J,j,k+1) \wedge rd(Q,j,k)) \vee$
$\qquad\qquad\qquad\qquad\qquad\qquad\quad (rd(P,j,\lambda) \wedge rd(J,j,k) \wedge rd(Q,j,k)))))) \wedge$
$\quad ln(P,l) \wedge ln(J,l) \wedge ln(Q,l) \wedge ln(S,l))$

$genc_5(s(P,J,Q,S)) \equiv_{def}$
$\quad \exists i,k,l(2 \leq k < l \wedge ((rd(P,i,w) \wedge rd(J,i,k+1) \wedge rd(Q,i,k) \wedge rd(S,k,i)) \vee$
$\qquad\qquad\qquad\qquad (rd(P,i,\lambda) \wedge rd(J,i,k) \wedge rd(Q,i,k) \wedge rd(S,k,i))) \wedge$
$\qquad \exists m(1 \leq m \leq k \wedge$
$\qquad\qquad \forall u(1 \leq u \leq m \rightarrow$
$\qquad\qquad\qquad \exists j(rd(P,j,\lambda) \wedge rd(J,j,u) \wedge rd(Q,j,u) \wedge rd(S,u,j))) \wedge$
$\qquad\qquad \forall n((1 \leq n \leq l \wedge \neg(n=i)) \rightarrow$
$\qquad\qquad\qquad ((rd(P,n,ncs) \wedge rd(Q,n,0)) \vee$
$\qquad\qquad\qquad\quad \exists r(1 \leq r \leq m \wedge$
$\qquad\qquad\qquad\qquad ((rd(P,n,w) \wedge rd(J,n,r+1) \wedge rd(Q,n,r)) \vee$
$\qquad\qquad\qquad\qquad\quad (rd(P,n,\lambda) \wedge rd(J,n,r) \wedge rd(Q,n,r))))))) \wedge$
$\quad ln(P,l) \wedge ln(J,l) \wedge ln(Q,l) \wedge ln(S,l))$

$genc_6(s(P,J,Q,S)) \equiv_{def}$
$\quad \exists i,l,u(rd(P,i,cs) \wedge rd(J,i,u+1) \wedge rd(Q,i,u) \wedge rd(S,u,i) \wedge u+1=l \wedge$
$\qquad \forall j((1 \leq j \leq l \wedge \neg(j=i)) \rightarrow ((rd(P,k,ncs) \wedge rd(Q,k,0)) \vee$
$\qquad\qquad\qquad\qquad\qquad\qquad\qquad (rd(P,k,w) \wedge rd(J,k,1) \wedge rd(Q,k,0)))) \wedge$
$\quad ln(P,l) \wedge ln(J,l) \wedge ln(Q,l) \wedge ln(S,l))$

$genc_7(s(P, J, Q, S)) \equiv_{def}$
$\quad \exists i, l, u(rd(P, i, cs) \wedge rd(J, i, u+1) \wedge rd(Q, i, u) \wedge u+1=l \wedge$
$\qquad \forall k(1 \leq k < l \rightarrow \exists i(rd(P, i, \lambda) \wedge rd(J, i, k) \wedge rd(Q, i, k) \wedge rd(S, k, i))) \wedge$
$\qquad ln(P, l) \wedge ln(J, l) \wedge ln(Q, l) \wedge ln(S, l))$

$genc_8(s(P, J, Q, S)) \equiv_{def}$
$\quad \exists i, l, u(rd(P, i, cs) \wedge rd(J, i, u+1) \wedge rd(Q, i, u) \wedge u+1=l \wedge$
$\qquad \exists m(1 \leq m \leq l \wedge \forall n(1 \leq n < m \rightarrow$
$\qquad\qquad\qquad \exists j(rd(P, j, \lambda) \wedge rd(J, j, n) \wedge rd(Q, j, n) \wedge rd(S, n, j))) \wedge$
$\qquad \forall j((1 \leq j \leq l \wedge \neg(j=i)) \rightarrow$
$\qquad\quad ((rd(P, j, ncs) \wedge rd(Q, j, 0)) \vee$
$\qquad\quad \exists k(1 \leq k < m \wedge$
$\qquad\qquad ((rd(P, j, w) \wedge rd(J, j, k+1) \wedge rd(Q, j, k)) \vee$
$\qquad\qquad (rd(P, j, \lambda) \wedge rd(J, j, k) \wedge rd(Q, j, k))))))) \wedge$
$\qquad ln(P, l) \wedge ln(J, l) \wedge ln(Q, l) \wedge ln(S, l))$

Design and Implementation of $\mathcal{A}_T$: A Real-Time Action Description Language

Luke Simon, Ajay Mallya, and Gopal Gupta

Department of Computer Science,
University of Texas at Dallas

Abstract. Real world applications of action description languages involve systems that have real-time constraints. The occurrence of an action is just as important as the time at which the action occurs. In order to be able to model such real-time systems, the action description language A is extended with real-time clocks and constraints. The formal syntax and semantics of the extended language are defined, and the use of logic programming as a means to an implementation of real-time A is discussed.

1 Introduction

Non-monotonic reasoning has been an area of intense study in the recent past [2]. Within non-monotonic reasoning, considerable attention has been paid to reasoning with action and change [4]. Actions induce non-monotonic behavior since they cause a change in the state of the world. Research in this area has included the design of *action description languages (ADLs)*: high level languages that allow systematic reasoning about actions and state change in dynamic environments [2]. An example of such a language is the language $\mathcal{A}$ designed by Gelfond and Lifschitz. The language $\mathcal{A}$ has been used to elegantly specify and reason about a number of classical problems such as the Yale shooting problem [4], and it has also been applied to a number of practical situations [15].

Action description languages describe the effect of actions on the truth value of logical propositions. Given a system description in $\mathcal{A}$, one can reason to find out the state(s) that results from a sequence of actions, or given a resultant state, deduce the sequence of actions that will lead us there. These actions are assumed to occur in a sequential (i.e., non-concurrent) manner, with the time intervals between two consecutive actions being arbitrary. Thus, the exact time at which the actions occur, or the elapsed time interval between two actions is of no consequence in such a language.

In practice, however, one has to reason about actions and change in a time-bound world, where actions may have to be performed within a certain time, or actions may have to be performed after a certain amount of time has elapsed. For instance, if we consider the classical Yale shooting problem, one may wish to model the fact that if the shooting does not take place within 30 seconds then the person being shot may go out of range. A difficulty with modeling

P.M. Hill (Ed.): LOPSTR 2005, LNCS 3901, pp. 44–60, 2006.

such time-dependent actions is that real-time is continuous, making its modeling and reasoning hard. Recently, however, constraint logic programming over the domain of real numbers has been shown to be suitable for modeling and reasoning with such continuous time [6].

In this paper, we show how action description languages can be extended to *real-time action description languages*. The notion of *timed actions*—an action with time constraints attached—is introduced. Timed ADLs can be used to systematically reason about actions and state-change in dynamic environments in the presence of real-time constraints. Thus, if the action of dropping a glass causes it to be broken, then with the added ability to reason with real-time, one can reason that dropping a glass causes it to be broken, unless it is caught within half a second (i.e., before it hits the floor).

In the rest of the paper we describe how we've extended the language $\mathcal{A}$ with real-time to obtain the language $\mathcal{A}_T$. The complete syntax and semantics of $\mathcal{A}_T$ is given, along with a description of its prototype implementation that we have recently completed. The model-theoretic semantics of action description languages is given in terms of a labeled transition system [4]. Similarly, the model-theoretic semantics of real-time systems is given in terms of timed automata [1]. We combine these two notions and give the semantics of $\mathcal{A}_T$ in terms of *timed transition systems*. Next, we render this semantics executable by denotationally mapping it to Constraint Logic Programming over reals (CLP($\mathcal{R}$)) [7]. This executable semantics serves as an implementation of $\mathcal{A}_T$.

This paper makes a number of contributions: (i) it presents the Real-timed Action Description Language $\mathcal{A}_T$ that can be used to elegantly model actions and change in the presence of real-time constraints; (ii) it presents the semantics of this new language, along with its implementation, based on constraint logic programming over reals; and, (iii) it paves the way for further constraint-based extensions of action description languages (such as action description languages where actions are constrained by the amount of resource, not just the presence or absence of a resource), and the incorporation of continuous real-time in planning applications.

We assume that the reader is familiar with CLP($\mathcal{R}$) as well as with timed automata. A detailed exposition can be found in [7] and [1] respectively.

2   Action Description Languages

Action description languages are high-level languages used to systematically reason about actions and state change in dynamic environments. These languages have proved to be a useful tool for solving various aspects of planning problems, such as plan specification and verification, planning with domain specific constraints and plan diagnosis and explanation [15, 2]. Given a partial description of the state of the world, and a sequence of actions and their properties, it is possible to deduce the state induced by the action sequence. Also, given a state that results from a sequence of actions, it is required to deduce information about past states. In the next section, we describe the action description language

$\mathcal{A}$ [4], with a discussion of its syntax and semantics. The language has a simple syntax that is used to specify properties of actions and an automata-theoretic semantics to reason about sequences of actions.

2.1   The Action Description Language $\mathcal{A}$

The action description language $\mathcal{A}$ provides a mechanism for describing action domains. Before we delve into the details of the language, we will introduce the notion of *fluents*. Intuitively, a fluent is something whose value depends upon the state, for example, the position of the ball on a soccer field. In this paper, we will use *propositional* fluents that take on the truth values *true* and *false* according to the state of the world. The language provides two different kinds of propositions: (i) a *value proposition*, that describes the truth value of a fluent in a particular state where the state can either be an initial state or a state resulting from a sequence of actions; (ii) an *effect proposition*, that describes the effect a given action has on a fluent.

The language $\mathcal{A}$ provides two different sets of symbols, *fluent names* and *action names*. Fluents that might be optionally preceded by a ¬ are called *fluent expressions*. A *value proposition* has the following syntax

$$F \textbf{ after } A_1; \ldots; A_m,$$

where F is a fluent expression and $A_1, \ldots, A_m$ $(m \geq 0)$ are action names. If $m = 0$, the above value proposition is written as

$$\textbf{initially } F.$$

An *effect proposition* has the syntax

$$A \textbf{ causes } F \textbf{ if } P_1, \ldots, P_n,$$

where A is an action name, and each of $F, P_1, \ldots, P_n$ $(n \geq 0)$ is a fluent expression. The effect proposition describes the effect that the action A has on the fluent F, subject to the *preconditions* $P_1, \ldots, P_n$. If $n = 0$, the above effect proposition is written as

$$A \textbf{ causes } F$$

We say that a *domain* consists of a possibly infinite set of value propositions and a finite set of effect propositions.

Example 1. The Yale Shooting domain [4], consists of the fluents *Loaded* and *Alive*. The action names are *Load*, *Shoot* and *Wait*. The propositions constituting the domain are

> **initially** ¬*Loaded*,
> **initially** *Alive*,
> *Load* **causes** *Loaded*,
> *Shoot* **causes** ¬*Alive* **if** *Loaded*,
> *Shoot* **causes** ¬*Loaded*.

A state consists of a set of fluents. A fluent name F holds in state σ if $F \in \sigma$ and ¬F holds in σ if $F \notin \sigma$. A *transition function* is a mapping Φ from the set of pairs (A, σ) to states. A *structure* is a tuple (σ_0, Φ), where σ_0 is called the *initial state* and Φ is a transition function.

A structure (σ_0, Φ) is a *model* of a domain D if every value proposition in D is true in the structure, and for every action name A, every fluent name F and every state σ, the following hold [4]:

1. if D includes an effect proposition describing the effect of A on F, whose preconditions are valid in σ, then $F \in \Phi(A, \sigma)$.
2. if D includes an effect proposition describing the effect of A on $\neg F$ whose preconditions are valid in σ, then $F \notin \Phi(A, \sigma)$.
3. if D does not include such effect propositions, then $F \in \Phi(A, \sigma)$ iff $F \in \sigma$.

3   Real-Time Systems

An important application of computing systems is in domains where response within a hard time bound is critical for success. These systems are called *real-time systems*. Examples include controllers for aircraft, industrial machinery and robots. These domains, by their very nature, have certain constraints, which if violated, can cause unacceptable consequences. Therefore it is essential to have a systematic framework to reason about properties of actions in real-time domains. The design of real-time systems has traditionally been studied from the perspective of scheduling [9]. However, this approach has the limitation that the only properties one can reason about are those which can be formulated in terms of task execution times. Also, due to the safety critical nature of the domain, the scheduling strategy is usually conservative, assuming that all task execution times are known in advance, thereby precluding its application in dynamic environments.

Due to these problems, it is fruitful to look at real-time systems from the planning perspective and explore the use of action description languages to reason about real-time properties of actions. This requires action description languages to be extended with the notion of *continuous time*. Time is modeled as a continuous entity, because in most real-time systems, the delay between events can be arbitrarily small. The theory of *timed automata* [1] has become the standard for analysis of real-time systems with continuous time.

3.1   Timed Automata

Timed automata are finite state automata with a finite set of *clocks*, which take values over the reals. While the clocks advance their values in the states of the timed automaton, transitions are assumed to be instantaneous. However, a transition may reset some of the clocks to zero (thus these clocks can be thought of as stopwatches). At any instant of time, the reading on a clock shows the time that has elapsed since the clock was last reset. Time is assumed to advance at the same rate on all of the clocks. A clock constraint is associated with each transition of the timed automaton. The transition occurs only if the clock constraint is satisfied. A clock constraint is also associated with each state of the timed automaton. The automaton can remain in a state as long as the clock constraint associated with that state is satisfied. Given a set X of clocks, the set of clock constraints $\mathcal{C}(X)$ is given by the following grammar:

$$\varphi := x \leq c \mid c \leq x \mid x < c \mid c < x \mid \varphi_1 \wedge \varphi_2$$

Formally, a timed automaton is defined as a tuple $(S, S_0, \Sigma, X, I, E)$, where

- S is a finite set of *states*
- $S_0 \subseteq S$ is a set of *initial states*
- Σ is a finite *alphabet*
- $I : S \rightarrow \mathcal{C}(X)$ is a mapping that maps states in S to clock constraints
- $E \subseteq S \times \Sigma \times \mathcal{C}(X) \times 2^X \times S$ is a set of transitions. Each tuple $(s, a, \varphi, \lambda, s')$ in E corresponds to a transition from location s to location s' labeled with a, a constraint φ that specifies when the transition is enabled, and a set of clocks $\lambda \subseteq X$, which are reset by the transition.

A comprehensive survey of Timed Automata can be found in [1].

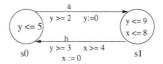

Fig. 1. A simple timed automaton

Consider the example timed automaton in Fig. 1. It consists of two states s_0 and s_1, s_0 being the initial state. There is a transition from s_0 to s_1 on the symbol a subject to the clock y being greater than or equal to 2 time units, while resetting the clock y, and a transition from s_1 to s_0 labeled by the symbol b, subject to the clock x being greater than or equal to 4 units and the clock y being greater than or equal to 3 units. The clock x is reset by this transition.

3.2   Shortcomings of $\mathcal{A}$

The language $\mathcal{A}$ allows one to reason about properties of temporal sequences of actions. In other words, time is dealt with in a qualitative manner. On the other hand, for real-time domains, it is essential to reason about time in a quantitative manner, i.e., in addition to reasoning about sequences of actions, it is also essential to reason about the deadlines that these actions have to meet. To the best of our knowledge, current action description languages do not have the capability to reason about real-time in this manner. There are many situations where this capability is needed. For example, if we consider the Yale shooting problem, we may want to reason that if a loaded gun is shot, then $\neg Alive$ will become true only if the shot is fired within 30 seconds of loading the gun (otherwise the person will get away, or the ammunition will not work). Similarly, we may want to reason that the drop action will cause a breakable object to shatter, unless it is caught within 0.5 seconds, thus preventing it from hitting the ground and breaking.

Action description languages can be used for specifying controllers and developing plans for machines, plants, and robots [15]. In these real-life situations, most actions will have severe time constraints attached. One can argue that an action description language, augmented with the capability to reason with time, will have significantly more applications; for example, in safety-critical systems. We next propose an extension to the action description language $\mathcal{A}$, which provides the machinery to specify and reason about real-time actions.

4   The Timed Action Description Language $\mathcal{A}_T$

We would like to be able to apply action description languages such as language $\mathcal{A}$ to real-time systems. Extending action description language $\mathcal{A}$ with real-time involves augmenting actions with clock constraints describing when the action occurs, and effect propositions must be augmented with preconditions on clocks and the ability to mutate clocks. These extensions give rise to a language we call $\mathcal{A}_T$, which is a conservative extension of language $\mathcal{A}$ in the sense that language $\mathcal{A}$ is a syntactic and semantic subset of $\mathcal{A}_T$. The following subsections cover $\mathcal{A}_T$ syntax and semantics.

4.1   Syntax

A real-time action α is defined as the pairing of an action name with a list of its clock constraints. In $\mathcal{A}_T$, this is written as

$$A \textbf{ at } T_1, \ldots, T_n$$

where $T_1 \ldots, T_n$ $(n \geq 0)$ are clock constraints of the form $C \leq E$, $C \geq E$, $C < E$, and $C > E$, where C is a clock name and E is a clock name or a clock name plus or minus a real valued constant, and when $n = 0$ the **at** clause can be dropped.

Now that we can explicitly state when an action occurs, value propositions are extended in a straightforward manner, given fluent expressions $F_1, \ldots, F_m$ $(m > 0)$ and real-time actions $\alpha_1, \ldots, \alpha_n$ $(n \geq 0)$ then a real-time value proposition is of the form:

$$F_1, \ldots, F_m \textbf{ after } \alpha_1; \ldots; \alpha_n$$

Note how inconsistent descriptions can arise from a real-time value proposition including a sequence of actions occurring at inconsistent times. However, even a language as simple as language $\mathcal{A}$ allowed for inconsistent descriptions, so clock constraints are simply another source of inconsistency. Furthermore, the typical abbreviation when the sequence of actions is empty, i.e., $n = 0$ is still written

$$\textbf{initially } F_1, \ldots, F_m$$

These degenerate forms of real-time value propositions simply serve as a means to describe the start state of a real-time system by asserting which fluents are true or false in the start state. Hence these degenerate real-time value propositions serve the exact same purpose as in language $\mathcal{A}$. As will be discussed in section 4.3, all clocks are assumed to be reset when initially entering the start state of a real-time system.

The most significant extension occurs with the effect proposition. Real-time effect propositions, also sometimes referred to as action rules, must be able to describe the fluent preconditions as well as the clock preconditions for the rule to apply. Moreover, in addition to describing how fluents are mutated, real-time effect propositions must also be able to describe how clocks are changed, by resetting some subset of them. So real-time effect propositions are of the form

$$A \textbf{ causes } F_1, \ldots, F_m \textbf{ resets } C_1, \ldots C_n \textbf{ when } T_1, \ldots, T_k \textbf{ if } P_1, \ldots, P_i$$

for action name A, fluent expressions $F_1 \ldots, F_m, P_1, \ldots, P_i$ $(m, i \geq 0)$, clock names $C_1, \ldots, C_n$ $(n \geq 0)$, and clock constraints $T_1, \ldots, T_k$ $(k \geq 0)$, where $m + n + k + i > 0$. As usual, when m, n, k, or i is zero the keywords **causes**, **resets**, **when**, or **if** respectively, can be dropped. The **resets** clause denotes the clocks that are to be reset assuming the fluent preconditions and **when** clause are satisfied. Clocks that are not reset continue to advance.

One last extension is needed [4]: A special action name **wait** denotes the action of waiting for time to elapse. Therefore it acts as a sort of wild-card that matches all other action names. This is demonstrated in the following examples.

4.2   Examples

Example 2. The Real-time Falling Object domain, a modification of an example from [4] with the notion that a dropped object can be caught before it hits the ground assuming the object takes 1 second to hit the ground.

> *Drop* **causes** $\neg Holding$, *Falling* **resets** *Clock* **if** *Holding*, $\neg Falling$
> *Catch* **causes** *Holding*, $\neg Falling$ **when** $Clock \leq 1$ **if** $\neg Holding$, *Falling*
> **wait causes** *Broken*, $\neg Falling$ **when** $Clock > 1$ **if** $\neg Holding$, *Falling*

Firstly, note that the assumption that units are in seconds is merely a convention used in this example. As far as the language $\mathcal{A}_T$ is concerned, all clocks are simply real valued variables. Furthermore, as is the case with language A, the language $\mathcal{A}_T$ possibly describes many possible worlds. In one of these worlds **initially** $Holding, \neg Falling, \neg Broken$ is true, and therefore $Broken$ **after** $Drop$; **wait at** $Clock = 2$ also holds as the object is dropped and then allowed to fall to the ground. Similarly, in that same world, if one takes too long to catch the object, the object still shatters on the ground. Hence in the aforementioned world $Broken$ **after** $Drop$; $Catch$ **at** $Clock = 2$ is also true. However, if the object is dropped and then is successfully caught, say half a second after dropping and therefore before it hits the ground, then as expected, the object is not broken by the sequence of events, i.e., $\neg Broken$ **after** $Drop$; $Catch$ **at** $Clock = 0.5$ is true.

Other possible worlds include the object starting out already in a falling state, while another world could even have the object already broken. The more information given in a description, the fewer possible worlds exist that satisfy the description. For example, assume that in addition to the original Real-time Falling Object domain description, it is also given that *Broken* **after** *Drop; Catch* **at** *Clock* = 0.5 is true, then it can safely be deduced that the object was broken to begin with, i.e., according to this new description it is true that **initially** *Broken*.

Example 3. Similarly, the real-time Soccer Playing domain is a modification of a domain described in [20]. It has the following domain description:

$ShotTaken$ **causes** $\neg HasBall$, $\neg ClearShot$, $Goal$ **when** $Clock \leq 0.5$
　　　　　　if $HasBall$, $ClearShot$, $\neg Goal$
$PassBall$ **causes** $ClearShot$ **resets Clock when** $Clock \leq 1$
　　　　　　if $\neg ClearShot$
wait causes $\neg HasBall$, $\neg ClearShot$ **when** $Clock > 0.5$
　　　　　　if $HasBall$, $ClearShot$
wait causes $\neg HasBall$, **when** $Clock > 1$ **if** $HasBall$

In the real-time Soccer Playing domain, a player has the ball and has a clear shot at the goal, then it is assumed that a goal is scored if the player can take a shot within 0.5 time units. If the player does not take the shot within this time, the ball gets stripped by an opponent. Also, a player who has possession of the ball, but no clear shot at the goal can pass the ball to a team-mate who has a clear shot. The pass has to be completed within 1 time unit. Failure to do so results in the ball getting intercepted by an opponent.

In one possible world, **initially** $HasBall$, $ClearShot$, $\neg Goal$ holds and therefore $Goal$ **after** $ShotTaken$ **at** $Clock = 0.2$ is also true. However, in an alternative world, if the player does not have a clear shot, and the ball is passed to a teammate who has a clear shot, then if the teammate does not take the shot within 0.5 time units, possession of the ball is lost. Therefore the statement $\neg HasBall$ **after** $PassBall; wait$ **at** $Clock = 1$ is true.

4.3   Semantics of $\mathcal{A}_T$

Now that the language $\mathcal{A}_T$ has been informally introduced, we can more formally specify its semantics. This should not only aid in the understanding of the language, but should also serve as a measure of the correctness of its implementations. As is the case for action language $\mathcal{A}$, the semantics of $\mathcal{A}_T$ is given in terms of a transition system. However, $\mathcal{A}_T$'s transition system is timed and therefore is technically a timed automaton with a finite region graph [1].

The semantics of $\mathcal{A}_T$ is an extension of the semantics for language $\mathcal{A}$. A state σ is a pair (Φ, Θ) where Φ is a subset of fluents and Θ is a function assigning to each clock name a non-negative real value. Let F be a fluent, then F holds in Φ if $F \in \Phi$, and $\neg F$ holds in Φ if $F \notin \Phi$. This truth valuation can be extended to sets of fluent expressions S as follows. S holds in Φ if every $F \in S$ holds in Φ.

A clock valuation Θ satisfies a set of time constraints Ω (see section 4.1), written $S(\Theta, \Omega)$ if and only if replacing every clock name C in Ω with $\Theta(C)$ results in a consistent set. This can be extended to states in a straightforward manner, $S((\Phi, \Theta), \Omega) \equiv S(\Theta, \Omega)$.

A real-time action α is simply a pairing (A, Ω) of an action name A with a set of time constraints Ω, which denotes the time constraints on the occurrence of a specific instantiation of the action named A. In the definition of a model we will also need to enforce the notion that the clocks monotonically increase during a state transition unless they are explicitly reset, and so we say that one clock valuation Θ is less than another valuation Θ' except for the reset clocks Π, written $\Theta \leq_{\Pi} \Theta'$ whenever $\forall C. \Theta(C) \leq_{\Pi} \Theta'(C)$. This can be extended to states such that $(\Phi, \Theta) \leq_{\Pi} (\Phi, \Theta')$ if and only if $\Theta \leq_{\Pi} \Theta'$.

Let $\longrightarrow$ be a ternary relation between egress states, actions, and ingress states such that $\sigma \xrightarrow{\alpha} \sigma'$ if and only if $\sigma \leq_{\emptyset} \sigma''$, $\alpha = (A, \Omega)$, and $S(\sigma'', \Omega)$, then $\longrightarrow$ is called a transition relation. Informally, $\sigma \xrightarrow{\alpha} \sigma'$ means that in state σ executing action α causes the current state to mutate into σ'. Given a start state $\sigma_0 = (\Phi_0, \Theta_0)$ for some set of fluents Φ_0 and clock valuation function Θ_0 such that $\forall C. \Theta_0(C) = 0$, i.e., all clocks are initially reset, a transition relation $\longrightarrow$ determines a system $M = (\sigma_0, \longrightarrow)$. Let $M^{\alpha_1; \dots; \alpha_n}$ denote the possible set of states that a system could be in after executing the sequence of actions $\alpha_1; \dots; \alpha_n$ in system M. The set of states $s = M^{\alpha_1; \dots; \alpha_n}$ where $M = (\sigma_0, \longrightarrow)$ is recursively defined as

$$\begin{array}{ll} \{\sigma_0\} & \text{if } n = 0 \\ \{\sigma' \mid \sigma \in M^{\alpha_1; \dots; \alpha_{n-1}} \wedge \sigma \xrightarrow{\alpha_n} \sigma'\} & \text{otherwise} \end{array}$$

Let $s = M^{\alpha_1; \dots; \alpha_n}$, then if $M^{\alpha_1; \dots; \alpha_n}$ is empty then the sequence of actions is said to be inconsistent. Otherwise if s is nonempty, then real-time value proposition

$$F_1, \dots, F_m \textbf{ after } \alpha_1; \dots; \alpha_n$$

is true (false) in a system M, if for all $(\Phi, \Theta) \in s$, $\{F_1, \dots, F_m\}$ holds (does not hold) in Φ. Otherwise the truth value of such a proposition is unknown, written $\perp$, as in some possible states the system fluents hold and in others they do not hold. We write $V_M(P)$ to denote this truth valuation of real-time value propositions P in system M. The truth valuation can be extended to sets of systems Γ, also known as "possible worlds", in the following manner. Firstly, let Γ be a set of systems, then $\Gamma^{\alpha_1; \dots; \alpha_n} = \{M^{\alpha_1; \dots; \alpha_n} \mid M \in \Gamma\}$. Given a set of systems Γ, then a real-time value proposition $P \equiv F_1, \dots, F_m \textbf{ after } \alpha_1; \dots; \alpha_n$ is assigned a truth value $V_\Gamma(P)$ as follows

$$\begin{array}{ll} inconsistent\,, & \text{if } \Gamma = \emptyset \text{ or } \emptyset \in \Gamma^{\alpha_1; \dots; \alpha_n} \\ true & , \text{ otherwise if } \forall M \in \Gamma. V_M(P) = true \\ false & , \text{ otherwise if } \forall M \in \Gamma. V_M(P) = false \\ \perp & , \text{ otherwise.} \end{array}$$

Again, inconsistency arises when there are no possible worlds corresponding to the proposition and $\perp$ arises when the proposition holds in some worlds but does not hold in other worlds, as is the case in [4].

Before we can define the models of a domain description, we need the following additional nomenclature. Let $reset(\Phi, \Theta, A)$ be the set of all clocks reset by effects propositions in D with preconditions satisfied in state σ. Furthermore, we say that an action A in state σ causes fluent expression F whenever there exists an effects proposition P in D with preconditions satisfied in state σ such that F occurs in the **causes** clause of P.

Now we can define the models of a real-time domain description D. A system M is said to be a model for D when every real-time value proposition P in D is true in M, i.e., $V_M(P) = true$. Furthermore, the transitions in a model must also satisfy the constraints imposed by the domain description's effect propositions. Hence $(\Phi_1, \Theta_1) \xrightarrow{(A,\Omega)} (\Phi_2, \Theta_2)$ in M if and only if there exists a Θ' such that $S(\Theta', \Omega)$, $\Theta_1 \leq_\emptyset \Theta' \leq_{reset(\Phi_1, \Theta', A)} \Theta_2$, and according to the domain description D one of the following holds:

1. action A in state (Φ_1, Θ') causes F and $F \in \Phi_2$
2. action A in state (Φ_1, Θ') causes $\neg F$ and $F \notin \Phi_2$
3. action A in state (Φ_1, Θ') does not cause F or $\neg F$, and $F \in \Phi_2$ if and only if $F \in \Phi_1$

Now we can define entailment. Let Γ be the set of all models of D, then a real-time domain description D entails a real-time value proposition P, if $V_\Gamma(P) = true$, D does not entail P, if $V_\Gamma(P) = false$, and it is unknown if D entails P, if $V_\Gamma(P) = \perp$.

Discussion. The semantics do not prevent different clocks from advancing at different rates, as is the case in the real world. However, it is up to the specific domain description whether or not clocks are further constrained to be synchronized. These semantics are general enough to be applied to other hybrid planning domains, not necessarily involving time, e.g., continuously consumed resources such as battery power or fuel, where it is even more important to be able to model various resources that are consumed at different rates.

4.4 Examples Formalized

The semantics of the real-time Soccer Playing and the real-time Falling Object domains is shown in Fig. 2. These domains were introduced in Section 4.2. The semantics of the real-time Falling Object domain and the real-time Soccer Playing domain are defined by the timed transition systems shown in Fig. 2(a) and Fig. 2(b) respectively. These transition systems define the transition relation $\longrightarrow$ corresponding to the definitions of these domains given in Section 4.2. Note that in the figure, t denotes the clock variable.

Choosing an initial state for a transition system, yields a timed automaton M, which defines a possible world specified by the $\mathcal{A}_T$ description of the corresponding real-time domain. Each possible choice of an initial state yields a different timed automaton and the set of all such timed automata is the set of possible worlds specified by the real-time domain description.

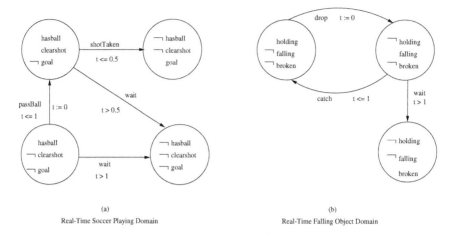

(a)
Real-Time Soccer Playing Domain

(b)
Real-Time Falling Object Domain

Fig. 2. Examples of Real-Time Domains

5   Implementation

The language A_T can easily be implemented using constraint logic programming over the real numbers (CLP($\mathcal{R}$)). The implementation has been done using SIC-Stus Prolog system. A top-level driver is used to parse an input file and then provide an interactive prompt for the user to submit queries against the description in the form of real-time value propositions. The design pattern used is to directly model both the syntax using a Definite Clause Grammar (DCG) and the denotational semantics, using syntax-directed valuation functions written as Horn clauses with real constraints that map A_T description parse trees to their denotations. As the predicates that implement these valuation functions are more or less a straightforward encoding of the formal semantics of A_T into CLP($\mathcal{R}$), proofs of the soundness and completeness of the implementation are also straightforward, yet tedious. Therefore due to lack of space such proofs are omitted.

If Fs is a list of fluent expressions and As is a sequence of real-time actions, then an evaluation of a query of the form

$$Fs \textbf{ after } As$$

is implemented by the following predicate

```
after( PT, Fs, As, V ) :-
    PT = parseTree( VPs, EPs, GCs, GFs ),
    setof( W, execute( VPs, EPs, GCs, GFs, As, W ), Ws ),
    val( Fs, Ws, V ).
```

where PT is the parse tree of the A_T domain description that the query is against and V is the response to the query, with values: *yes* when the query is entailed by the description, *no* when the query is not entailed, *unknown* when the description describes at least one world, i.e., model, in which the query is *true* and another in which it is *false*. The implementation is also capable of recognizing when a description or query is inconsistent and can also respond to such queries as being *inconsistent*. The higher-order *setof* is used to get a set of possible worlds Ws corresponding to the domain description and queried action sequence. The value V is calculated from these possible worlds using the val predicate, which mirrors the denotational semantics valuation function $V_\Gamma(P)$ defined in section 4.3. However, in the implementation, the set of worlds is actually a set of possible residual states, i.e., the possible resultant states that could arise according to the domain description P and action sequence As.

A residual state is defined by the predicate execute which takes the query's sequence of actions As and generates a possible residual state W according to the pertinent elements of the domain description: the list of value propositions VPs, the list of effects propositions EPs, the list of global clock names GCs, and the list of global fluent names GFs.

```
execute( VPs, EPs, GCs, GFs, As, W ) :-
        applyAfterConstraints( VPs, EPs, GCs, GFs, SS ),
        transitionClosure( EPs, GCs, GFs, SS, As, W ),
        validState( GFs, W ).
```

The predicate execute first determines the constraints on a possible start state SS from the domain description's value propositions and effects propositions, using the applyAfterConstraints predicate. Then the transitionClosure predicate is used to determine the constraints on the state reached via a path determined by the sequence of actions $\hat{As}$ and the domain's effect propositions. Finally, the term representing the residual state is grounded using the validState predicate.

The predicate transitionClosure implements a transitive closure of the transition predicate, which implements the transition relation $\longrightarrow$ defined in section 4.3.

```
transition( EPs, GCs, GFs, S1, C1, A, TCs, S2, C2 ) :-
      satisfiesAllTimeConstraints( GCs, TCs, C1 ),
      applyEffectsRules(GCs,GFs,EPs,S1,C1,A,S2,C2,FFs,RCs),
      inertia( GFs, S1, S2, FFs ),
      increasingTime( GCs, C1, C2, RCs ).
```

The egress state of the transition is represented by two lists S1 and C1 of fluent values (*true* and *false*) and clock values respectively, while the ingress state is similarly represented by S2 and C2. The list of fluent values represents the truth value table for the state, which is more efficient than a set representation due to the multiple physical representations of a set, which unnecessarily complicates search. The clock values are similarly implemented as a value table using CLP($\mathcal{R}$) variables, which allows for a declarative implementation, yet efficient constraint solving. The predicate is implemented by first checking that all time constraints on the time of occurrence of the action $\hat{A}$ can be satisfied. Then the set of effects propositions which can apply in such a situation are used to determine some of the fluent constraints (i.e., forced fluents FFs) on the ingress state in the main goal applyEffectsRules. The remaining fluent constraints are determined by the set difference of global fluent names GFs and forced fluents FFs in the inertia predicate. Finally, the increasingTime predicate uses CLP($\mathcal{R}$) constraints to force the clocks in the egress state C1 to be less than or equal to the respective clocks in the ingress state C2, with exceptions for the clocks that are listed in RCs as being reset.

The main goal applyEffectsRules enforces that every effects proposition either applies or does not apply by traversing through the list of effects propositions. Because of the issues involved in using negation alongside CLP($\mathcal{R}$), negation is implicitly used by defining a predicate and its dual as follows

```
effectRuleApplies( GCs, GFs, EP, S1, C1, A1, S2 ) :-
    EP = causes( A2, _, TCs, EFs, CFs ),
    equalNames( A1, A2 ),
    satisfiesAllTimeConstraints( GCs, TCs, C1 ),
    satisfiesAllFluents( GFs, S1, CFs ),
    satisfiesAllFluents( GFs, S2, EFs ).

effectRuleDoesNotApply( _, _, EP, _, _, A1 ) :-
    EP = causes( A2, _, _, _, _ ),
    not( equalNames( A1, A2 ) ).
effectRuleDoesNotApply( GCs, _, EP, _, C1, A1 ) :-
    EP = causes( A2, _, TCs, _, _ ),
    equalNames( A1, A2 ),
    notSatisfiesAllTimeConstraints( GCa, TCs, C1 ).
effectRuleDoesNotApply( _, GFs, EPs, S1, _, A1 ) :-
    EP = causes( A2, _, _, _, CFs ),
    equalNames( A1, A2 ),
    notSatisfiesAllFluents( GFs, S1, CFs ).
```

Hence while effectRuleApplies is true when the given effects proposition EP's preconditions are satisfied by egress state S1 and the action named A1, the dual predicate effectRuleDoesNotApply is true when some precondition is not satisfied. Also note that the explicit use of negation of equalNames is not necessary, but since A1 and A2 are always ground and the predicate's definition does not make use of CLP($\mathcal{R}$), this limited use of negation by failure simplifies the implementation. Effects propositions are represented by terms of the form

```
causes( A, RCs, TCs, EFs, CFs )
```

where A is the action name, RCs is the list of reset clocks, TCs is the list of time constraint preconditions, EFs is the list of effected fluent expressions, and CFs is the list of fluent preconditions.

The implementation of the condition satisfaction predicates and their duals are relatively straightforward, where the predicates involving real-time are implemented using CLP($\mathcal{R}$) constraints and the other predicates are implemented as pure Horn clauses, with the exception of a limited use of negation as failure on ground goals.

```
satisfiesAllFluents( [], [], _ ).
satisfiesAllFluents( [ N | Ns ], [ _ | Fs ], CFs ) :-
     not( member( N, CFs ) ),
     not( member( -N, CFs ) ),
     satisfiesAllFluents( Ns, Fs, CFs ).
satisfiesAllFluents( [ N | Ns ], [ true | Fs ], CFs ) :-
     member( N, CFs ),
     satisfiesAllFluents( Ns, Fs, CFs ).
satisfiesAllFluents( [ N | Ns ], [ false | Fs ], CFs ) :-
     member( -N, CFs ),
     satisfiesAllFluents( Ns, Fs, CFs ).
```

Again, while this use of negation as failure could be eliminated via explicit definition of a dual predicate, doing so is unnecessary as the negated predicate is ground and does not involve the use of CLP($\mathcal{R}$) or negation in its definition. satisfiesAllFluents simultaneously recurses through a list of global fluent names Ns and a given state's fluent value table Fs, verifying that the fluents are either not mentioned in the preconditions CFs or that their occurrence in CFs is satisfiable.

The definition of satisfiesAllTimeConstraints and its dual is more complicated, as it involves the manifestation of CLP($\mathcal{R}$) constraints, which are then applied to the clocks in question. The predicate satisfiesAllTimeConstraints recurses through the list of time constraints on clocks, and asserts them. Their satisfiability is determined by the CLP($\mathcal{R}$) engine.

```
satisfiesAllTimeConstraints( _, [], _ ).
satisfiesAllTimeConstraints( GCs, [ T | Ts ], Cs ) :-
     satisfiesTimeConstraint( GCs, T, Cs ),
     satisfiesAllTimeConstraints( GCs, Ts, Cs ).
```

In other words, the top-level implementation traverses through the list of time constraints Ts, so that each time constraint can be individually applied to the given set of clocks Cs. Each individual time constraint is represented as a term and only manifested into actual CLP($\mathcal{R}$) constraints when needed, so that subsequent applications of the constraints do not alter the original definition of effects propositions. Note that w.r.t. checking for satisfiability, the exact time at which a particular action happened is unimportant, what matters is that the accumulated constraints are consistent.

A prototype based on the ideas above is operational and has been tested on a number of benchmarks. Note that the current prototype implementation can be used only for computing states that result after a series of timed-actions are performed. For these kinds of computations a Prolog system extended with CLP($\mathcal{R}$) suffices (thus the SICStus Prolog system is sufficient). We are currently working on extending the system so that one can pose queries to determine a sequence of actions that causes a desired property to hold. Note that these kinds of (non-timed) queries are hard to specify and compute in $\mathcal{A}$ as well. Implementing these extensions will require more advanced implementations of logic programming such as those based on tabling. Note however, that if a time bound is imposed on the sequence of actions to be queried, then one can still avoid the use of tabled logic programming since the time bound constraints will ensure that cycles are not traversed infinitely.

6   Related Work

Several frameworks have been proposed to reason about the real-time aspects of actions. Most of them are extensions of the Situation Calculus or the Event Calculus, with features like occurrences and narratives, and some representation of real-time. Though these techniques provide a powerful formal mechanism for reasoning about real-time actions, there is a dearth of tools implementing them. This is because these techniques are usually axiomatized in terms of first-order logic and therefore do not allow for a tractable implementation.

Logic programming has been extensively studied in the context of implementation of the Event Calculus and its extensions. It has also been demonstrated that logic programming is a viable means for implementing action description languages, which are fragments of the Situation Calculus. In this paper, we show how CLP($\mathcal{R}$) can be used as an elegant framework for implementing reasoning tools based on the Situation and Event Calculi.

We now survey related work in the area: [17, 18] provide a method for reasoning about concurrent, real-time actions in the Situation Calculus, using a solution to the frame problem. [10] describes methods to reason about narratives with real-time in the Situation Calculus. [16] generalizes the approach in [18] to the Situation Calculus with narratives and occurrences. All these formalisms are based on axiomatic reasoning using first-order logic. Implementing a reasonable model of continuous real-time, which is essential to develop a practical reasoning tool becomes difficult in these frameworks due to decidability issues. We use CLP($\mathcal{R}$) to realize a simple and elegant model of real-time, which allows us to develop a working implementation of a reasoning tool for real-time actions.

Other techniques for reasoning with real-time include [12], which models time as being discrete, whereas our method provides a more general continuous model of time. [13] describes a method for reasoning about time in a temporal rather than a numerical manner. [11] presents real-time extensions of the Event Calculus, but does not provide an implementable model of real-time. Though our technique has been developed in the context of action description languages, it can also be extended to the Situation Calculus, the Event Calculus and their various extensions.

Action description languages have traditionally been used for reasoning about the effect of actions and change of state in various domains in [2, 5, 8, 19]. However these languages do not provide the ability to reason about actions in real-time domains.

7 Conclusions

Practical applications of action description languages require the ability to describe and reason about real-time, especially in safety-critical domains. We have presented a method of extending the syntax and semantics of action description languages with real-time. We have also presented an implementation of $\mathcal{A}_T$, a real-time extension of action description language $\mathcal{A}$.

We are currently investigating the integration of techniques developed for handling concurrent actions in action description languages [2] with the methods described in this paper. This is because a large class of safety-critical systems consist of multiple concurrent subsystems, which exhibit real-time behavior. We would also like to provide the ability to query for a sequence of actions that causes a desired property to hold. Future work also includes investigating generalized constraint action description languages, in which actions may have arbitrary constraints (e.g., resource constraints) attached. A timed ADL is a special case of such a constraint ADL.

References

1. R. Alur Timed Automata, *NATO-ASI 1998 Summer School on Verification of Digital and Hybrid Systems.*
2. C. Baral, Knowledge Representation, Reasoning and Declarative Problem Solving, Cambridge University Press, 2003.
3. E. Clarke, O. Grumberg, D. Peled. Model Checking. MIT Press. 1999.
4. M. Gelfond and V. Lifschitz Representing Action and Change by Logic Programs *Journal of Logic Programming,*Vol. 17, pp. 301-321, 1993.
5. M. Gelfond and V. Lifschitz Action Languages, *Electronic Transactions on AI*, vol. 3, No. 16, 1998
6. G. Gupta and E. Pontelli A Constraint based Approach to the Specification and Verification of Real-Time Systems, In *Proc. IEEE RTSS*, pp. 230-239, 1997.
7. K. Marriott and P. Stuckey. Constraint Programming. MIT Press. 1998.
8. V. Lifschitz, Answer set planning, In *Proc. ICLP '99*, LNCS, 1999.
9. Jane W.S. Liu, Real-Time Systems, Prentice Hall, NJ, 2000.
10. R. Miller and M. Shanahan, Narratives in the Situation Calculus, In *Journal of Logic and Computation*, 1994.
11. R. Miller and M. Shanahan, Some Alternative Formulations of the Event Calculus, In *Computational Logic*, LNAI vol 2408, Springer, 2002.
12. E. Sandewall, Features and Fluents (vol. 1): The Representation of Knowledge about Dynamic Systems, *Oxford University Press*, 1995.
13. P. Doherty et al., TAL: Temporal Action Logics Language, `http://www.ep.liu.se/ea/cis/1998/015/`
14. S. Mukhopadhyay and A. Podelski, Model Checking for Timed Logic Processes, *Computational Logic 2000*, pp. 598-612.
15. M. Nogueira, M. Balduccini, M. Gelfond, R. Watson, M. Barry, An A-Prolog decision support system for the Space Shuttle, In *Proc. PADL '01*, LNCS, pp. 169-183.
16. J. Pinto, Occurrences and narratives as constraints in the branching structure of the Situation Calculus, In*Journal of Logic and Computation*, 8:777-808, 1994.

17. R. Reiter, Natural actions, concurrency and continuous time in the situation calculus, In *Proc. KR '96*, Morgan-Kauffman,pp. 2-13.
18. J. Pinto, R. Reiter, Reasoning about time in the situation calculus. In *Annals of Mathematics and Artificial Intelligence*, 14:251-268.
19. H. Turner, Representing actions in logic programs and default theories: A situation calculus approach, *Journal of Logic Programming*, vol. 31, pp. 245-298, 1997.
20. U.D. Ulusar and H.L. Akin Design and Implementation of a Real Time Planner for Robots *Proc. TAINN 2004*, pp. 263-270.

An Algorithm for Local Variable Elimination in Normal Logic Programs

Javier Álvez and Paqui Lucio

Faculty of Computer Science, Basque Country University,
San Sebastián, Spain
{jibalgij, jiplucap}@si.ehu.es

Abstract. A variable is *local* if it occurs in a clause body but not in its head. Local variables appear naturally in practical logic programming, but they complicate several aspects such as negation, compilation, memoization, static analysis, program approximation by neural networks etc. As a consequence, the absence of local variables yields better performance of several tools and is a prerequisite for many technical results. In this paper, we introduce an algorithm that eliminates local variables from a wide proper subclass of normal logic programs. The proposed transformation preserves the Clark-Kunen semantics for normal logic programs.

1 Introduction

Local variables are very often used —as auxiliaries— to store intermediate results in logic programs. Their values are passed from one atom to another in a clause body, but they are not lifted to the head. Whilst they are useful in practical logic programming, the occurrence of local variables could cause inefficiency or even prevent the satisfaction of some properties. In the area of *negation in logic programming*, several results are restricted to *local variable free* (*lvf*, for short) programs or are less efficiently applicable when local variables are present. For instance, local variables lead to *floundering* problems in *negation as failure* [8]. In addition, their presence prevents completeness results for more recent techniques like *intensional negation* [5] and other transformational negation techniques [20, 25]. In several computational mechanisms proposed for *constructive negation* [2, 6, 7, 11, 23], local variables force one to deal with universal quantification, which is not easy to compute in an efficient manner. Other logic programming areas where local variables lead to technical problems are related to compilation, memoization, static analysis, program approximation by neural networks etc. Moreover, in equational logic programming, local variables cause problems since, in their presence, narrowing may become incomplete. In [12], some transformations of definite (equational) logic programs into *lvf* ones are presented. Unfortunately, these methods do not preserve failure.

It is well known that every computable function can be computed by a definite logic program [3, 24]. Besides, the program built in [24] is an *lvf* definite program. Therefore, from the theoretical point of view, the function that is computed by

P.M. Hill (Ed.): LOPSTR 2005, LNCS 3901, pp. 61–79, 2006.

any given normal logic program (according to the Clark-Kunen semantics) can also be computed by an *lvf* definite program (in PROLOG). The question is how to automatically generate an *lvf* program from any given program with local variables. In particular, the *lvf* program given in [24] simulates the computation of a universal Turing machine over the Turing machine that computes the recursive function. This is not the program that we try to generate by transformation. Besides, each *lvf* normal program can be transformed into a definite one (see, for instance, [5]). Hence, the automatic removing of local variables from normal programs is a plausible and encouraging goal.

In this paper, we present an algorithm for eliminating the local variables from normal logic programs while preserving the Clark-Kunen semantics. This method is applicable, in particular, to the class of well-moded logic programs ([9, 10, 19]). We explain the algorithm, prove its correctness and give illustrative examples.

Outline of the paper. In the next section, we fix notation and terminology. In Section 3, we present a preliminary adjustment of the variable occurrences. Section 4 is devoted to partition the arguments of literals depending on the local variables, called mode, and to the notion of tail recursion w.r.t. a mode. In Section 5, we explain how to eliminate the local variables of a literal and the necessary conditions for doing this. The transformation to tail recursion w.r.t. a mode is shown in Section 6. In Section 7, we discuss the algorithm and its termination. Finally, we summarize conclusions and briefly discuss related work.

2   Preliminaries

We assume that the reader is familiar with the basic concepts and notation of logic programming, see e.g. [4]. In this section, we recall some basic terminology and introduce some notational conventions used throughout the paper.

A bar is used to denote tuples, or finite sequences, of objects. For example, $\bar{x}$ denotes an n-tuple of variables $x_1, \ldots, x_n$. Throughout the paper, tuples of variables are assumed to be pairwise distinct. As a consequence, we treat them as sets and use the constant $\emptyset$ and the operators $\smallsetminus$ (set difference), $\cup$ and $\cap$ for tuples of variables with their usual meaning over sets. However, tuples of terms and tuples of literals may have repeated elements. In such cases, concatenation of tuples is denoted by the infix operator $\cdot$ and $\langle \, \rangle$ stands for the empty tuple.

In clauses, we split the variables into *global* and *local*. A variable is *local* in a clause if it occurs in its body but not in its head. Otherwise, it is *global*. For α which is a clause —or any syntactic object inside a clause like atom, term, etc— we denote by $\mathsf{LVar}(\alpha)$ ($\mathsf{GVar}(\alpha)$) the set of *local* (*global*) variables in α. An *lvf* clause/program is a clause/program free of local variables.

A literal is either an atom $p(\bar{t})$ (positive literal) or a negated atom $\neg p(\bar{t})$ (negative literal), where p and $\neg p$ are the *predicate (symbol)* of the literal and $\bar{t}$ is a tuple of terms. We usually denote literals by $L(\bar{t})$, $M(\bar{t})$, $N(\bar{t})$, ... and L, M, N, ... are used to denote the predicate of a literal. In a literal, when we do not need to specify the arguments, we simply omit the tuple of terms, and then L, M, N, ... denote a literal. Throughout the paper, the context always makes it clear whether a capital letter stands for a literal or a predicate symbol.

Our program transformations preserve the Clark-Kunen semantics of normal programs, which is given by Clark's program completion [8] interpreted in three-valued logic [13]. Note that the logical Clark-Kunen semantics is independent of the order in which the literals appear in the clause bodies.

Given a normal program P and a predicate symbol p, $\mathtt{Def}_P(p)$ is the set of all clauses from P whose head literal begins with p. From Clark's completion, we have that $\neg p(\overline{x}) \leftrightarrow \neg\varphi$ where φ is the disjunction of the body clauses, which are existentially quantified on its local variables. If $\mathtt{Def}_P(p)$ has no local variables, then $\neg p(\overline{x}) \leftrightarrow \neg\varphi$ can be easily reduced to a set of clauses that have a normal body and a negative head.[1] In this case, we say that this is a *normal definition* called $\mathtt{Def}_P(\neg p)$. Otherwise, the universal quantification in clauses with head $\neg p(\overline{x})$ can not be avoided and we say that $\mathtt{Def}_P(\neg p)$ is a *complex definition*. In our transformations, only normal definitions are handled. Complex definitions are delayed until they become normal or, otherwise, they are delayed forever.

We make use of the fold/unfold transformation system described in [17] (see also [15]) where equivalence w.r.t. the Clark-Kunen semantics for definite programs is ensured by forbidding unfolding on direct recursion and requiring that a clause C should be folded with another clause, different from C, taken from the current program. Besides, this result can be extended to normal programs with the proviso that only normal (not complex) definitions of negated predicates are used. However, the fold/unfold technique is not powerful enough to prove some of our results and we complement it with direct induction on the bottom-up computation of the Clark-Kunen semantics.

Given a program P and two predicates L and M, we say that M *directly depends on* L if L occurs in $\mathtt{Def}_P(M)$. By the reflexive transitive closure of this relation, we obtain the set $\mathsf{Dpd}_P(L)$ of all predicates on which L depends. Besides, we define the set of all mutually recursive predicates with L by:

$$\mathsf{MR}_P(L) = \{M \mid M \in \mathsf{Dpd}_P(L) \text{ and } L \in \mathsf{Dpd}_P(M)\}.$$

The induced equivalence relation —given by $(L, M) \in R \Longleftrightarrow L \in \mathsf{MR}_P(M)$— partitions the set of all predicates into a finite number of equivalence classes. Classes are $\mathsf{MR}_P(L)$ where L is the class representative predicate. Then, the set consisting of all the equivalence classes (or factor set) can be partially ordered by the following relation:

$$\mathsf{MR}_P(L) \preceq \mathsf{MR}_P(M) \Longleftrightarrow \text{There exists } N \in \mathsf{MR}_P(L) \text{ and } Q \in \mathsf{MR}_P(M)$$
$$\text{such that } N \in \mathsf{Dpd}_P(Q).$$

Moreover, given a program P, its set of mutually recursive classes does not contain any infinite decreasing chain with respect to $\preceq$. That is, $\preceq$ is a well-founded order. For technical reasons, we need to distinguish the body literals

---

[1] Of course, disequality is needed.

that are mutually recursive with the clause head. Hence, when convenient, a clause will be written in the following Dpd-*form*:

$$H \leftarrow \overline{L}^1, K_1, \overline{L}^2, \ldots, \overline{L}^n, K_n, \overline{L}^{n+1}$$

to denote that $K_i \in \mathsf{MR}_P(H)$ for each $1 \leq i \leq n$ and $M \notin \mathsf{MR}_P(H)$ for each $M \in \overline{L}^i$ and each $1 \leq i \leq n+1$. Note that $n = 0$ when no body literal belongs to $\mathsf{MR}_P(H)$. Besides, every $\overline{L}^i$ could be an empty tuple.

In what follows, we assume a program, always called P, that is being transformed into an *lvf* program. We would like to emphasize that, although our method chooses some ordering on the clause bodies and the target programs depend on that ordering, we always preserve the Clark-Kunen semantics.

3 Local-Regulation

Local-regulation (LR, for short) is a preliminary treatment of the variable occurrences in the clause bodies. Roughly speaking, it is an adjustment for enabling local variable elimination. First, we define some syntactic conditions, called term-apartness, and show that it can be achieved by program transformation.

Definition 1. *Let $L(\overline{t})$ be an n-ary literal in a given clause $H \leftarrow \overline{M}, L(\overline{t}), \overline{N}$ and $\overline{x} \subseteq \mathsf{Var}(L(\overline{t}))$. The variables $\overline{x}$ are term-apart in $L(\overline{t})$ iff for every $1 \leq i \leq n$ (at least) one of the following two conditions holds:*

(a) $\mathsf{Var}(t_i) \cap \overline{x} \cap \mathsf{Var}(\overline{M}) = \emptyset$
(b) $\mathsf{Var}(t_i) \cap \overline{x} \cap \mathsf{Var}(\overline{N}) = \emptyset$.   □

For example, given the clause $h(x) \leftarrow p(x), q(x, f(x,y), y), \neg h(y)$, the variables (x, y) are not term-apart in $q(x, f(x,y), y)$ due to the term $f(x,y)$ in the second argument, but each variable individually is term-apart in that literal. The intuition behind term-apartness is that it allows us to partition the terms $\overline{t}$ of a literal $L(\overline{t})$ in two tuples $\overline{t}_1$ and $\overline{t}_2$ such that the variables that occur in $\overline{t}_1$ ($\overline{t}_2$) only occur in the left-hand side literals $\overline{M}$ (right-hand side literals $\overline{N}$). This partition facilitates the dataflow analysis of the clause.

Lemma 1. *Every normal program P can be transformed into a Clark-Kunen equivalent normal program P' such that all its variables are term-apart in the literals occurring in P'.*

Proof. Let $\overline{x} \subseteq \mathsf{Var}(L(\overline{t}))$ in a clause $C = H \leftarrow \overline{M}, L(\overline{t}), \overline{N} \in P$ such that $\overline{w} = \mathsf{Var}(t_i) \cap \overline{x} \cap \mathsf{Var}(\overline{M}) \neq \emptyset$ and $\mathsf{Var}(t_i) \cap \overline{x} \cap \mathsf{Var}(\overline{N}) \neq \emptyset$ for some i. We define a new predicate p by $D = p(\overline{z} \cdot \overline{w} \cdot \overline{w}) \leftarrow L(\overline{z})$ and substitute the clause $C' = H \leftarrow \overline{M}, p(\overline{t}' \cdot \overline{w} \cdot \overline{w}'), \overline{N}[\overline{w}'/\overline{w}]$ for C, where $\overline{w}'$ is a tuple of fresh variables and $\overline{t}'$ is obtained by replacing t_i with $t_i[\overline{w}'/\overline{w}]$ in $\overline{t}$. In the resulting program, D is an *lvf* clause since only a literal occurs in its body and, besides, we have that $\mathsf{Var}(t_i') \cap \overline{x} \cap \mathsf{Var}(\overline{M}) = \emptyset$ in the clause C'. Furthermore, it is easy to see that the new literal $p(\bar{t}' \cdot \bar{w} \cdot \bar{w}')$ in C' will not be affected by any subsequent transformation. After this process, equivalence is preserved since we obtain the program P by unfolding the new literal $p(\bar{t}' \cdot \bar{w} \cdot \bar{w}')$ in C' with the clause D. □

Now, we formulate the condition of local-regularity on clauses and extend it to programs in an obvious way.

Definition 2. *A clause C:*

$$H \leftarrow \overline{L}^1(\bar{r}^1),\ K_1(\bar{s}^1),\ \overline{L}^2(\bar{r}^2),\ \ldots\ ,\ \overline{L}^n(\bar{r}^n),\ K_n(\bar{s}^n),\ \overline{L}^{n+1}(\bar{r}^{n+1})$$

in Dpd-*form is* local-regular *iff $n = 0$ or it satisfies the following two conditions:*

(a) LVar$(K_i(\bar{s}^i))$ *are term-apart in $K_i(\bar{s}^i)$ for every $1 \leq i \leq n$*
(b) *every local variable occurs in $\bar{s}^{i-1} \cdot \bar{r}^i \cdot \bar{s}^i$ for some $1 \leq i \leq n+1$ and does not occur anywhere in the clause (by convention, $\bar{s}^0 = \bar{s}^{n+1} = \langle\ \rangle$).*

A program P is local-regular *iff every clause $C \in P$ is local-regular.* □

Next, we show a method to transform any program into a local-regular one.

Lemma 2. *Every normal program P can be transformed into a Clark-Kunen equivalent local-regular normal program P'.*

Proof. Due to Lemma 1, we can always transform P into an equivalent program that satisfies the first condition. Therefore, we only focus on the second condition. Let $C = H \leftarrow \overline{L}^1(\bar{r}^1),\ K_1(\bar{s}^1),\ \ldots\ ,\ K_n(\bar{s}^n),\ \overline{L}^{n+1}(\bar{r}^{n+1}) \in P$ be a clause in Dpd-form such that the leftmost occurrence of a local variable y that violates the second condition is either in $K_{i-1}(\bar{s}^{i-1})$ for $2 \leq i \leq n$ or in $\overline{L}^i(\bar{r}^i)$ for $1 \leq i \leq n$ and let C be rewritten as $H \leftarrow \overline{M},\ \overline{L}^i(\bar{r}^i),\ K_i(\bar{s}^i),\ \overline{N}$. Then, we replace C with:

$$C' = H \leftarrow \overline{M},\ \overline{L}^i(\bar{r}^i),\ p_i(\bar{s}^i \cdot y \cdot y'),\ \overline{N}[y'/y]$$

where y' is a new local variable and p_i is a new predicate defined by the clause $D = p_i(\bar{z} \cdot x \cdot x) \leftarrow K_i(\bar{z})$. Now, y satisfies the second condition since it exactly occurs in the tuple of literals $K_{i-1}(\bar{s}^{i-1}) \cdot \overline{L}^i(\bar{r}^i) \cdot p_i(\bar{s}^i \cdot y \cdot y')$ in C'. The iteration of this process ends because either the number of local variables that violate the condition decreases (that is, y' satisfies it) or y' occurs closer to the end of the clause body in C' than y in C: the leftmost occurrence of y is either in $K_{i-1}(\bar{s}^{i-1})$ or in $\overline{L}^i(\bar{r}^i)$ in the clause C whereas the leftmost occurrence of y' is in $p_i(\bar{s}^i \cdot y \cdot y')$ in the clause C'. Also, the new predicate p_i is mutually recursive to H and, therefore, the clause C' is in Dpd-form. Besides, it is easy to see that the first condition of local regulation is always preserved by the above transformation. We have that the resulting program P' is equivalent to P because we obtain P by unfolding the new literals in P'. □

The following example describes the transformation of a one-clause program into a local-regular program consisting of three clauses and using two fresh predicates.

Example 1. Let us consider the following clause of some program P:

$$E1.1: \quad p(f(x_1, x_2)) \leftarrow q_1(f(x_2, w_1)),\ p_1(g(w_1, w_2)),$$
$$q_2(f(w_2, w_1)),\ p_2(g(w_3, x_1)),\ q_3(f(w_2, w_3))$$

such that $\mathsf{MR}_P(p) = \{p,\ p_1,\ p_2\}$. The clause is not local-regular because the local variable w_1 violates both conditions of Def. 2 and w_2 violates the second one. Considering w_1, we define a new predicate p_1' and replace $E1.1$ with the following clauses:

$$E1.2: \quad p_1'(z, w, w) \leftarrow p_1(z)$$
$$E1.3: \quad p(f(x_1, x_2)) \leftarrow q_1(f(x_2, w_1)),\ p_1'(g(w_1', w_2), w_1, w_1'),$$
$$q_2(f(w_2, w_1')),\ p_2(g(w_3, x_1)),\ q_3(f(w_2, w_3))$$

Now, w_1 and w_1' violate neither the first condition nor the second one. With regard to w_2, its leftmost occurrence is in the literal $p_1'(g(w_1', w_2), w_1, w_1')$. Therefore, we define a new predicate p_2' and substitute the following clauses for $E1.3$:

$$E1.4: \quad p_2'(z, w, w) \leftarrow p_2(z)$$
$$E1.5: \quad p(f(x_1, x_2)) \leftarrow q_1(f(x_2, w_1)),\ p_1'(g(w_1', w_2), w_1, w_1'),$$
$$q_2(f(w_2, w_1')),\ p_2'(g(w_3, x_1), w_2, w_2'),\ q_3(f(w_2', w_3))$$

All the resulting clauses are local-regular. Thus, the source and target programs are shown to be equivalent by unfolding the literals of predicates p_1' and p_2'.   □

4   Input/Output Modes for Literals

Input/output modes were introduced in [16] and further extensively studied from many points of view and for many applications. In the classical view, the mode of a predicate indicates how its arguments will be used in the sense of identifying arguments which belong to the input and to the output. In this paper, in order to eliminate the local variable y, it might be necessary to consider as output the second argument in $p(x_1, y)$ and as input the second argument in $p(x_2, y)$. However, for the sake of clarity, we allow to assign a unique mode to each predicate. Hence, instead of assigning multiple modes to predicates, we consider a different but equivalent program where the predicates are conveniently renamed and different copies of the same predicate are provided, one for each different mode.

Definition 3. *A* mode *for an n-ary predicate L, denoted by $\mathsf{m} : L$, is an n-tuple $\mathsf{m} \in \{\mathsf{in}, \mathsf{out}\}^n$, where the position i ($1 \leq i \leq n$) such that $\mathsf{m}_i = \mathsf{in}$ ($\mathsf{m}_i = \mathsf{out}$) is considered as an* input *(*output*) position.*   □

Throughout this paper, we will use the following notation:

Remark 1. Given a mode m for a predicate L and a literal $L(\bar{t})$, the expression $\bar{t}_\mathrm{I} \overset{\mathsf{m}}{\triangleright} \bar{t}_\mathrm{O}$ means the unique partition of $\bar{t}$ into the order-preserving subsequences consisting of the input ($\bar{t}_\mathrm{I}$) and output ($\bar{t}_\mathrm{O}$) arguments of $L(\bar{t})$ according to m. Besides, the expression $L(\bar{t}_\mathrm{I} \overset{\mathsf{m}}{\triangleright} \bar{t}_\mathrm{O})$ is called the IO-*form* of $L(\bar{t})$, which implicitly represents m in $L(\bar{t})$. Whenever the upper mode name m is irrelevant, we simply omit it and write $L(\bar{t}_{\mathrm{I}} \vartriangleright \bar{t}_0)$. If (all or some of) the literals of a clause are in IO-form, then we say that the clause is in IO-form. From now on, the literals of any clause (in particular, in Dpd-form) can be written in IO-form.   □

Definition 4. *Let C be a clause:*

$$H \leftarrow \overline{M}, L(\bar{t}), K_1(\overline{u}^1), \ \ldots \ , K_n(\overline{u}^n), \overline{N}$$

where:

- $\overline{y} \subseteq \mathsf{Var}(L(\bar{t}))$,
- $\overline{y} \cap \mathsf{Var}(\overline{N}) = \emptyset$, *and*
- $\overline{y} \cap \mathsf{Var}(K_i(\overline{u}^i)) \neq \emptyset$ *for each $1 \leq i \leq n$*

such that the variables $\overline{y}$ are term-apart in $L(\bar{t})$. Then, the collection of modes $\{\mathtt{m} : L, \mathtt{m}^1 : K_1, \mathtt{m}^2 : K_2, \ \ldots, \ \mathtt{m}^n : K_n\}$, denoted by $\mathsf{VarMode}(C, L(\bar{t}), \overline{y})$, is defined by:

(a) $\mathtt{m}_i = \mathtt{in}$ *if* $\mathsf{Var}(t_i) \cap \overline{y} \subseteq \mathsf{Var}(\overline{M})$ *and* $\mathtt{m}_i = \mathtt{out}$ *otherwise.*
(b) For each $1 \leq j \leq n$: $\mathtt{m}_i^j = \mathtt{in}$ *if* $\mathsf{Var}(u_i^j) \cap \overline{y} \neq \emptyset$ *and* $\mathtt{m}_i^j = \mathtt{out}$ *otherwise.*   □

Note that, by the term-apartness of $\overline{y}$, the variables in $\mathsf{Var}(\bar{t}_{\mathrm{I}}) \cap \overline{y}$ do not occur in $K_1(\overline{u}^1), \ \ldots, K_n(\overline{u}^n)$.

Example 2. Let C be the following clause in a program P:

$$p(x_1, x_2) \leftarrow q(f(x_1, y_1), y_1), \ r(y_1, f(x_2, y_2)), \ r(x_2, f(y_2, x_2)), \ q(x_1, x_1).$$

First, we need to rename the second literal $r(x_2, f(y_2, x_2))$, which is replaced with $r'(x_2, f(y_2, x_2))$, and provide a copy of $\mathtt{Def}_P(r)$ for the definition of the new predicate r':

$$C' = p(x_1, x_2) \leftarrow q(f(x_1, y_1), y_1), \ r(y_1, f(x_2, y_2)), \ r'(x_2, f(y_2, x_2)), \ q(x_1, x_1).$$

Then, the set of modes $\mathsf{VarMode}(C', r(y_1, f(x_2, y_2)), (y_1, \ y_2))$ is:

$$\{(\mathtt{in}, \mathtt{out}) : r, \ (\mathtt{out}, \mathtt{in}) : r'\}$$

which yields the following IO-form of C':

$$p(x_1, x_2) \leftarrow q(f(x_1, y_1), y_1), \ r(y_1 \vartriangleright f(x_2, y_2)), \ r'(f(y_2, x_2) \vartriangleright x_2), \ q(x_1, x_1).$$

By contrast, $\mathsf{VarMode}(C', r(y_1, f(x_2, y_1)), x_2)$ gives:

$$p(x_1, x_2) \leftarrow q(f(x_1, y_1), y_1), \ r(y_1 \vartriangleright f(x_2, y_2)), \ r'(x_2, f(y_2, x_2) \vartriangleright \langle \, \rangle), \ q(x_1, x_1).$$

Note that we have not assigned a mode to the literals on q since r is not mutually recursive with the predicate q.   □

Our intention is to eliminate the local variables that occur in the terms $\bar{t}_0$ of a given $L(\bar{t}_I \overset{\mathtt{m}}{\triangleright} \bar{t}_0)$. For $(\mathtt{in}, \mathtt{out}) : r$ (see Example 2), that variable is y_2. For this purpose, we must associate modes with the clauses in the definition of L according to $\mathtt{m}$. That is, we first fix $\mathtt{m}$ as the mode for the head literal of each clause C in $\mathtt{Def}_P(L)$. Then, taking into account the input/output partition of the head literal and the local variables of C, we associate a mode with every body literal of C that is mutually recursive with L.

Definition 5. *Let $\mathtt{m}$ be the mode assigned to a predicate L and C be the following normal local-regular[2] clause in Dpd-form:*

$$L(\bar{u}_I \overset{\mathtt{m}}{\triangleright} \bar{u}_0) \leftarrow \overline{L}^1(\bar{r}^1), \ K_1(\bar{s}^1), \ \overline{L}^2(\bar{r}^2), \ \ldots \ , \ \overline{L}^n(\bar{r}^n), \ K_n(\bar{s}^n), \ \overline{L}^{n+1}(\bar{r}^{n+1})$$

where each $K_i(\bar{s}^i)$ is an n_i-ary literal. Then, the mode for the clause C, denoted by $\mathtt{ClauseMode}(C, \mathtt{m})$, is given by the set of modes $\{\mathtt{m} : L, \ \mathtt{m}^1 : K_1, \ \ldots \ , \ \mathtt{m}^n : K_n\}$, where each $\mathtt{m}^i$ is defined as follows:

$$\mathtt{m}^i_j = \begin{cases} \mathtt{in} & \textit{if } \mathsf{LVar}(s^i_j) \cap \mathsf{LVar}(\bar{r}^{i-1}) \neq \emptyset \quad \textit{or} \\ & \quad \mathsf{LVar}(s^i_j) = \emptyset \ \textit{and} \ (\mathsf{Var}(s^i_j) \cap \mathsf{Var}(\bar{u}_I) \neq \emptyset \ \textit{or} \ \mathsf{Var}(s^i_j) \cap \mathsf{Var}(\bar{u}_0) = \emptyset) \\ \mathtt{out} & \textit{otherwise} \end{cases}$$

for every $1 \leq j \leq n_i$. Besides, assuming that $\mathtt{Def}_P(L) = \{C_1, \ldots, C_k\}$, the mode for the definition of L, denoted by $\mathtt{DefMode}(P, L, \mathtt{m})$, is given by the set of clause modes $\{\mathtt{ClauseMode}(C_1, \mathtt{m}), \ldots, \mathtt{ClauseMode}(C_k, \mathtt{m})\}$. □

Example 3. Let P be the following program:

    $E3.1 :$ $h(x) \leftarrow p(x, y), \ q(y), \ r(x)$
    $E3.2 :$ $p(a, b)$
    $E3.3 :$ $p(f(v), z) \leftarrow h(v), \ r(z)$

such that $\mathsf{MR}_P(p) = \{h, \ p\}$. Then, the set of modes $\mathtt{VarMode}(E3.1, p(x, y), y)$ yields the following IO-form for the clause $E3.1$:

$$h(x) \leftarrow p(x \triangleright y), \ q(y \triangleright \langle \, \rangle), \ r(x)$$

Besides, since $(\mathtt{in}, \mathtt{out})$ is the mode for the predicate p, the set of clause modes $\mathtt{DefMode}(P, p, (\mathtt{in}, \mathtt{out}))$ yields the following clauses:

$$p(a \triangleright b)$$
$$p(f(v) \triangleright z) \leftarrow h(v \triangleright \langle \, \rangle), \ r(z)$$

where the mode $(\mathtt{in})$ is assigned to the predicate h. Finally, the set of clause modes $\mathtt{DefMode}(P, h, (\mathtt{in}))$ gives the clause:

$$h(x \triangleright \langle \, \rangle) \leftarrow p(x \triangleright y), \ q(y \triangleright \langle \, \rangle), \ r(x)$$

Note that, in this example, we have assigned a unique mode to the predicates h and p without renaming. □

---

[2] By Lemma 2, we can assume local-regularity.

Now, starting with a mode m assigned to a predicate L, we collect the modes that are assigned to all the predicates that are mutually recursive with L.

Definition 6. *Let* m *be the mode assigned to a predicate L in a program P. The relation $\prec$ is defined by:*

$$\mathtt{m} : L \prec \mathtt{m}' : M \iff \mathtt{m}' : M \in \mathtt{DefMode}(P, L, \mathtt{m}).$$

Besides, the mode *for the predicates that are mutually recursive with L, denoted by* $\mathtt{ModeMR}(P, L, \mathtt{m})$, *is given by the least set of modes that contains the singleton* $\{\mathtt{m} : L\}$ *and is upwards closed with respect to the relation $\prec$.* □

Example 4. In the program of Example 3, the set of modes $\mathtt{ModeMR}(P, p, (\mathtt{in}, \mathtt{out}))$ is given by:

$$\{(\mathtt{in}, \mathtt{out}) : p,\ (\mathtt{in}) : h\ \}$$

Note that, since we assign a unique mode to each predicate, we have that $\mathtt{ModeMR}(P, p, (\mathtt{in}, \mathtt{out})) = \mathtt{ModeMR}(P, h, (\mathtt{in}))$. □

Next, we present the notion of tail recursion, which is relative to a mode.

Definition 7. *The definition of a predicate L in a program P is* tail recursive *w.r.t. a mode* m *iff the following two conditions hold:*

(a) $\mathtt{MR}_P(L) = \{L\}$
(b) the set of clause modes $\mathtt{DefMode}(P, L, \mathtt{m})$ *yields clauses of the following two forms:*

$$\begin{aligned}
&(1)\ \ L(\bar{r}_{\mathtt{I}} \overset{\mathtt{m}}{\triangleright} \bar{r}_0) \leftarrow \overline{E} \\
&(2)\ \ L(\bar{s}_{\mathtt{I}} \overset{\mathtt{m}}{\triangleright} \bar{z}) \leftarrow \overline{F},\ L(\bar{s}'_{\mathtt{I}} \overset{\mathtt{m}}{\triangleright} \bar{z})
\end{aligned}$$

where $N \notin \mathtt{MR}_P(L)$ for each $N \in \overline{E} \cdot \overline{F}$ and $\bar{z}$ is a tuple of fresh variables. □

This notion of tail recursion is more restrictive than the classical one. Intuitively stated, it means that, besides the fact that only the rightmost literal is head-dependent, all the recursive calls return exactly the same value.

5   Elimination of the Local Variables of a Literal

When $\mathtt{Def}_P(L)$ is tail recursive w.r.t. a mode, we are able to eliminate the local variables that occur in the output arguments of the selected literal $L(\bar{t})$. This is done by substituting a set of clauses, called $\mathtt{LVF}_P(C, L(\bar{t}))$, for the clause C.

Definition 8. *Let* $\mathtt{VarMode}(C, L(\bar{t}), \bar{y})$ *yield the following IO-form for C:*

$$C = H \leftarrow \overline{M},\ L(\bar{t}_{\mathtt{I}} \overset{\mathtt{m}}{\triangleright} \bar{t}_0),\ K_1(\bar{u}^1_{\mathtt{I}} \overset{\mathtt{m}^1}{\triangleright} \bar{u}^1_0),\ \ldots\ ,\ K_n(\bar{u}^n_{\mathtt{I}} \overset{\mathtt{m}^n}{\triangleright} \bar{u}^n_0),\ \overline{N}$$

where $\bar{y} = \mathtt{LVar}(L(\bar{t}))$ are term-apart in $L(\bar{t})$ and $\bar{y} \cap \mathtt{Var}(\overline{N}) = \emptyset$. If $\mathtt{Def}_P(L)$ is tail recursive w.r.t. m, *then $\mathtt{LVF}_P(C, L(\bar{t}))$ consists of the following clauses:*

(a) One single clause of the form:

$$H \leftarrow \overline{M}, \; p(\overline{t}_I, \overline{w}_I \triangleright \overline{u}_0, \overline{w}_0), \; \overline{N}$$

where $\overline{u}_0 = \overline{u}_0^1 \cup \ldots \cup \overline{u}_0^n$.

(b) For each non-recursive clause $L(\overline{r}_I \overset{m}{\triangleright} \overline{r}_0) \leftarrow \overline{E} \in \mathsf{Def}_P(L)$, a clause:

$$p(\overline{r}_I \sigma, \overline{w}_I \sigma \triangleright \overline{v}, \overline{w}_0 \sigma) \leftarrow \overline{E}\sigma, \; K_1(\overline{u}_I^1 \sigma \overset{m^1}{\triangleright} \overline{v}^1), \; \ldots, \; K_n(\overline{u}_I^n \sigma \overset{m^n}{\triangleright} \overline{v}^n)$$

where $\sigma = mgu(\overline{r}_0, \overline{t}_0)$ and $\overline{v} = \overline{v}^1 \cup \ldots \cup \overline{v}^n$.

(c) For each recursive clause $L(\overline{s}_I \overset{m}{\triangleright} \overline{z}) \leftarrow \overline{F}, L(\overline{s}_I' \overset{m}{\triangleright} \overline{z}) \in \mathsf{Def}_P(L)$, a clause:

$$p(\overline{s}_I, \overline{w}_I \triangleright \overline{v}, \overline{w}_0) \leftarrow \overline{F}, \; p(\overline{s}_I', \overline{w}_I \triangleright \overline{v}, \overline{w}_0)$$

where p is a fresh predicate symbol, $\overline{v}$ is a fresh tuple of variables of the size of $\overline{u}_0$, $\overline{w}_I = \mathsf{GVar}(\overline{t}_0) \smallsetminus \mathsf{GVar}(\overline{t}_I \cdot \overline{u}_0)$ and $\overline{w}_0 = \mathsf{GVar}(\overline{u}_I) \smallsetminus \mathsf{GVar}(\overline{t}_I \cdot \overline{u}_0)$. □

In the above definition, $\overline{w}_I$ and $\overline{w}_0$ are used to keep the links between literals through global variables. Note that, in the original clause C, the exact variables $\overline{y}$ occur in $\overline{t}_0$ and $\overline{u}_I^j$ for $1 \leq j \leq n$, but do not occur in $\mathsf{LVF}_P(C, L(\overline{t}))$. Hence, $\overline{y}$ has been eliminated from C. Some occurrences of local variables could remain in the clauses of the form *(b)*, but they are in literals that do not depend on the head. We will return to this matter for a discussion about termination.

Theorem 1. *Let $\mathsf{LVF}_P(C, L(\overline{t}))$, $L(\overline{t})$ and the clause C be as in Definition 8. The programs P and $P' = P \smallsetminus \{C\} \cup \mathsf{LVF}_P(C, L(\overline{t}))$ are Clark-Kunen equivalent.*

Proof. Let us assume that $\mathsf{VarMode}(C, L(\overline{t}), \overline{y})$ yields the following IO-form:

$$C: \quad H \leftarrow \overline{M}, \; L(\overline{t}_I \overset{m}{\triangleright} \overline{t}_0), \; K_1(\overline{u}_I^1 \overset{m^1}{\triangleright} \overline{u}_0^1), \; \ldots, \; K_n(\overline{u}_I^n \overset{m^n}{\triangleright} \overline{u}_0^n), \; \overline{N}$$

where $\overline{y} = \mathsf{LVar}(L(\overline{t}))$. A program P_0 is obtained by introducing the new predicate p in P. In P_0, p is defined by the single clause:

$$D: \quad p(\overline{x}, \overline{w}_I \triangleright \overline{z}, \overline{w}_0) \leftarrow L(\overline{x} \overset{m}{\triangleright} \overline{t}_0), \; K_1(\overline{u}_I^1 \sigma \overset{m^1}{\triangleright} \overline{z}^1), \; \ldots, \; K_n(\overline{u}_I^n \sigma \overset{m^n}{\triangleright} \overline{z}^n)$$

where $\overline{x}$, $\overline{z}^1$, $\ldots$, $\overline{z}^n$ are tuples of fresh variables, the sets $\overline{w}_I$ and $\overline{w}_0$ are obtained as in Definition 8 and $\overline{z} = \overline{z}^1 \cup \ldots \cup \overline{z}^n$. The programs P and P_0 are trivially equivalent. Next, we obtain P_1 from P_0 by folding C using D:

$$C': \quad H \leftarrow \overline{M}, \; p(\overline{t}_I, \overline{w}_I \triangleright \overline{u}_0, \overline{w}_0), \; \overline{N}$$

where $\overline{u}_0 = \overline{u}_0^1 \cup \ldots \cup \overline{u}_0^n$. Then, the program P_2 is obtained by unfolding the literal $L(\overline{x} \triangleright \overline{t}_0)$ in the clause D. Since $\mathsf{Def}_P(L)$ (and therefore, $\mathsf{Def}_{P_1}(L)$) is tail recursive w.r.t. m, it consists of clauses of the following two forms:

$$T1.1: \; L(\overline{r}_I \overset{m}{\triangleright} \overline{r}_0) \leftarrow \overline{E}$$
$$T1.2: \; L(\overline{s}_I \overset{m}{\triangleright} \overline{z}) \leftarrow \overline{F}, \; L(\overline{s}_I' \overset{m}{\triangleright} \overline{z})$$

and, hence, after the unfolding step, we get clauses of the form:

$$T1.3: \; p(\overline{r}_I \sigma, \overline{w}_I \sigma \triangleright \overline{z}, \overline{w}_0 \sigma) \leftarrow \overline{E}\sigma, \; K_1(\overline{u}_I^1 \sigma \overset{m^1}{\triangleright} \overline{z}^1), \; \ldots, \; K_n(\overline{u}_I^n \sigma \overset{m^n}{\triangleright} \overline{z}^n)$$
$$T1.4: \; p(\overline{s}_I, \overline{w}_I \triangleright \overline{z}, \overline{w}_0) \leftarrow \overline{F}, \; L(\overline{s}_I' \overset{m}{\triangleright} \overline{t}_0), \; K_1(\overline{u}_I^1 \overset{m^1}{\triangleright} \overline{z}^1), \ldots, K_n(\overline{u}_I^n \sigma \overset{m^n}{\triangleright} \overline{z}^n)$$

where $\sigma = mgu(\overline{r}_0, \overline{t}_0)$. The programs P_2 and P' are syntactically equal except for the clauses $T1.4$, where $L(\overline{s}'_I \overset{\mathtt{m}}{\triangleright} \overline{t}_0)$, $K_1(\overline{u}^1_I \sigma \overset{\mathtt{m}^1}{\triangleright} \overline{z}^1)$, $\ldots$, $K_n(\overline{u}^n_I \sigma \overset{\mathtt{m}^n}{\triangleright} \overline{z}^n)$ correspond with the literal $p(\overline{s}'_I, \overline{w}_I \triangleright \overline{z}, \overline{w}_0)$ in the program P'. It is easy (but tedious) to prove that P_2 and P' are equivalent using induction on bottom-up computation of the Clark-Kunen semantics. The interested reader may find the details in [1]. Therefore, the programs P and P' are also equivalent.   □

Example 5. Let P be the following program:

$E5.1:$ $\quad q(x_1, x_2) \leftarrow member(y, x_1),\ \neg\, member(y, x_2)$
$E5.2:$ $\quad member(x, [x|\_])$
$E5.3:$ $\quad member(x_1, [\_|x_2]) \leftarrow member(x_1, x_2)$

In order to eliminate the local variable y, we first obtain the set of modes $\mathtt{VarMode}(E5.1, member(y, x_1), y)$, that yields the following IO-form of $E5.1$:

$$q(x_1, x_2) \leftarrow member(x_1 \triangleright y),\ \neg\, member(y \triangleright x_2)$$

where the mode $(\mathtt{out}, \mathtt{in})$ is assigned to $member$. Besides, the set of clause modes $\mathtt{DefMode}(P, member, (\mathtt{out}, \mathtt{in}))$ gives the following clauses:

$$member([x|\_] \triangleright x)$$
$$member([\_|x_2] \triangleright x_1) \leftarrow member(x_2 \triangleright x_1)$$

Since $\mathtt{Def}_P(member)$ is tail recursive w.r.t. the mode $(\mathtt{out}, \mathtt{in})$, then the set of clauses $\mathtt{LVF}_P(E5.1, member(y, x_1))$ is a compound of:

$E5.4:$ $\quad q(x_1, x_2) \leftarrow p(x_1 \triangleright x_2)$
$E5.5:$ $\quad p([x|\_] \triangleright z) \leftarrow \neg\, member(x \triangleright z)$
$E5.6:$ $\quad p([\_|x] \triangleright z) \leftarrow p(x \triangleright z)$ □

6   Tail Recursive Transformation

We use the well known technique of the *call stack* for transforming recursion into tail recursion. The method in [21] also uses the call stack to convert a definite program into a continuation passing style program which, in particular, is a binary program (clauses have at most one literal in the body). We perform a similar, but simpler, treatment since our target program is not required to be binary. For the sake of readability, consider that the clauses to be transformed have (at most) two head-dependent literals in the body (see (1) below). Generalization to n literals is not difficult but unnecessarily complicates the description of the transformation we explain below.

A given $\mathtt{Def}_P(L)$, that is not tail recursive with respect to a mode $\mathtt{m}$, is transformed into a new definition formed by the single clause:

$$L(\overline{x} \overset{\mathtt{m}}{\triangleright} \overline{z}) \leftarrow q(\overline{x}, [c_L] \triangleright \overline{z}).$$

where q is a fresh predicate and c_L is a constant that stands for L. This new definition is obviously tail recursive w.r.t. any mode (in particular w.r.t. m).

Then, we use the original definition of L for providing a tail recursive definition of q w.r.t. the mode in $q(\overline{x}, [c_L] \triangleright \overline{z})$, which is the extension of $\mathtt{m}$ by adding an input position. The definition of q is given by:

- the single clause $q(\overline{z}, [\,] \triangleright \overline{z})$,
- plus, for each element $\mathtt{m}' : K \in \mathsf{ModeMR}(P, L, \mathtt{m})$ and each clause from $\mathsf{Def}_P(K)$ (in Dpd-form):

$$K(\overline{t}_\mathrm{I} \overset{\mathtt{m}'}{\triangleright} \overline{t}_0) \leftarrow \overline{L}^1, \ K_1(\overline{s}_\mathrm{I}^1 \overset{\mathtt{m}^1}{\triangleright} \overline{s}_0^1), \ \overline{L}^2, \ K_2(\overline{s}_\mathrm{I}^2 \overset{\mathtt{m}^2}{\triangleright} \overline{s}_0^2), \ \overline{L}^3 \tag{1}$$

the following four clauses:

(i) $q(\overline{t}_\mathrm{I}, [c_K|S] \triangleright \overline{z}) \leftarrow q(\overline{t}_\mathrm{I}, [\overline{w}^1, c_1^C, \overline{w}^2, c_2^C, \overline{w}^C, c^C|S] \triangleright \overline{z})$
(ii) $q(\overline{t}_\mathrm{I}, [\overline{w}^1, c_1^C|S] \triangleright \overline{z}) \leftarrow \overline{L}^1, \ q(\overline{s}_\mathrm{I}^1, [c_{K_1}|S] \triangleright \overline{z})$
(iii) $q(\overline{s}_0^1, [\overline{w}^2, c_2^C|S] \triangleright \overline{z}) \leftarrow \overline{L}^2, \ q(\overline{s}_\mathrm{I}^2, [c_{K_2}|S] \triangleright \overline{z})$
(iv) $q(\overline{s}_0^2, [\overline{w}^C, c^C|S] \triangleright \overline{z}) \leftarrow \overline{L}^3, \ q(\overline{t}_0, S \triangleright \overline{z})$

where $\overline{z}$ is a tuple of fresh variables, $\overline{w}^1 = \mathsf{GVar}(\overline{L}^1 \cdot \overline{s}_\mathrm{I}^1), \ \overline{w}^2 = \mathsf{GVar}(\overline{s}_0^1 \cdot \overline{L}^2 \cdot \overline{s}_\mathrm{I}^2)$ and $\overline{w}^C = \mathsf{GVar}(\overline{s}_0^2 \cdot \overline{L}^3 \cdot \overline{t}_0) \cap (\overline{w}^1 \cup \overline{w}^2)$.

The sets of variables in the stack are used to keep the links between literals through global variables. As defined, these sets are not minimal. A more sophisticated analysis would produce smaller sets of variables. Note that the fresh predicate q is used with tuples of terms of different sizes in the input arguments and, therefore, we are really defining several predicates, one for each arity. This is not a minor difference if we consider the dependences of predicates, especially in Definition 8. By contrast, the size of the tuple of fresh variables $\overline{z}$ is equal in all the clauses and it coincides with the number of output positions in $\mathtt{m}$.

Example 6. Let P be the following program:

E6.1 : $k(a \overset{m}{\triangleright} b)$
E6.2 : $k(f(x_1) \overset{m}{\triangleright} f(x_2)) \leftarrow q(x_1 \overset{m}{\triangleright} x_2)$
E6.3 : $q(x_1 \overset{m}{\triangleright} x_2) \leftarrow \neg h(x_1, x_2)$
E6.4 : $q(f(x_1) \overset{m}{\triangleright} f(x_2))) \leftarrow k(x_1 \overset{m}{\triangleright} y), \ q(g(y, x_1) \overset{m}{\triangleright} x_2)$

where $\mathsf{ModeMR}(P, k, \mathtt{m}) = \{\mathtt{m} : k, \ \mathtt{m} : q\}$ for $\mathtt{m} = (\mathtt{in}, \mathtt{out})$. Since $\mathsf{Def}_P(k)$ is not tail recursive w.r.t. $\mathtt{m}$, a tail recursive definition of k w.r.t. $\mathtt{m}$ consists of the following clauses. First, the initial clauses:

E6.5 : $k(x \overset{m}{\triangleright} z) \leftarrow p(x, [c_k] \triangleright z)$
E6.6 : $p(z, [\,] \triangleright z)$

where the constant c_k stands for the predicate k. Since E6.1 is non-recursive, the above clauses (ii) and (iii) are not necessary (c^1 corresponds with E6.1):

E6.7 : $p(a, [c_k|S] \triangleright z) \leftarrow p(a, [c^1|S] \triangleright z)$
E6.8 : $p(a, [c^1|S] \triangleright z) \leftarrow p(b, S \triangleright z)$

In the clause $E6.2$, there is one recursive literal. Hence, (iii) is not necessary:

$E6.9:\ p(f(x_1),[c_k|S] \triangleright z) \leftarrow p(f(x_1),[c_1^2,c^2|S] \triangleright z)$
$E6.10:\ p(f(x_1),[c_1^2|S] \triangleright z) \leftarrow p(x_1,[c_q|S] \triangleright z)$
$E6.11:\ p(x_2,[c^2|S] \triangleright z) \leftarrow p(f(x_2),S \triangleright z)$

where c^2 stands for the clause $E6.2$, c_1^2 for the literal $q(x_1 \triangleright x_2)$ and c_q for the predicate q. The clause $E6.3$ is non-recursive (c^3 corresponds to $E6.3$), then:

$E6.12:\ p(x_1,[c_q|S] \triangleright z) \leftarrow p(x_1,[c^3|S] \triangleright z)$
$E6.13:\ p(x_1,[c^3|S] \triangleright z) \leftarrow \neg\, h(x_1,y),\ p(y,S \triangleright z)$

Finally, the clause $E6.4$ has two recursive literals, where c^4, c_1^4 and c_2^4 respectively stand for the clause itself and the literals $k(x_1 \triangleright x_2)$ and $q(g(y,x_1) \triangleright x_2)$:

$E6.14:\ p(f(x_1),[c_q|S] \triangleright z) \leftarrow p(f(x_1),[c_1^4,x_1,c_2^4,c^4|S] \triangleright z)$
$E6.15:\ p(f(x_1),[c_1^4|S] \triangleright z) \leftarrow p(x_1,[c_k|S] \triangleright z)$
$E6.16:\ p(f(x),[x_1,c_2^4|S] \triangleright z) \leftarrow p(g(x,x_1),[c_q|S] \triangleright z)$
$E6.17:\ p(x_2,[c^4|S] \triangleright z) \leftarrow p(f(x_2),S \triangleright z)$ □

It is easy to see that, in the above example, the transformed program uses the stack to simulate the computation of the original program for any goal. In general, the transformation works similarly for clauses with any arbitrary number of head-dependent body literals and it preserves the Clark-Kunen equivalence. The proof of this result is omitted for brevity and it can be found in [1].

Theorem 2. *Let* m *be a mode for a predicate L in a program P. Then, the definition of L can be transformed into a Clark-Kunen equivalent definition that is tail recursive w.r.t.* m.   □

7   An Algorithm for Elimination of Local Variables

Now, we present our algorithm —see Figure 1— for eliminating local variables. In previous sections, we have shown the basic transformations that our algorithm performs. These are: local-regulation (LR), elimination of a tuple of local variables (LVF) and tail-recursive transformation (TR). These three basic operations have different effects on the set of local variable occurrences in the transformed program. Sometimes, new local variables could arise in the new clauses and, at the same time, other local variables are erased. In this section, we show that it is possible to give decidable conditions that guarantee termination. Such conditions are concerned with the notion of a literal candidate, which we will make precise after a brief introduction of the algorithm itself.

The algorithm outlined in Figure 1 first collects all the literals that contain some local variables in the set $\mathsf{Lit}(P)$. Then, until $\mathsf{Lit}(P)$ becomes empty, we select any literal $L(\bar{t})$ from that set. Let assume that $L(\bar{t})$ occurs in a clause C such that m is the mode assigned to the predicate L by $\mathsf{VarMode}(C, L(\bar{t}), \mathsf{LVar}(L(\bar{t})))$ and H is the literal in the clause head. On the one hand, if the selected literal is not a candidate (line 5), then we simply delete it from $\mathsf{Lit}(P)$ and proceed to the next iteration. On the other hand, if $L(\bar{t})$ is a candidate, then there are two main cases. If $\text{Def}_P(L)$ is tail recursive w.r.t. m (line 7), we substitute $\text{LVF}_P(C, L(\bar{t}))$ for C. Besides, we delete from $\text{Lit}(P)$ all the literals that occur in C and add to $\text{Lit}(P)$ all the literals from $\text{LVF}_P(C, L(\bar{t}))$ that contain some local variables. Otherwise, if the definition of L is not tail recursive w.r.t. m (line 12), we transform $\text{Def}_P(L)$ into tail recursive w.r.t. that mode. Besides, we delete from $\text{Lit}(P)$ the literals that occur in $\text{Def}_P(L)$ and add to $\text{Lit}(P)$ the literals that contain some local variables in the new clauses. In the former case (line 7), we directly eliminate the subset of local variables from the clause C. In the latter case (line 12), the definition of L is adapted for fulfilling the condition of the first case. Note that, in the last case (line 12), the clause C is removed from P only if L depends on H, because $\text{Def}_P(L) = \text{Def}_P(H)$. Therefore, we have to select a different candidate in the next step. Otherwise, $L(\bar{t})$ can be selected as a candidate in the next step and the subset of local variables will be eliminated.

```
1    collect in Lit(P) all the literals that contain some local variables
2    while Lit(P) ≠ ∅ loop
3        select a literal L(t̄) in a clause C = H ← M̄, L(t̄), N̄
4        let m : L ∈ VarMode(C, L(t̄), LVar(L(t̄)))
5        if L is not a candidate then
6            delete L from Lit(P)
7        elsif Def_P(L) is tail recursive w.r.t. m then
8            substitute LVF_P(C, L) for the clause C in P
9            delete from Lit(P) the literals in C
10           add to Lit(P) the literals in LVF_P(C, L) that contain
11                             some local variables
12       else
13           transform Def_P(L) into tail recursive w.r.t. m
14           delete from Lit(P) the literals in Def_P(L)
15           add to Def_P(L) the literals in the new clauses that
16                             contain some local variables
17       end if
18   end loop
```

Fig. 1. An Algorithm for Elimination of Local Variables

The algorithm in Figure 1 terminates when there is no candidate, although the resulting program may not necessarily be *lvf*. With regard to termination, the transformation LR introduces new local variables but, since local-regularity is preserved by the other two transformations, LR is applied only finitely many times. The transformation LVF does not introduce new local variables, but the local variables $\bar{y}$ to be removed could be only partially eliminated in some cases. In particular, a clause of the form *(b)* of Definition 8 could contain some variables from $\bar{y}$. However, they necessarily occur in literals that do not depend on the clause head. This fact ensures termination because the set of all mutually recursive components of a program is well-foundedly ordered w.r.t. predicate dependencies. The transformation TR, explained in Section 6, could introduce new local variables, which could lead to non-termination problems through clauses **(i)** and **(iv)** (see Section 6). The problem arises when new local variables exactly occur in literals which depend on the clause head because, in that case, the resulting definition is never tail recursive w.r.t that is given by `VarMode` with respect to the new local variables. Therefore, we would transform the definition of a predicate into tail recursive w.r.t. the corresponding mode infinitely many times. On the one hand, since clauses **(i)** are binary, they must be *lvf* in order to avoid that problem. On the other hand, let us illustrate the problem of clauses **(iv)** by the following example.

Example 7. Consider the following program P:

E7.1 : $perfectsq(v) \leftarrow mult(y, y, v)$
E7.2 : $mult(0, x, 0)$
E7.3 : $mult(s(x_1), x_2, x_3) \leftarrow mult(x_1, x_2, y),\ sum(x_2, y, x_3)$

To eliminate the local variable y in the first clause, $\texttt{VarMode}(E7.1, mult(y, y, v), y)$ assigns the mode (out, out, in) to the predicate $mult$. Since $\texttt{Def}_P(mult)$ is not tail recursive w.r.t. (out, out, in), we transform the definition of the predicate $mult$ as explained in Section 6. Then, the clause **(iv)** obtained from $E7.2$ is:

$$q(0, [c^{E7.2}|S] \triangleright z_1, z_2) \leftarrow q(0, y', S \triangleright z_1, z_2)$$

where y' is a new local variable that occurs in a literal that depends on the clause head. However, if the clause $E7.2$ is replaced with the following two clauses:

E7.4 : $mult(0, 0, 0)$
E7.5 : $mult(0, s(x), 0) \leftarrow mult(0, x, 0)$

then, the respective clauses **(iv)** are *lvf* (therefore, not problematic):

$$q(0, [c^{E7.4}|S] \triangleright z_1, z_2) \leftarrow q(0, 0, S \triangleright z_1, z_2)$$
$$q(0, x, [c^{E7.5}|S] \triangleright z_1, z_2) \leftarrow q(0, s(x), S \triangleright z_1, z_2)$$

Note that the programs P and $P \setminus \{E7.2\} \cup \{E7.4, E7.5\}$ are not Clark-Kunen equivalent. □

In order to avoid the termination problem, we can establish syntactic conditions to ensure that the clauses **(i)** are *lvf* and also that the new local variables of **(iv)** occur in literals which do not depend on the head. This is a sufficient condition for termination assuming that the literal selection rule (line 3 in Figure 1) is fair, although the resulting program might be not *lvf*. This condition is formally stated in the following definition.

Definition 9. *Let P be a program and $N(\overline{u})$ be a literal in a clause C such that $\texttt{VarMode}(C, N(\overline{u}), \texttt{LVar}(N(\overline{u})))$ assigns the mode $\texttt{m}$ to the predicate N and $\overline{u}_I \triangleright \overline{u}_0$ is the unique partition of the tuple of terms $\overline{u}$ w.r.t. $\texttt{m}$. Then, the literal $N(\overline{u})$ is called* candidate *iff:*

(a) $\mathsf{LVar}(N(\overline{u}))$ *are term-apart in* $N(\overline{u})$
(b) $\mathsf{Def}_P(K)$ *is local-regular for every* $K \in \mathsf{MR}_P(N)$
(c) $\mathsf{LVar}(\overline{u}_0) \neq \emptyset$
(d) for each element $\mathsf{m}' : K \in \mathsf{ModeMR}(P, N, \mathsf{m})$ *and each clause in* $\mathsf{Def}_P(K)$ *of the form* $K(\overline{t}_{\mathrm{I}} \overset{\mathsf{m}'}{\triangleright} \overline{t}_0) \leftarrow \overline{L}^1, K_1(\overline{s}_{\mathrm{I}}^1 \triangleright \overline{s}_0^1), \ldots, \overline{L}^n, K_n(\overline{s}_{\mathrm{I}}^n \triangleright \overline{s}_0^n), \overline{L}^{n+1}$[3]:
  (d.1) $\mathsf{GVar}(\overline{L}^1 \cdot \overline{s}_{\mathrm{I}}^1 \cdot \overline{s}_0^1 \cdot \ldots \cdot \overline{L}^n \cdot \overline{s}_{\mathrm{I}}^n) \subseteq \mathsf{GVar}(\overline{t}_{\mathrm{I}})$
  (d.2) $\mathsf{GVar}(\overline{t}_0) \subseteq \mathsf{GVar}(\overline{t}_{\mathrm{I}} \cdot \overline{L}^{n+1} \cdot \overline{s}_0^n)$
(e) $\mathsf{Def}_P(K)$ *is a normal definition for every* $K \in \mathsf{MR}_P(N)$ □

The conditions $(d.1)$ and $(d.2)$ in the above definition respectively ensure that the clauses **(i)** and **(iv)** are not problematic. Note that, in Example 7, the literal $mult(y, y, v)$ is not a candidate because $(d.2)$ does not hold for $E7.2$ and mode $(\mathsf{out}, \mathsf{out}, \mathsf{in})$, since $\mathsf{GVar}(\overline{t}_0) = \{x\}$ and $\mathsf{GVar}(\overline{t}_{\mathrm{I}} \cdot \overline{L}^{n+1} \cdot \overline{s}_0^n) = \emptyset$. On the contrary, the clauses $E7.4$ and $E7.5$ avoid this problem, because the former does not have any global variable, whereas for the latter $\mathsf{GVar}(\overline{t}_0) = \{x\}$ and $\mathsf{GVar}(\overline{t}_{\mathrm{I}} \cdot \overline{L}^{n+1} \cdot \overline{s}_0^n) = \{x\}$. Besides, the condition (e) ensures that, dealing with normal logic programs, the transformations LVF and LR are applicable to the involved definition. Note that the elimination of some local variables could turn a non-candidate literal into a candidate one when its complex definition becomes normal.

We have verified that the algorithm in Figure 1 successfully works for most of the programs in Sterling and Shapiro [22] (about 35 definite programs and 6 normal programs). The interested reader may find them and their *lvf* version in the URL: http://www.sc.ehu.es/jiwlucap/LVF.html. Outstanding exceptions are the programs that use difference-lists. Let us give an example.

Example 8. Let P be the following program:

$E8.1:$ $flatten(x_1, x_2) \leftarrow flatten\_dl(x_1, x_2 \setminus [\,])$
$E8.2:$ $flatten\_dl([\,], x \setminus x)$
$E8.3:$ $flatten\_dl(x_1, [x_1|x_2] \setminus x_2) \leftarrow constant(x_1), x_1 \neq [\,]$
$E8.4:$ $flatten\_dl([x_1|x_2], x_3 \setminus x_4) \leftarrow flatten\_dl(x_1, x_3 \setminus y),$
$ flatten\_dl(x_2, y \setminus x_4)$

that flattens a list of lists using difference-lists. The algorithm in Figure 1 cannot eliminate the local variable y in the clause $E8.4$. In order to eliminate y, the mode $(\mathsf{in}, \mathsf{out}) : flatten\_dl$ is given by $\mathsf{VarMode}(E8.4, flatten\_dl(x_1, x_3 \setminus y), y)$. However, the clause $E8.2$ does not hold the condition $(d.2)$ in Definition 9 with respect to this mode.   □

In spite of this drawback, our algorithm successfully eliminates all the local variables from a wide subclass of normal logic programs. That is, many pograms satisfy the conditions in Definition 9. In order to provide some more intuitition on the Definition 9, we would like to point out that any well-moded program ([9, 10, 19]) satisfy it. Roughly speaking, in a well-moded program, each predicate

---

[3] For technical reasons, we assume that $\overline{s}_0^0$ is the tuple $\overline{t}_{\mathrm{I}}$.

has assigned a unique mode such that the literals (in clause bodies) satisfy a left-to-right *producer-consumer* relation. For mostly well-moded clauses, that relation directly ensures the conditions $(d.1)$ and $(d.2)$ of Definition 9. Some exceptions are due to the fact that we only assign modes to some predicates (the ones that are mutually recursive with the predicate in the clause head). This shortcoming can be avoided by requiring local-regulation (see Definition 2) in the global variables as it is required for the local ones. Notice that, in Example 7, the clauses $E7.4$ and $E7.5$ are well-moded. The first one is trivially well-moded because its body is empty and all the terms in its head are ground. In the clause $E7.5$, there is a well-moded *producer-consumer* relation since the literal in the clause body *produces* the output variable x of the head. Notice also that, on the contrary, the clause $E7.2$ cannot be well-moded because the output variable x is neither *produced* by the clause body (it is empty), nor is it also an input variable.

8   Conclusions and Related Work

We have introduced an algorithm that removes local variables from normal programs while preserving Clark-Kunen semantics and show that our algorithm eliminates all the local variables from a wide range of normal logic programs. However, it is still an open problem to decide whether any normal (or, even, definite) program can be transformed into an *lvf* one, despite the result of [24].

Since our transformation includes fresh symbols and new literals, a real implementation should clean up the target program to prevent a hypothetical performance deterioration. Superfluous literals can be removed by unfolding. Note that unfolding in an *lvf* program preserves the *lvf* feature. Furthermore, we can reduce the blow-up of new symbols and literals by keeping the original definition of predicates in the program, although their tail recursive versions are used for performing the local variable elimination.

The work most closely related to our own is [21], where a continuation passing style (CPS, for short) transformation is introduced for definite programs. The CPS conversion is also related to both the call stack technique and the notion of mode. Moreover, the authors introduce the possibility of local variable elimination through CPS conversion and give a sufficient condition for successful elimination, called *ground I/O condition*, in a definite program. The ground I/O condition of a clause depends on some (arbitrary) mode for every predicate occurring in it. Anyway, there are marked differences in our approach and results. First, we deterministically assign one mode to each literal taking into account the local variables to be eliminated, whereas the transformation of [21] depends on an arbitrary mode. Second, we only manage the clauses that belong to the predicate definition (and the mutually recursive ones) of the selected literal. By contrast, in the approach of [21], the definition of all the literals in the affected clause are handled and all of them must satisfy the ground I/O condition.

The aim of [18] is to yield more efficient SLD-computations of definite programs by the elimination of redundant computations caused by the so-called *unnecessary* variables. Local variables are a special kind of such unnecessary variables, because that method also considers as unnecessary those variables that occur more than once in the clause body (called *multiple* variables), even when they occur in the head. Different strategies for guiding the application of unfold/fold transformations are presented in order to eliminate such unnecessary variables. These strategies guarantee the complete elimination of unnecessary variables for a syntactically characterized subclass of definite programs.

Other significant related work is [14], which introduces an algorithm, called RAF, for eliminating *redundant arguments* from definite programs. Actually, RAF is intended as a post-processing phase for program transformers, since automatic transformation produces many redundant arguments. Usually, local variables appear in redundant arguments. Hence, local variable elimination can be performed through a combination of some program transformation method (for instance, conjunctive partial deduction) and the RAF algorithm. This kind of system is closer in spirit to [18] than our own method.

Acknowledgment. We would like to thank the anonymous referees for their valuable comments, which aided in improving the quality of this paper and in clarifying the presentation. This work was partially supported by the Spanish Project TIN2004-079250-C03-03.

References

1. J. Álvez and P. Lucio. An algorithm for local variable elimination in normal logic programs. Technical Report LSI/TR 10-2005, Basque Country University, 2005.
2. J. Álvez, P. Lucio, F. Orejas, E. Pasarella, and E. Pino. Constructive negation by bottom-up computation of literal answers. In *SAC '04: Proceedings of the 2004 ACM symposium on Applied computing*, pages 1468–1475, New York, NY, USA, 2004. ACM Press.
3. H. Andréka and I. Németi. The generalized completeness of Horn predicate-logic as a programming language. *Acta Cybern.*, 4:3–10, 1980.
4. K. R. Apt. Logic programming. In *Handbook of Theoretical Computer Science, Volume B: Formal Models and Sematics (B)*, pages 493–574. Elsevier, 1990.
5. R. Barbuti, P. Mancarella, D. Pedreschi, and F. Turini. A transformational approach to negation in logic programming. *J. Log. Program.*, 8(3):201–228, 1990.
6. P. Bruscoli, F. Levi, G. Levi, and M. C. Meo. Compilative constructive negation in constraint logic programs. In *CAAP '94: Proceedings of the 19th International Colloquium on Trees in Algebra and Programming*, pages 52–67, London, UK, 1994. Springer-Verlag.
7. D. Chan. An extension of constructive negation and its application in coroutining. In *NACLP*, pages 477–493, 1989.
8. K. L. Clark. Negation as failure. In H. Gallaire and J. Minker, editors, *Logic and Data Bases*, pages 293–322, New York, 1978. Plenum Press.
9. P. Dembinski and J. Maluszynski. And-parallelism with intelligent backtracking for annotated logic programs. In *SLP*, pages 29–38, 1985.
10. W. Drabent. Do logic programs resemble programs in conventional languages? In *SLP*, pages 289–396, 1987.
11. W. Drabent. What is failure? an approach to constructive negation. *Acta Inf.*, 32(1):27–29, 1995.

12. M. Hanus. On extra variables in (equational) logic programming. In *ICLP*, pages 665–679, 1995.
13. K. Kunen. Negation in logic programming. *J. Log. Program.*, 4(4):289–308, 1987.
14. M. Leuschel and M. H. Sørensen. Redundant argument filtering of logic programs. In J. Gallagher, editor, *Logic Program Synthesis and Transformation, Proceedings of LoPSTr '96, Stockholm, Sweden*, Lecture Notes in Computer Science 1207, pages 83–103. Springer-Verlag, 1996.
15. M. J. Maher. Correctness of a logic program transformation system. Technical Report RC 13496, IBM T.J. Watson Research Center, 1988.
16. C. S. Mellish. The automatic generation of mode declarations for prolog programs. Technical Report 163, Dept. of Artificial Intelligence, University of Edinburgh, Scotland, 1981.
17. A. Pettorossi and M. Proietti. Transformation of logic programs. In D. M. Gabbayand, C. J. Hogger, and J. A. Robinson, editors, *Handbook of Logic in Artificial Intelligence and Logic Programming, Vol. 5*, pages 697–787. Oxford University Press, 1998.
18. M. Proietti and A. Pettorossi. Unfolding - definition - folding, in this order, for avoiding unnecessary variables in logic programs. *Theor. Comput. Sci.*, 142(1): 89–124, 1995.
19. D. A. Rosenblueth. Chart parsers as proof procedures for fixed-mode logic programs. In *FGCS*, pages 1125–1132, 1992.
20. T. Sato and H. Tamaki. Transformational logic program synthesis. In *FGCS*, pages 195–201, 1984.
21. T. Sato and H. Tamaki. Existential continuation. *New Generation Comput.*, 6(4):421–438, 1989.
22. L. Sterling and E. Shapiro. *The art of Prolog: advanced programming techniques.* MIT Press, Cambridge, MA, USA, 1986.
23. P. J. Stuckey. Negation and constraint logic programming. *Inf. Comput.*, 118(1):12–33, 1995.
24. S.-Å. Tärnlund. Horn clause computability. *BIT*, 17(2):215–226, 1977.
25. H. C. Wasserman, K. Yukawa, and Z. Shen. An alternative transformation rule for logic programs. In *SAC '95: Proceedings of the 1995 ACM symposium on Applied computing*, pages 364–368, New York, NY, USA, 1995. ACM Press.

Removing Superfluous Versions in Polyvariant Specialization of Prolog Programs

Claudio Ochoa[1], Germán Puebla[1], and Manuel Hermenegildo[1,2]

[1] School of Computer Science, Technical U. of Madrid
{cochoa, german, herme}@fi.upm.es
[2] Depts. of Comp. Sci. and El. and Comp. Eng., U. of New Mexico
herme@unm.edu

Abstract. Polyvariant specialization allows generating multiple versions of a procedure, which can then be separately optimized for different uses. Since allowing a high degree of polyvariance often results in more optimized code, polyvariant specializers, such as most partial evaluators, can generate a large number of versions. This can produce unnecessarily large residual programs. Also, large programs can be slower due to cache miss effects. A possible solution to this problem is to introduce a minimization step which identifies sets of *equivalent* versions, and replace all occurrences of such versions by a single one. In this work we present a unifying view of the problem of superfluous polyvariance. It includes both partial deduction and abstract multiple specialization. As regards partial deduction, we extend existing approaches in several ways. First, previous work has dealt with pure logic programs and a very limited class of builtins. Herein we propose an extension to traditional characteristic trees which can be used in the presence of calls to external predicates. This includes all builtins, libraries, other user modules, etc. Second, we propose the possibility of collapsing versions which are not strictly equivalent. This allows trading time for space and can be useful in the context of embedded and pervasive systems. This is done by residualizing certain computations for external predicates which would otherwise be performed at specialization time. Third, we provide an experimental evaluation of the potential gains achievable using minimization which leads to interesting conclusions.

1 Introduction and Motivation

Partial evaluation (PE) of logic programs [3, 13] aims at obtaining code which is as optimized as possible by performing aggressive unfolding at the local control level, and by being as accurate as possible (generalize the least possible) at the global control level, as long as termination is guaranteed. We refer to [7] for a survey on control issues. In particular, given a fixed local control rule, different global control rules will have different effects on the polyvariance level of partial evaluation, i.e., the number of versions produced for each procedure. In general, a common heuristic is to produce as many different versions as possible, as long as termination is not compromised, the idea being that by considering different versions separately, further optimizations may be uncovered. This heuristic

P.M. Hill (Ed.): LOPSTR 2005, LNCS 3901, pp. 80–97, 2006.

```
(1) main(A,B,C,D,E,F,G,H,I,J,K,L,M,N,O):-        (2) addlists([],[],[]).
        write(C),                                 (3) addlists([A|B],[C|D],[H|T]):-
        addlists([4,4|A],[0,3|B],[4,7|C]),            H is A+C,
        addlists([3,3|D],[1,4|E],[4,7|F]),            addlists(B,D,T).
        addlists([3,3|G],[1,4|H],I),
        addlists([1,1|J],[3,6|K],L),
        addlists([7,1|M],[1,5|N],O).
```

Fig. 1. Adding pairs of lists

makes sense from the point of view of optimizing programs in terms of resolution steps, but it can produce unnecessarily large results, and may even slow down programs due to cache miss effects.

Example 1. Fig. 1 shows our running example. Predicate `addlists/3` adds the contents of two lists, using the builtin `is/2`. Clauses are numbered for later reference. A possible result of partial evaluation for the initial query `main/15` is shown in Fig. 2. Unfolding of `main/15` only performs one step since the leftmost literal `write(C)` has side-effects, and performing non-leftmost unfolding of any other literal may backpropagate bindings (as variables may be aliases) onto `write(C)`. Note that one version has been generated for each call to `addlists/3` within the body of `main/15`, plus one version for the general case. However, the four versions `addlists_2` through `addlists_5` are indeed equivalent and could be replaced by a single one, resulting in the program shown in Fig. 3.

The problem of superfluous polyvariance has been studied both in the context of abstract multiple specialization [18, 16] and in the context of partial evaluation of normal logic programs [9]. The common idea is to identify sets of versions which are *equivalent* and replace all occurrences of such versions by a single, canonical, one. This poses two questions which we address in this work: under which conditions can we consider two given versions as equivalent? And, how can we efficiently check for equivalence?

In this work, we provide a thorough analysis of these questions, comparing different approaches for controlling polyvariance, and we also extend previous

```
main(A,B,C,D,E,F,G,H,I,J,K,L,M,N,O) :- write(C),
    addlists_2([4,4|A],[0,3|B],[4,7|C]), addlists_3([3,3|D],[1,4|E],[4,7|F]),
    addlists_4([3,3|G],[1,4|H],I),       addlists_5([1,1|J],[3,6|K],L),
    addlists_6([7,1|M],[1,5|N],O).

addlists_1([],[],[]).
addlists_1([A|B],[C|D],[E|F]) :-            E is A+C, addlists_1(B,D,F).

addlists_2([4,4],[0,3],[4,7]).
addlists_2([4,4,A|B],[0,3,C|D],[4,7,E|F]) :- E is A+C, addlists_1(B,D,F).

addlists_3([3,3],[1,4],[4,7]).
addlists_3([3,3,A|B],[1,4,C|D],[4,7,E|F]) :- E is A+C, addlists_1(B,D,F).

addlists_4([3,3],[1,4],[4,7]).
addlists_4([3,3,A|B],[1,4,C|D],[4,7,E|F]) :- E is A+C, addlists_1(B,D,F).

addlists_5([1,1],[3,6],[4,7]).
addlists_5([1,1,A|B],[3,6,C|D],[4,7,E|F]) :- E is A+C, addlists_1(B,D,F).

addlists_6([7,1],[1,5],[8,6]).
addlists_6([7,1,A|B],[1,5,C|D],[8,6,E|F]) :- E is A+C, addlists_1(B,D,F).
```

Fig. 2. Specialization of addlists/3 via partial evaluation

```
main(A,B,C,D,E,F,G,H,I,J,K,L,M,N,O) :- write(C),
  addlists_5([4,4|A],[0,3|B],[4,7|C]), addlists_5([3,3|D],[1,4|E],[4,7|F]),
  addlists_5([3,3|G],[1,4|H],I), addlists_5([1,1|J],[3,6|K],L),
  addlists_6([7,1|M],[1,5|N],O) .

addlists_1([],[],[]).
addlists_1([A|B],[C|D],[E|F]) :-  E is A+C, addlists_1(B,D,F) .

addlists_5([A,A],[_1,_2],[4,7]).
addlists_5([A,A,B|C],[_1,_2,D|E],[4,7,F|G]) :- F is B+D, addlists_1(C,E,G).

addlists_6([7,1],[1,5],[8,6]).
addlists_6([7,1,A|B],[1,5,C|D],[8,6,E|F]) :- E is A+C, addlists_1(B,D,F).
```

Fig. 3. Specialization of addlists/3 after minimization

approaches in two ways. First, we tackle in an accurate way the case in which programs contain *external predicates*, i.e., predicates whose code is not defined in the program being specialized, and thus it is not available to the specializer. This includes predicates defined in other user modules, library predicates, builtins, predicates implemented in other languages, etc. Note that external predicates may have *impure* features. The minimization shown in Figure 3 is not possible in previous works such as [9] as it involves calls to the builtin predicate is/2, which is not *safe* in the sense that it may produce bindings during its execution.

Second, previously proposed minimization techniques do not provide any degrees of freedom at the minimization stage. We propose the possibility of collapsing versions which are not *strictly* equivalent. This is achieved by residualizing certain computations for external predicates which would otherwise be performed at specialization time. This allows automatically trading time for space and can be of interest in the context of embedded and pervasive systems, where computing resources and storage are often limited.

A completely different approach to that studied in this paper is to incorporate within the global control certain heuristics which limit polyvariance based for example on characteristic trees [2, 6, 12]. Such approach has both advantages and disadvantages. The advantage is that there is no need to perform a post minimization phase, such as that discussed in this paper. On the other hand, the disadvantage of that approach is that it sometimes produces results which are suboptimal, since the fact that characteristic trees are equal not always means that the corresponding versions should be merged.

We argue that a minimization phase is important in specialization algorithms, since it allows using very accurate global control rules while limiting the risk of generating large residual code. Rather than deciding *a priori* the best global control possible, this technique allows using aggressive control strategies. We can minimize the program *a posteriori* and eliminate those specialized versions which are redundant.

2   Background

We assume some basic knowledge on the terminology of logic programming. See for example [14] for details. Very briefly, an *atom A* is a syntactic construction of the form $p(t_1, \ldots, t_n)$, where p/n, with $n \geq 0$, is a predicate symbol and $t_1, \ldots, t_n$ are terms. The function $pred$ applied to atom A, i.e., $pred(A)$, returns the predicate symbol p/n for A. A *clause* is of the form $H \leftarrow B$ where its head H is an atom and its body B is a conjunction of atoms. A *definite program* is a finite set of clauses. A *goal* (or query) is a conjunction of atoms. We denote by $\{X_1 \mapsto t_1, \ldots, X_n \mapsto t_n\}$ the *substitution* σ with $\sigma(X_i) = t_i$ for all $i = 1, \ldots, n$ (with $X_i \neq X_j$ if $i \neq j$) and $\sigma(X) = X$ for any other variable X, where t_i are terms. We denote with ϵ the empty substitution. Also, $dom(\sigma)$ denotes the set of variables affected by substitution σ, i.e., $dom(\{X_1 \mapsto t_1, \ldots, X_n \mapsto t_n\}) = \{X_1, \ldots, X_n\}$.

A term t is *more general* than s (or s is an *instance* of t), in symbols $t \leq s$, if $\exists \sigma.\ t\sigma = s$. Two terms t and t' are *variants*, denoted $t \approx t'$, if there exists a renaming ρ such that $t\rho = t'$. A *unifier* of a pair of terms $\{t_1, t_2\}$ is a substitution σ such that $t_1\sigma = t_2\sigma$. A unifier σ is called *most general unifier* (*mgu*) if $\sigma \leq \sigma'$ for every other unifier σ'. A *generalization* of a set of terms $\{t_1, \ldots, t_n\}$ is another term t such that $\exists \theta_1, \ldots, \theta_n$ with $t_i = t\theta_i$, $i = 1, \ldots, n$. A generalization t is the *most specific generalization* (*msg*) of $\{t_1, \ldots, t_n\}$ if for every other term t' s.t. t' is a generalization of $\{t_1, \ldots, t_n\}$, $t' \leq t$. Given a set of clauses $\{Cl_1 = H_1 \leftarrow B_1, \ldots, Cl_n = H_n \leftarrow B_n\}$, $n \geq 0$, we denote by $instantiate(\{Cl_1, \ldots, Cl_n\}, A)$ the set of clauses $\{Cl_1\theta_1, \ldots, Cl_n\theta_n\}$ where each $\theta_i = mgu(H_i, A)$.

2.1 Basics of Partial Evaluation

Traditional algorithms for on-line partial evaluation of logic programs (known as *partial deduction* (PD) [13, 3]) usually include two control levels: *local control* and *global control* [3]. Local control defines an unfolding rule. Given an atom A, an *unfolding rule* computes a set of finite SLD derivations $D_1, \ldots, D_n$ (i.e., a possibly incomplete SLD tree) of the form $D_i = A, \ldots, G_i$ with computed answer substitution θ_i for $i = 1, \ldots, n$. We use $U(P, G) = \tau$ to denote the fact that the unfolding rule U when applied to goal G in program P returns the SLD tree τ. The global control rule decides when and how to generalize atoms before applying the unfolding rule to them. Such generalization steps are necessary in order to guarantee that the number of atoms to which the unfolding rule is applied remains finite. We refer to [7] for a survey on both control issues.

3   A General View of Polyvariance and Minimization

We now present a very general description of a polyvariant specialization process which includes both partial evaluation [13, 3, 7] and abstract multiple specialization [16]. Given a program P and a set of atoms $\mathcal{Q} = \{A_1, \ldots, A_m\}$, which describe the possible initial queries to P, polyvariant specialization performs the following three steps:

1. *Analysis.* In this phase, we compute a set of call patterns $\{A_1, \ldots, A_n\} \supseteq \mathcal{Q}$ which cover all calls in the specialized program. We write $Analysis(P, \mathcal{Q})$

$= \{A_1, \ldots, A_n\}$ to denote that the result of analysis for P and Q is the set of call patterns $\{A_1, \ldots, A_n\}$.

2. *Code Generation.* The aim of this phase is, for each call pattern $A_i \in$ *Analysis*(P, Q), to compute properly optimized residual code. We denote by $code(A_i)$ the code (set of clauses) associated to A_i. In partial evaluation, an unfolding rule U is used for generating code, i.e., $code(A_i) = U(P, A_i)$.

3. *Renaming.* In this phase we assign a fresh predicate name to each atom in $\{A_1, \ldots, A_n\}$. Then, for each $code(A_i)$, we perform appropriate renamings in the head and body atoms so that each program point uses a correct (and as optimized as possible) version. *Ren* denotes the renaming function.

The polyvariant specialized program P_Q is then defined as:

$$P_Q = \bigcup_{A_i}^{Analysis(P, Q)} Ren(code(A_i))$$

3.1   Minimizing the Results of Polyvariant Specialization

The aim of minimization is to group the call patterns (or *versions*) in $\{A_1, \ldots, A_n\}$ into *equivalence classes*, obtaining a minimal program that allows the same set of optimizations, and that can be implemented without introducing run-time tests to select amongst different versions of a predicate.

Deciding whether two versions A_i and A_j with $pred(A_i) = pred(A_j)$ are equivalent is not straightforward, as we have to consider not only the code of A_i and A_j, but also the code of all other versions which are reachable from them. In the case of the *main* predicate in a program, we would have to take the code of all the specialized program into account. Thus, we will split the notion of equivalence into a *local equivalence* and a *global equivalence* level. Local equivalence concentrates on comparing the code for A_i and A_j only, without worrying about the other predicates which are reachable from them. Global equivalence will only hold if A_i and A_j are locally equivalent and all reachable versions for the corresponding program points are also locally equivalent.

The minimization algorithm (called *Minimize* from now on) consists of two phases. In [17], the first phase is called *reunion* and the second phase is called *splitting*. The reunion phase is concerned with local equivalence only and it places together all versions for the same predicate which are considered locally equivalent according to some criteria. The splitting phase is concerned with global equivalence. It splits sets of versions which are not globally equivalent until no more splitting is needed, i.e., until we have reached a partition where all sets contain versions which are globally equivalent. This minimization process is isomorphic to the minimization of deterministic finite automata (DFA) [5], by considering each call pattern A_i as a *state* and each program point in $code(A_i)$ as a *symbol*.

A crucial point thus is, given a pair of atoms A and A', to decide whether they can be safely considered locally equivalent. The decision criteria has to satisfy two properties: (1) it must produce correct results, and (2) it must be effective, i.e. it must be possible to efficiently decide whether A and A' are candidates for equivalence based on syntactic, local conditions. For this purpose, in this work we introduce *structural equivalence*.

Definition 1 (structurally equivalent). *Let A_1 and A_2 be two call patterns such that $pred(A_1)=pred(A_2)$. We say that A_1 and A_2 are* structurally equivalent *iff*

$$C = msg(code(A_1), code(A_2))$$
$$\wedge\ instantiate(C, A_1) \approx code(A_1)$$
$$\wedge\ instantiate(C, A_2) \approx code(A_2)$$

Clearly, if $code(A_1) \approx code(A_2)$ then A_1 and A_2 are structurally equivalent. However the definition above allows also considering as structurally equivalent call patterns whose code only differs in constants which are input arguments to the predicate but which do not play an important role for local optimization. Note that structural equivalence is just a syntactic characterization which guarantees that two call patterns are locally equivalent. In fact, there can be call patterns which are locally equivalent in the sense that their behaviours under the semantics of interest are identical but which our definition of structural equivalence would not capture. Also, structural equivalence in particular, and local equivalence in general do not guarantee global equivalence. It often happens that two call patterns which are structurally equivalent end up in different equivalence classes after the splitting phase. Only after this phase terminates we can be sure that two call patterns are globally equivalent.

The polyvariant specialized program with minimization $P_{\mathcal{Q}}^{Min}$ is defined as:

$$P_{\mathcal{Q}}^{Min} = \bigcup_{V_i}^{Minimize(Analysis(P,\mathcal{Q}))} Ren_{\equiv}(code(V_i))$$

where given a set of atoms $\{A_1, \ldots, A_n\}$, we partition them in equivalence classes $\{V_1, \ldots, V_k\}$, $k \geq n$ s.t. $\forall A, A' \in V_i$. A and A' are structurally equivalent. We use $code(\{A_1, \ldots, A_i\})$ to denote $msg(\{code(A_1), \ldots, code(A_i)\})$. Also, $Ren_{\equiv}$ is a new renaming function which always uses the same (*canonical*) predicate name for any atom in $\{A_1, \ldots, A_i\}$.

Our definition of structural equivalence plays several roles. It underlies the notions of local equivalence used both in abstract multiple specialization and partial deduction, thus allowing us to present a unified view of both minimization processes. Furthermore, it can also be used in order to determine whether two versions are locally equivalent. Existing approaches to minimization do not compare the syntactic structure of the residual code directly (as this definition would require) but rather use the specialization history in order to decide local equivalence. In [16] two call patterns are considered locally equivalent iff (1) they correspond to the same predicate in the original program and (2) the set of optimizations in both call patterns is the same. In [9] two call patterns are locally equivalent iff they have the same characteristic tree.

4   Characteristic Trees with External Predicates

A *characteristic tree* [2] is a data structure which encapsulates the evaluation behaviour of an atom, i.e., a trace of the unfolding process. The following definitions are taken from [9], which in turn were derived from [2].

Definition 2 (characteristic path). *Let G_0 be a goal, and let P be a definite program whose clauses are numbered. Let $G_0, \ldots, G_n$ be the goals of a finite, possibly incomplete SLD-derivation D of $P \cup \{G_0\}$. The characteristic path of the derivation D is the sequence $\langle l_0 : c_0, \ldots, l_{n-1} : c_{n-1} \rangle$, where l_i is the position of the selected atom in G_i, and c_i is the number of the clause chosen to resolve with G_i.*

Now that we have characterized derivations, we can characterize goals through the derivations in their associated SLD-trees.

Definition 3 (characteristic tree). *Let G be a goal, P a definite program, and τ a finite SLD-tree for $P \cup \{G\}$. Then the characteristic tree $\hat{\tau}$ of τ is the set containing the characteristic paths of the nonfailing SLD-derivations associated with the branches of τ.*
Let U be an unfolding rule such that $U(P, G) = \tau$. Then $\hat{\tau}$ is also called the characteristic tree of G (in P) via U. We introduce the notation $ch\_tree(G, P, U) = \hat{\tau}$.

Although existing partial evaluation systems such as SP [1] and ECCE [10] perform some limited handling of builtins within characteristic trees, the existing formal definitions of characteristic trees do not contemplate the existence of builtins nor of external predicates. We now extend the standard definitions in order to accurately include external predicates.

Definition 4 (chpath with external predicates). *Let G_0 be a goal, and let P be a program whose clauses are numbered. Let $G_0, \ldots, G_n$ be the goals of a finite, possibly incomplete SLD-derivation D of $P \cup \{G_0\}$. Let $A_0, \ldots, A_{n-1}$ be the selected atoms in D. The characteristic path with external predicates of the derivation D is the sequence $\langle l_0 : c_0, \ldots, l_{n-1} : c_{n-1} \rangle$, where l_i is the position of A_i in G_i, and c_i is defined as follows:*

- *if $pred(A_i)$ is defined in P, then c_i is the number of the clause in P chosen to resolve with G_i;*
- *if $pred(A_i)$ is an external predicate, then let θ be a computed answer generated when performing $exec(A_i)$. Then, c_i is a pair (A_i, θ).*

In the definition above, $exec(A_i)$ represents the execution of A_i. For this, the external call A_i has to be *evaluable* [15], i.e., A_i is both well-moded and well-typed, it does not produce any side-effect, and it universally terminates. Note that $exec(A_i)$ can succeed more than once and possibly with different computed answers. Reconsidering characteristic paths, each pair $(l_i : c_i)$ in a characteristic path must uniquely identify: (1) the position of the selected atom A_i, (2) the bindings introduced by this step on the current goal, and (3) the atoms which

$$\tau_2 = \{\langle 1:3,1:(4\ is\ 4+0,\epsilon),1:3,1:(7\ is\ 4+3,\epsilon),1:2\rangle,$$
$$\langle 1:3,1:(4\ is\ 4+0,\epsilon),1:3,1:(7\ is\ 4+3,\epsilon),1:3\rangle\},$$
$$\tau_3 = \{\langle 1:3,1:(4\ is\ 3+1,\epsilon),1:3,1:(7\ is\ 3+4,\epsilon),1:2\rangle,$$
$$\langle 1:3,1:(4\ is\ 3+1,\epsilon),1:3,1:(7\ is\ 3+4,\epsilon),1:3\rangle\},$$
$$\tau_4 = \{\langle 1:3,1:(A\ is\ 3+1,\{A\mapsto 4\}),1:3,1:(B\ is\ 3+4,\{B\mapsto 7\}),1:2\rangle,$$
$$\langle 1:3,1:(C\ is\ 3+1,\{C\mapsto 4\}),1:3,1:(D\ is\ 3+4,\{D\mapsto 7\}),1:3\rangle\},$$
$$\tau_5 = \{\langle 1:3,1:(E\ is\ 1+3,\{E\mapsto 4\}),1:3,1:(F\ is\ 1+6,\{F\mapsto 7\}),1:2\rangle,$$
$$\langle 1:3,1:(G\ is\ 1+3,\{G\mapsto 4\}),1:3,1:(H\ is\ 1+6,\{H\mapsto 7\}),1:3\rangle\}.$$
$$\tau_6 = \{\langle 1:3,1:(I\ is\ 7+1,\{I\mapsto 8\}),1:3,1:(J\ is\ 1+5,\{J\mapsto 6\}),1:2\rangle,$$
$$\langle 1:3,1:(L\ is\ 7+1,\{L\mapsto 8\}),1:3,1:(M\ is\ 1+5,\{M\mapsto 6\}),1:3\rangle\}.$$

Fig. 4. Characteristic trees for addlists/3 versions

must be introduced in the goal in place of the selected atom A_i. An important obvious difference between external and regular predicates is that the code for external predicates may not be available, so it is not possible, as done with regular predicates, to assign clause numbers to them or to unfold them. Instead of unfolding external predicates, we will fully execute them. As a result, no atoms will be introduced in the current goal and, thus, (3) is not needed in this case.

In the case of external predicates, we introduce in the characteristic tree an *external success*, i.e., a pair (A_i, θ) containing the call pattern A_i and the bindings θ generated during evaluation for each external predicate. Note that, in contrast to the handling of builtins within characteristic trees in SP and ECCE, this makes it possible to reconstruct the residual code for an atom without the need for (re-)evaluating external predicates, even if the external predicates succeed several times with (possibly) different computed answers. The notion of characteristic paths with external predicates is indeed consistent with traditional characteristic paths. In the case of regular predicates, the same *implicit* representation as in traditional characteristic paths is used. This representation is efficient in space since rather than introducing (an instantiated version of) the clause chosen for resolving the selected atom directly in the characteristic tree, only the number of the clause used for unfolding is stored. This suffices since the actual instantiation can be performed later if needed using the actual clause. In the case of external predicates, this implicit representation is no longer possible, since the clauses are not available. Instead, the call pattern and the corresponding bindings are *explicitly* stored.

Characteristic trees are extended to handle external predicates by simply considering characteristic paths with external predicates. Fig. 4 shows the characteristic trees with external predicates τ_2, τ_3, τ_4, τ_5 and τ_6 for versions addlists_2/3, addlists_3/3, addlists_4/3, addlists_5/3, and addlists_6/3, respectively.

5   Isomorphic Characteristic Trees

In this section we define the notion of *isomorphic* characteristic trees with external predicates, which guarantees that the corresponding code is structurally equivalent. We assume that predicate names cannot be numbers, as is the case in most existing logic programming systems. Also, *number(X)* succeeds iff X is a number.

First, we introduce the concept of *quasi-isomorphic characteristic trees*, for identifying characteristic trees which only (possibly) differ in the input and/or output values of arguments in calls to external predicates:

Definition 5 (quasi-isomorphic characteristic trees). *Two characteristic paths* $\delta^1 = \langle l_0 : c_0^1, \ldots, l_m : c_m^1 \rangle$ *and* $\delta^2 = \langle l_0 : c_0^2, \ldots, l_m : c_m^2 \rangle$ *are quasi-isomorphic and we denote it* $\delta^1 \approx_q \delta^2$ *iff* $\forall i \in \{1..m\}$. $number(c_i^1) \Rightarrow c_i^1 = c_i^2$. *Two characteristic trees* τ_1 *and* τ_2 *are* quasi-isomorphic, *denoted* $\tau_1 \approx_q \tau_2$, *iff* $\forall \delta^1 \in \tau_1$. $\exists \delta^2 \in \tau_2$ *s.t.* $\delta^1 \approx_q \delta^2$ *and* $\forall \delta^2 \in \tau_2$. $\exists \delta^1 \in \tau_1$ *s.t.* $\delta^2 \approx_q \delta^1$.

Note that quasi-isomorphic characteristic paths must have the same length and the selected atom must be in the same position in each resolution step. Furthermore, if the atom is not for an external predicate, then the atom must have been resolved against the same clause. In Fig. 4, $\tau_2 \approx_q \tau_3 \approx_q \tau_4 \approx_q \tau_5 \approx_q \tau_6$.

Now we define some relationships among external successes, after some auxiliary definitions. A *position* uniquely determines a subterm within a term.

Definition 6 (Position). *A position* ω *is either the empty position* ε, *or* $n.\omega'$, *where* n *is a natural number and* ω' *is a position.*

Definition 7 (getval, Pos, and Allpos). *Let* $A = f(\overline{t_n})$ *be a term. Let* ω *be a position. Let* X *be a variable s.t.* $X \in vars(A)$. *Let* θ *be a substitution.*

- *We define* $getval(\omega, A)$ *as* A *if* $\omega = \varepsilon$ *and as* $getval(\omega', t_i)$ *if* $\omega = i.\omega'$.
- *We define* $Pos(A, X)$ *as* $\{\omega \mid getval(\omega, A) = X\}$.
- *We define* $Allpos(A, \theta)$ *as* $\cup_{X \in dom(\theta)} \{\omega\}, s.t.\ \omega \in Pos(A, X)$.

Example 2. $getval(2.1.\varepsilon, f(a, g(b, c))) = b$, and $Pos(f(a, g(b, Y)), Y) = \{2.2.\varepsilon\}$. If A is not linear, then for some X, the set $Pos(A, X)$ may have more than one element. E.g., $Pos(f(Z, g(Z)), Z) = \{1.\varepsilon, 2.1.\varepsilon\}$. In such case, any $\omega \in Pos(A, X)$ can be used for our purposes. Also $Allpos(A\ is\ 3 + 1, \{A \mapsto 4\}) = \{1.\varepsilon\}$.

Definition 8 (isomorphic external successes). *Let* $c = (A, \theta)$ *and* $c' = (A', \theta')$ *be external successes. Then* c *and* c' *are* isomorphic external successes, *denoted by* $c \simeq c'$, *iff* $\forall \omega \in Allpos(A, \theta) \cup Allpos(A', \theta')$. $getval(\omega, A\theta) = getval(\omega, A'\theta')$.

Example 3. This definition tries to consider as isomorphic as many pairs of external successes as possible. A particular subcase of this definition corresponds to the case where the calls to external predicates generate no bindings. For example, the pair $(4\ is\ 4+0, \epsilon)$ and $(4\ is\ 3+1, \epsilon)$ is isomorphic, whereas the notion of equivalence in [9] cannot capture this since the builtin predicate is/2 potentially generates bindings, though in this case it does not. Note that $(4is4 + 0, \epsilon)$ and $(8is2*4, \epsilon)$ are also considered as isomorphic although their syntactic structure is very different. Another interesting subcase is when the external successes have different levels of instantiation but on success they are variants. This happens with $(A\ is\ 3+1, \{A \mapsto 4\})$ and $(4\ is\ 3+1, \epsilon)$. Furthermore, it allows considering as isomorphic external successes which have the same values in all positions which are instantiated in either external success. For example $(A \; is \; 3+1, \{A \mapsto 4\})$ and $(4 \; is \; 4+0, \epsilon)$ are considered isomorphic since $Allpos(A \; is \; 3+1, \{A \mapsto 4\}) = \{1.\varepsilon\} \wedge Allpos(4 \; is \; 4+0, \epsilon) = \emptyset \wedge getval(1.\varepsilon, 4 \; is \; 3+1) = getval(1.\varepsilon, 4 \; is \; 4+0) = 4$. However, $(E \; is \; 1+3, \{E \mapsto 4\}) \not\approx (I \; is \; 7+1, \{I \mapsto 8\})$, since $Allpos(E \; is \; 1+3, \{E \mapsto 4\}) = Allpos(I \; is \; 7+1, I) = \{1.\varepsilon\}$, but $getval(1.\varepsilon, 4 \; is \; 1+3) = 4 \neq getval(1.\varepsilon, 8 \; is \; 7+1) = 8$.

Definition 9 (isomorphic characteristic trees). *Two characteristic paths* $\delta^1 = \langle l_0 \; : \; c_0^1, \ldots, l_m \; : \; c_m^1 \rangle$ *and* $\delta^2 = \langle l_0 \; : \; c_0^2, \ldots, l_m \; : \; c_m^2 \rangle$ *are isomorphic and we denote it* $\delta^1 \approx \delta^2$ *iff* $\delta^1 \approx_q \delta^2 \wedge \forall i \in \{1..m\}$. $c_i^1 = (A_i^1, \theta_i^1) \Rightarrow c_i^2 = (A_i^2, \theta_i^2) \wedge c_i^1 \simeq c_i^2$. *Two characteristic trees* τ_1 *and* τ_2 *are isomorphic, denoted* $\tau_1 \approx \tau_2$, *iff* $\forall \delta^1 \in \tau_1$. $\exists \delta^2 \in \tau_2$ *s.t.* $\delta^1 \approx \delta^2$ *and* $\forall \delta^2 \in \tau_2$. $\exists \delta^1 \in \tau_1$ *s.t.* $\delta^2 \approx \delta^1$.

The following proposition provides the basis for our minimization approach.

Proposition 1 (structural equivalence). *Let P be a program with external predicates, let U be an unfolding rule, let A_1 and A_2 be two call patterns such that $\tau_1 = ch\_tree(A_1, P, U)$ and $\tau_2 = ch\_tree(A_2, P, U)$. If $\tau_1 \approx \tau_2$ then A_1 and A_2 are structurally equivalent.*

A difficulty with our notion $\approx$ of isomorphic characteristic trees and its usage as a condition for local equivalence is that though the $\approx$ relation is reflexive and symmetric, it is not transitive. This means that $(\tau_1 \approx \tau_2 \wedge \tau_2 \approx \tau_3) \not\rightarrow \tau_1 \approx \tau_3$. As a result, in order to be able to state that all characteristic trees in a set $\{\tau_1, \ldots, \tau_n\}$ are isomorphic we have to check that $\forall \tau, \tau' \in \{\tau_1, \ldots, \tau_n\}$. $\tau \approx \tau'$.

Example 4. Let us consider again the characteristic trees in Fig. 4. We have already noticed that all of them are quasi-isomorphic. If we take the quasi-isomorphic paths of τ_2, τ_3, τ_4 and τ_5, and extract their external successes, we can see that they are isomorphic. For example, if we take $c_{21} = (4 \; is \; 4+0, \epsilon)$, $c_{31} = (4 \; is \; 3+1, \epsilon)$, $c_{41} = (A \; is \; 3+1, \{A \mapsto 4\})$ and $c_{51} = (C \; is \; 1+3, \{C \mapsto 4\})$, we can compute $\cup_{i \in \{2\ldots5\}} Allpos(c_{i1}) = \{1.\epsilon\}$. Since $getval(1.\epsilon, 4 \; is \; 4+0) = getval(1.\epsilon, 4 \; is \; 3+1) = getval(1.\epsilon, 4 \; is \; 1+3) = 4$, we can conlude that they are isomorphic.

Finally, note that even though $\tau_5 \approx_q \tau_6$, they are not (fully) isomorphic since, for instance, $(E \; is \; 1+3, \{E \mapsto 4\}) \not\approx (I \; is \; 7+1, \{I \mapsto 8\})$. Indeed, addlists_5/3 and addlists_6/3 are not structurally equivalent. As a result, the sets which are identified as locally equivalent during the reunion phase are: {{main/15}, {addlists_1/3}, {addlists_2/3, addlists_3/3, addlists_4/3, addlists_5/3}, {addlists_6/3}}. This is also the final partition after applying the splitting phase. This produces the minimized program which was shown in Fig. 3.

6 Minimization Via Residualization of External Calls

There are situations in which even the minimized program is too large and/or where we would like to trade space for time efficiency. This would mean achieving programs which are smaller, but at the cost of introducing some efficiency penalty. In cases like this, we propose as candidates for minimization, call patterns with *quasi-isomorphic* characteristic trees. An important observation is that if $\delta^1 \approx_q \delta^2$ then the associated resultants have the same structure. However, this is not a sufficient condition for structural equivalence. This is because part of the bindings needed for structural equivalence cannot be achieved by the operation *instantiate*, as in Def. 1, but rather they originate from the execution of calls to external predicates. Thus, the second important observation is that if the calls to external predicates involved succeed only once, i.e. they are deterministic, such missing bindings can be recovered at run-time by residualizing (part of the) calls to external predicates which had in principle taken place during specialization time. Note that for detecting determinacy, no static analysis is actually required. We can simply check whether the calls which are to be residualized succeed just once by directly executing the calls as they appear in the different characteristic trees, i.e., before applying the msg to them. After the required external predicates have been residualized, the corresponding versions will be structurally equivalent.

The strategy we propose is the following: for any pair of versions A_1 and A_2 with $\tau_1 = ch\_tree(A_1, P, U)$ and $\tau_2 = ch\_tree(A_2, P, U)$ s.t. $\tau_1 \approx_q \tau_2$ we

1. Compute $(C, T) = msg((code(A_1), \overline{\tau}_1), (code(A_2), \overline{\tau}_2))$, where $\forall i \in \{1..2\}.\overline{\tau}_i$ is obtained from τ_i by *evaluating* all external successes, i.e., $\forall (B, \theta)$ we replace it by $B\theta$.
2. **If** $\forall i \in \{1..2\} . instantiate(C, A_i) \approx code(A_i)$
   - **then** A_1 and A_2 are structurally equivalent. No need to residualize.
   - **else** if for every evaluated external success $c \in T$ such that c is no longer sufficiently instantiated to be executed we can determine that its corresponding $c_1 \in \tau_1$ and $c_2 \in \tau_2$ are both *deterministic*,
     • then *residualize* all $c \in T$ being no longer sufficiently instantiated.
     • otherwise we cannot collapse A_1 and A_2.

Note that without such residualization, the code generated by the *msg* is not directly usable, since there are bindings in the original versions which are lost if we apply the code produced by the *msg*.

$$msg \left(\begin{array}{l} \{addlists([4,4],[0,3],[4,7])., \langle 1:(4\ is\ 4+0), 1:(7\ is\ 4+3)\rangle\} \\ \{addlists([3,3],[1,4],[4,7])., \langle 1:(4\ is\ 3+1), 1:(7\ is\ 3+4)\rangle\} \\ \{addlists([3,3],[1,4],[4,7])., \langle 1:(4\ is\ 3+1), 1:(7\ is\ 3+4)\rangle\} \\ \{addlists([1,1],[3,6],[4,7])., \langle 1:(4\ is\ 1+3), 1:(7\ is\ 1+6)\rangle\} \end{array} \right)$$
$$\overline{\{addlists([X,X],[Y,Z],[4,7])., \langle 1:(4\ is\ X+Y), 1:(7\ is\ X+Z)\rangle\}}$$

$$msg \left(\begin{array}{l} \{addlists([4,4,A|B],[0,3,C|D],[4,7,E|F]):-E\ is\ A+C, addlists(B,D,F)., \\ \qquad \langle 1:(4\ is\ 4+0), 1:(7\ is\ 4+3)\rangle\} \\ \{addlists([3,3,A|B],[1,4,C|D],[4,7,E|F]):-E\ is\ A+C, addlists(B,D,F)., \\ \qquad \langle 1:(4\ is\ 3+1), 1:(7\ is\ 3+4)\rangle\} \\ \{addlists([3,3,A|B],[1,4,C|D],[4,7,E|F]):-E\ is\ A+C, addlists(B,D,F)., \\ \qquad \langle 1:(4\ is\ 3+1), 1:(7\ is\ 3+4)\rangle\} \\ \{addlists([1,1,A|B],[3,6,C|D],[4,7,E|F]):-E\ is\ A+C, addlists(B,D,F)., \\ \qquad \langle 1:(4\ is\ 1+3), 1:(7\ is\ 1+6)\rangle\} \end{array} \right)$$
$$\overline{\{addlists([X,X,R|S],[Y,Z,T|U],[4,7,V|W]):-V\ is\ R+T, addlists(S,U,W)., \\ \langle 1:(4\ is\ X+Y), 1:(7\ is\ X+Z)\rangle\}}$$

Fig. 5. *msg* of versions `addlists_2`, `addlists_3`, `addlists_4` and `addlists_5`

Example 5. As we have already mentioned, all characteristic trees in Fig. 4 are quasi-isomorphic. Therefore, they can be collapsed into one version. In Fig. 5 we show the *msg* of both the code and the characteristic trees for versions addlists_2, addlists_3, addlists_4 and addlists_5. In this figure, the scope of variables is local to each clause. Since $\tau_2 \approx \tau_3 \approx \tau_4 \approx \tau_5$, the *msg* does not produce any information loss. This can be easily verified by instantiating back the *msg* with any of the call patterns. For instance, if we take addlists([X,X], [Y,Z],[4,7]) and instantiate it with addlists([3,3|G],[1,4|H],I) we obtain the original clause (eighth clause of Fig. 2).

Example 6. Now, let us now compute the *msg* of the generalized code and characteristic tree obtained in Example 5 with addlists_6.

$$msg\left(\frac{\{addlists([X,X],[Y,Z],[4,7])., \langle 1:(4\ is\ X+Y),1:(7\ is\ X+Z)\rangle\}}{\{addlists([\ 7,\ 1],[\ 1,5],[8,6])., \langle 1:(8\ is\ \ 7+\ 1),1:(6\ \ is\ \ 1+5)\rangle\}}\right)$$
$$\frac{}{\{addlists([A,B],[C,D],[E,F])., \langle 1:(E\ is\ A+C),1:(F\ is\ B+D)\rangle\}}$$

$$msg\left(\begin{array}{c}\{addlists([X,X,R|S],[Y,Z,T|U],[4,7,V|W]):-V\ is\ R+T, addlists(S,U,W)., \\ \langle 1:(4\ is\ X+Y),1:(7\ is\ X+Z)\rangle\} \\ \{addlists([7,\ 1,R|S],[\ 1,5,T|U],[8,6,V|W]):-V\ is\ R+T, addlists(S,U,W)., \\ \langle 1:(8\ is\ \ 7+1),1:(6\ is\ \ 1+5)\rangle\}\end{array}\right)$$
$$\frac{}{\begin{array}{c}\{addlists([A,B,G|H],[C,D,I|J],[E,F,K|L]):-K\ is\ G+I, addlists(H,J,L)., \\ \langle 1:(E\ is\ A+C),1:(F\ is\ B+D)\rangle\}\end{array}}$$

Since addlists_6 is not (fully) isomorphic with the other versions, the *msg* introduces some information loss through the variables E and F in the new heads $addlists([A,B],[C,D],[E,F])$ and $addlists([A,B,G|H],[C,D,I|J],[E,F,K|L])$. This information loss cannot be recovered by *instantiate*, since, for example, when instantiating the *msg* addlists([A,B],[C,D],[E,F]) with the call pattern addlists([3,3|G],[1,4|H],I) we obtain addlists([3,3],[1,4],[E,F]), in which E and F are unbound variables. If we take the external successes which correspond to E is A+C and F is B+D we can verify that the original external successes were deterministic (indeed, all calls to is/2 are deterministic). Thus, it is possible to collapse by residualization. As both external calls are no longer sufficiently instantiated, they are residualized. Residualized atoms are always placed before any other atom in the generalized clause, guaranteeing that after execution of such residual atoms at run-time, the clause as a whole is actually a variant of the original definition of the clause. The resulting minimized program is shown in Fig. 6. Residual atoms are underlined to distinguish them from the rest of atoms in body clauses.

```
main(A,B,C,D,E,F,G,H,I,J,K,L,M,N,O) :- write(A),
    addlists_6([4,4|A],[0,3|B],[4,7|C]), addlists_6([3,3|D],[1,4|E],[4,7|F]),
    addlists_6([3,3|G],[1,4|H],I), addlists_6([1,1|J],[3,6|K],L),
    addlists_6([7,1|M],[1,5|N],O) .

addlists_1([],[],[]).
addlists_1([A|B],[C|D],[E|F]) :- E is A+C, addlists_1(B,D,F) .

addlists_6([A,B],[C,D],[E,F]) :-    E is A+C, F is B+D.
addlists_6([A,B,G|H],[C,D,I|J],[E,F,K|L]) :- E is A+C, F is B+D,
    K is G+I, addlists_1(H,J,L) .
```

Fig. 6. Specialization of addlists/3 after minimization with residualization

7   Experimental Results

In this section we assess experimentally the impact of our proposed minimization. Most of the benchmarks considered contain calls to builtins which possibly generate bindings, such as is/2, and thus the existing partial evaluators which perform minimization [10, 11] would not be able to minimize them optimally.

In our experiments we use an unfolding rule based on homeomorphic embedding (see, e.g., [7]) and which performs leftmost unfolding steps only. This guarantees the correctness of the partial evaluation process even in the presence of impure predicates. Note that the issue of redundant polyvariance may occur for any unfolding rule. The global control rule is based on homeomorphic embedding and global trees [8]. All benchmarks have been run on an Intel Pentium 4, 3.4 GHz processor, with 512 Mb of RAM, and running a 2.6 Linux kernel.

7.1   The Benefits of Minimization

Table 1 shows the size reduction introduced by the minimization step after partial evaluation. Each benchmark program is evaluated using five different minimization criteria, as shown in the *Min Crit* column. Specialization history is used in *pure*, *nobinds*, and *bindings*, in order to consider two versions as locally equivalent, while *codemsg* directly applies the definition of structural equivalence for the same purpose. In particular, *pure* considers two versions as locally equivalent when their characteristic trees are identical. Of course, if external successes are included, these must be identical too. The criteria *nobinds* and *bindings* check for isomorphism of external successes instead. *Nobinds* only considers two external successes c and c' as isomorphic when they generate no bindings, i.e., when $Allpos(c) = Allpos(c) = \emptyset$, while *bindings* applies the full power of Def. 8. Finally, *residual* considers two versions as candidates for minimization when their characteristic trees are quasi-isomorphic, possibly residualizing calls to external predicates in the resulting program.

The number of predicates in the original program is shown in the column *Orig Preds*. The number of predicates in the specialized programs are shown under the column *Versions*. *PE* shows both the number of versions which are generated after partial evaluation (i.e., the effects of polyvariance) and the number of sets of predicates with quasi-isomorphic characteristic trees. The latter provides a lower bound on the number of predicates which the minimized program may have. *Min* shows the number of elements in the partition generated by the reunion phase of the minimization algorithm (local equivalence) and the number of elements in the partition after the splitting phase (global equivalence). Finally, *Ratio* shows the reduction ratio for each criteria compared to the number of versions produced by partial evaluation. The column *Size* compares the sizes of the compiled bytecode of programs minimized using the different criteria.

The last row, *Overall*, shows the weighted geometric mean (*wgm*) for ratios in terms of number of versions and size. Weights are number of versions and size of the *PE* column, respectively. In both cases, under the column *Min* we find the *wgm* of the *codemsg* criterion, which achieves the best results while still

Table 1. Benchmarks (Minimization Ratios)

Benchmark	Min Crit	Orig Preds	Minimization					
			Versions			Size (bytes)		
			PE	Min	Ratio	PE	Min	Ratio
datetime	pure	15	56/31	36/36	1.78	131377	102651	1.28
	nobinds			36/36	1.78		102836	1.28
	bindings			34/35	1.83		102331	1.28
	codemsg			34/35	1.83		102295	1.28
	residual			31/33	1.94		100976	1.30
flattrees	pure	2	33/16	22/22	1.50	226390	223320	1.01
	nobinds			22/22	1.50		223435	1.01
	bindings			22/22	1.50		223389	1.01
	codemsg			17/19	1.74		221513	1.02
	residual			16/18	1.83		220796	1.03
freeof	pure	3	93/8	35/35	2.66	292642	245262	1.19
	nobinds			35/35	2.66		245442	1.19
	bindings			32/35	2.66		245370	1.19
	codemsg			18/35	2.66		245334	1.19
	residual			8/35	2.66		245370	1.19
mmatrix_2	pure	3	70/11	18/34	2.06	58323	37061	1.57
	nobinds			18/34	2.06		37236	1.57
	bindings			18/34	2.06		37166	1.57
	codemsg			18/34	2.06		37131	1.57
	residual			11/30	2.33		31781	1.84
nrev_38	pure	2	41/3	3/3	13.67	25115	5261	4.77
	nobinds			3/3	13.67		5281	4.76
	bindings			3/3	13.67		5273	4.76
	codemsg			3/3	13.67		5269	4.77
	residual			3/3	13.67		5273	4.76
qsort_33	pure	3	168/50	68/68	2.47	232079	166288	1.40
	nobinds			50/50	3.36		131650	1.76
	bindings			50/50	3.36		131548	1.76
	codemsg			50/50	3.36		131497	1.76
	residual			50/50	3.36		131548	1.76
sublists	pure	4	29/19	27/27	1.11	101969	99986	1.02
	nobinds			27/27	1.11		100121	1.02
	bindings			19/19	1.58		95815	1.06
	codemsg			19/19	1.58		95795	1.06
	residual			19/19	1.58		95815	1.06
Overall				2.88 / 2.96			1.32 / 1.33	

producing programs of maximal optimization. Under the column *Ratio* we find the *wgm* of the *residual* criterion, which achieves highest ratio.

As can be seen in the table, in most of the benchmarks considered, minimization is capable of considerably reducing the specialized program, both in terms of number of versions and of bytecode size. As it is to be expected, out of the four criteria which are guaranteed to produce programs of maximal optimization,

Table 2. Benchmarks (Minimization Times)

Benchmark	Minimization Criteria	Minimization Times (msec)				
		Total	Analysis	Minim	Codegen	Slowdown
datetime	nomin	556.52	475.33	0	81.19	1
	pure	632.90	486.13	61.19	85.59	1.14
	nobinds	634.30	476.13	72.79	85.39	1.14
	bindings	640.10	479.93	73.99	86.19	1.15
	codemsg	642.30	478.13	79.19	84.99	1.15
	residual	687.30	479.93	77.59	129.78	1.23
flattrees	nomin	299.55	232.56	0	66.99	1
	pure	395.14	230.97	107.78	56.39	1.32
	nobinds	396.34	231.57	108.58	56.19	1.32
	bindings	400.19	230.21	113.48	56.49	1.34
	codemsg	412.74	231.36	125.98	55.39	1.38
	residual	424.94	231.36	125.78	67.79	1.42
freeof	nomin	5732.93	5583.15	0	149.78	1
	pure	5833.11	5589.95	118.98	124.18	1.02
	nobinds	5844.11	5589.15	131.38	123.58	1.02
	bindings	5858.31	5573.35	160.38	124.58	1.02
	codemsg	5948.90	5595.15	230.97	122.78	1.04
	residual	6113.47	5613.95	221.97	277.56	1.07
mmatrix_2	nomin	316.15	271.76	0	44.39	1
	pure	356.55	272.76	48.39	35.39	1.13
	nobinds	367.14	274.56	57.39	35.19	1.16
	bindings	364.34	272.76	55.99	35.59	1.15
	codemsg	373.34	274.96	63.19	35.19	1.18
	residual	435.53	270.76	60.79	103.98	1.38
nrev_38	nomin	898.26	877.07	0	21.20	1
	pure	886.67	861.27	13.20	12.20	0.99
	nobinds	901.86	872.67	16.80	12.40	1.00
	bindings	898.86	870.27	16.40	12.20	1.00
	codemsg	903.86	874.67	17.20	12.00	1.01
	residual	916.26	873.87	17.20	25.20	1.02
qsort_33	nomin	9983.68	9745.12	0	238.56	1
	pure	10267.64	9778.91	282.96	205.77	1.03
	nobinds	10303.83	9768.12	337.75	197.97	1.03
	bindings	10339.03	9771.91	368.94	198.17	1.04
	codemsg	10401.82	9764.92	441.73	195.17	1.04
	residual	11241.69	9732.72	371.14	1137.83	1.13
sublists	nomin	401.94	293.56	0	108.38	1
	pure	647.70	295.35	278.56	73.79	1.61
	nobinds	651.90	297.75	281.36	72.79	1.62
	bindings	679.50	295.56	280.16	103.78	1.69
	codemsg	681.30	297.56	278.76	104.98	1.70
	residual	744.09	296.95	284.56	162.57	1.85

i.e., *pure, bindings, nobinds,* and *codemsg,* the one which produces the best results is the latter. Among the three of them which take the minimization history into account—and which are more efficient in terms of specialization time—, the best is *bindings,* but it sometimes does not produce as good results as *codemsg.* The effects of the splitting phase are clear in many benchmarks, showing that, in effect, local equivalence does not imply global equivalence. Finally, for `datetime`, `flattrees` and `mmatrix_2`, *residual* is able to further reduce code size.

7.2   The Cost of Minimization

In Table 2 we can observe the cost, in terms of specialization time, introduced by minimization, expressed in milliseconds. The (*Total*) time of the whole specialization process is shown, including the time taken by the partial evaluation (*Analysis*), minimization (*Minim*), and code generation (*Codegen*) steps. A new minimization criteria is introduced, *nomin,* showing the time employed by partial evaluation without minimization. The *Slowdown* column shows the cost of performing this minimization post-processing.

Interestingly, the table shows that when minimization is employed, the code generation phase takes less time in most cases, since fewer versions need to be generated. This lowers the burden introduced by minimization post-processing. However, even in the worst case the slowdown introduced is reasonable (1.85). As expected, using specialization history makes minimization faster than just applying the definition of structural equivalence. Given the fact that employing structural equivalence generates fewer versions than other criteria based on the specialization history, the *codemsg* criterion emerges as a very interesting one. Also, for the *residual* minimization criterion, the time spent in code generation is greater than for the rest of criteria, since it requires deciding which external successes need to be residualized.

7.3   Benefits of Minimization in Runtime

Table 3 shows how specialized programs behave in terms of runtime. Benchmark programs having residualized external predicates (for the *residual* minimization

Table 3. Benchmarks (Speedup)

Benchmark	PE Time	Speedup				
		Pure	No Binds	Bindings	CodeMsg	Residual
datetime*	167.77	1.01	1.02	1.01	1.01	1.01
flattrees*	81.39	1.03	1.01	1.01	1.03	1.01
freeof	246.96	1.04	1.04	1.05	1.04	1.05
mmatrix_2*	1920.11	1.02	1.02	1.02	1.02	1.00
nrev_38	141.38	1.20	1.18	1.18	1.19	1.19
qsort_33	457.33	1.05	1.04	1.04	1.05	1.04
sublists	15501.44	1.00	1.00	1.00	1.00	1.00

criterion) are marked with * in the table. Column *PE Time* shows the absolute run-time for the partially evaluated program. The rest of the columns show the speedup achieved for the minimized programs (for each different minimization criteria) w.r.t. *PE Time*. As can be seen in the table, in most benchmarks a small speedup is achieved (1.00 – 1.20), and no slowdown is produced in any case. As expected, in the case of programs with residualized external predicates, the speedup achieved is usually smaller than for the other minimization criteria.

8   Discussion and Related Work

The problem of superfluous polyvariance has been tackled in the context of abstract multiple specialization in [18, 16], and in the context of partial evaluation of normal logic programs in [9]. This work presents a unifying view under which the minimization problems in both contexts are isomorphic.

The work in [9], reflected in the ECCE [10] partial evaluator, uses an internal table of *safe* builtins which basically correspond to instantiation and type tests and which are guaranteed (1) not to generate any bindings, and (2) to be deterministic. The minimization phase then would only allow collapsing two predicates in the same version if their characteristic trees are quasi-isomorphic and all the builtins executed are listed in the table of pure predicates.

The approach presented herein, and implemented in the Ciao system preprocesor, CiaoPP [4], can handle any external predicate, including non-safe builtins, and the notion of isomorphic external predicates can be satisfied for builtins which generate bindings and which are non-deterministic. Also, there is no need for a static table of builtins. Additionally, the technique automatically applies to any external predicates, for example other modules written by the user.

To the best of our knowledge, this work presents the first experimental evaluation of the benefits of post-minimization in partial deduction. We have compared several criteria, with different cost and potential benefit. We have also applied directly the definition of structural equivalence and discovered that it is also applicable in practice, in addition to the other criteria based on the specialization history. Finally, we have proposed a criteria which allows residualizing external calls. The experiments show that it is also applicable in practice and provides some further program reduction.

Acknowledgments

The authors would like to thank Michael Leuschel and John Gallagher for useful discussions. This work was funded in part by the Information Society Technologies programme of the European Commission, Future and Emerging Technologies under the IST-2001-38059 *ASAP* project and by the Spanish Ministry of Science and Education under the MCYT TIC 2002-0055 *CUBICO* project. M. Hermenegildo is also supported by the Prince of Asturias Chair in Information Science and Technology at UNM.

References

1. J. Gallagher. A system for specialising logic programs. Technical Report TR-91-32, University of Bristol, November 1991.
2. J. Gallagher and M. Bruynooghe. The derivation of an algorithm for program specialisation. *New Generation Computing*, 9(1991):305–333, 1991.
3. J.P. Gallagher. Tutorial on specialisation of logic programs. In *Proc. of PEPM'93*, pages 88–98. ACM Press, 1993.
4. M. Hermenegildo, F. Bueno, G. Puebla, and P. López-García. Program Analysis, Debugging and Optimization Using the Ciao System Preprocessor. In *1999 ICLP*, pages 52–66. MIT Press, Nov 1999.
5. J. E. Hopcroft and J. D. Ullman. *Introduction to Automata Theory, Languages and Computation*. Addison-Wesley, 1979.
6. M. Leuschel. Ecological partial deduction: Preserving characteristic trees without constraints. In *Proc. of LOPSTR'95*, LNCS 1048, pages 1–16. Springer, 1995.
7. M. Leuschel and M. Bruynooghe. Logic program specialisation through partial deduction: Control issues. *TPLP*, 2(4 & 5):461–515, July & September 2002.
8. M. Leuschel and B. Martens. Global control for partial deduction through characteristic atoms and global trees. In *1996 Dagstuhl Seminar on Partial Evaluation*, LNCS 1110, pages 263–283, Schloß Dagstuhl, 1996.
9. M. Leuschel, B. Martens, and D. De Schreye. Controlling generalisation and polyvariance in partial deduction of normal logic programs. *ACM TOPLAS*, 20(1):208–258, 1998.
10. Michael Leuschel. The ECCE partial deduction system and the DPPD library of benchmarks. Obtainable via http://www.ecs.soton.ac.uk/~mal, 1996-2002.
11. Michael Leuschel. *Advanced Techniques for Logic Program Specialisation*. PhD thesis, K.U. Leuven, May 1997.
12. Michael Leuschel and Danny De Schreye. Constrained partial deduction and the preservation of characteristic trees. *New Generation Computing*, 16:283–342, 1998.
13. J. W. Lloyd and J. C. Shepherdson. Partial evaluation in logic programming. *The Journal of Logic Programming*, 11:217–242, 1991.
14. J.W. Lloyd. *Foundations of Logic Programming*. Springer, 2nd Ext. Ed., 1987.
15. G. Puebla, E. Albert, and M. Hermenegildo. Efficient Local Unfolding with Ancestor Stacks for Full Prolog. In *Proc. of LOPSTR'04*, pages 149–165. Springer LNCS 3573, 2005.
16. G. Puebla and M. Hermenegildo. Implementation of Multiple Specialization in Logic Programs. In *Proc. of PEPM'95*, pages 77–87. ACM Press, June 1995.
17. G. Puebla and M. Hermenegildo. Abstract Multiple Specialization and its Application to Program Parallelization. *JLP*, 41(2&3):279–316, November 1999.
18. W. Winsborough. Multiple Specialization using Minimal-Function Graph Semantics. *Journal of Logic Programming*, 13(2 and 3):259–290, July 1992.

Extension of Type-Based Approach to Generation of Stream-Processing Programs by Automatic Insertion of Buffering Primitives

Kohei Suenaga[1], Naoki Kobayashi[2], and Akinori Yonezawa[3]

[1] University of Tokyo
kohei@yl.is.s.u-tokyo.ac.jp
[2] Tohoku University
koba@kb.ecei.tohoku.ac.jp
[3] University of Tokyo
yonezawa@yl.is.s.u-tokyo.ac.jp

Abstract. In our previous paper, we have proposed a framework for automatically translating tree-processing programs into stream-processing programs. However, in writing programs that require buffering of input data, a user has to explicitly use *buffering primitives* which copy data from input stream to memory or copy constructed trees from memory to an output stream. Such explicit insertion of buffering primitives is often cumbersome and worsens the readability of the program. We overcome the above-mentioned problems by developing an algorithm which, given any simply-typed tree-processing program, automatically inserts buffering primitives. The resulting program is guaranteed to be well-typed under our previous ordered-linear type system, so that the program can be further transformed into an equivalent stream-processing program using our previous framework.

1 Introduction

There are two ways for processing tree-structured data such as XML [1]: one is to manipulate data using a tree representation (e.g., DOM API [16], XDuce [4,5], CDuce [15] in the case of XML processing), and the other is to use a stream representation (e.g., SAX, in the case of XML processing). Since large tree-structured data are typically stored in files using the stream representation, the former approach requires that the data be first loaded into memory and converted into the tree representation. On the other hand, the former approach has an advantage that it is easier to read and write programs.

To take the best of both approaches, in our previous paper [7], we have proposed a framework in which a user can write a tree processing program, which is then automatically transformed into an equivalent stream processing program. For example, consider the programs in Figure 1. A user writes the tree-processing program, which takes a binary tree t as an input, and returns the tree whose leaf values are incremented by 1. A system then automatically transforms the

P.M. Hill (Ed.): LOPSTR 2005, LNCS 3901, pp. 98–114, 2006.

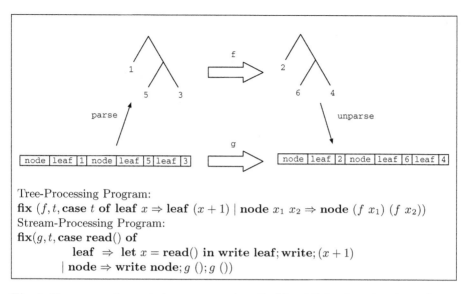

Tree-Processing Program:
fix $(f, t, \mathbf{case}\ t\ \mathbf{of\ leaf}\ x \Rightarrow \mathbf{leaf}\ (x + 1) \mid \mathbf{node}\ x_1\ x_2 \Rightarrow \mathbf{node}\ (f\ x_1)\ (f\ x_2))$
Stream-Processing Program:
fix$(g, t, \mathbf{case\ read}()\ \mathbf{of}$
$\qquad \mathbf{leaf} \Rightarrow \mathbf{let}\ x = \mathbf{read}()\ \mathbf{in\ write\ leaf}; \mathbf{write}; (x + 1)$
$\qquad \mid \mathbf{node} \Rightarrow \mathbf{write\ node}; g\ ();g\ ())$

Fig. 1. Tree-processing and stream-processing. **fix** (f, x, M) is a function that takes an argument to x and evaluates M in which the whole function is referred to by f.

program into the stream-processing program, which is more efficient for data stored in the stream representation since there is no need to construct trees on memory. We have implemented a generator of XML stream processing programs based on the framework, and confirmed that the approach works well for certain programs [6].

Our previous framework [7], however, imposes a severe restriction on tree-processing programs. The framework can deal with only programs that access each node of an input tree only once, in the depth-first, left-to-right order. For example, consider the program *swap_deep'* in Figure 2. It swaps the children of nodes whose depth is more than n. Stream-processing would be effective since the program traverses the input tree mostly in the depth-first, left-to-right order, but our previous framework simply rejects it. In principle, a user can write any tree-processing by explicitly inserting primitives for copying data from an input stream to memory or copying constructed trees from memory to an output stream (both of which are called *buffering primitives* below). For example, one can rewrite the program *swap_deep'* to the program *swap_deep* by inserting a buffering primitive *s2m*, which copies data from the input stream to memory. Our previous framework can then be applied to obtain a stream-processing program, which constructs only deep sub-trees on memory. Such explicit insertion of buffering primitives is, however, often cumbersome and worsens the readability of the program. Moreover, whether a program conforms to the access order restriction is checked by using a static type system with ordered linear types (inspired by ordered linear logic [12]), so a programmer has to understand the type system to insert buffering primitives in appropriate places.

Ill-typed tree-processing program:

$swap\_deep' \overset{\text{def}}{\equiv}$

let $swap$ =

  fix $(f, t, \textbf{case } t \textbf{ of leaf } x \Rightarrow \textbf{ leaf } x \mid \textbf{node } x_1\ x_2 \Rightarrow \textbf{node } (f\ x_2)\ (f\ x_1))$ **in**

    $\lambda n.\textbf{fix } (g, t,$

        if $n = 0$ **then** $swap\ t$

        else case t **of**

            leaf $x \Rightarrow$ **leaf** x

        $\mid$ **node** $x_1\ x_2 \Rightarrow$ **node** $(g\ (n-1)\ x_1)\ (g\ (n-1)\ x_2))$

Well-typed tree-processing program:

$swap\_deep \overset{\text{def}}{\equiv}$

let $swap$ =

  fix $(f, t,$

    mcase t **of mleaf** $x \Rightarrow$ **leaf** $x \mid$ **mnode** $x_1\ x_2 \Rightarrow$ **node** $(f\ x_2)\ (f\ x_1))$ **in**

      $\lambda n.\textbf{fix } (g, t,$

          if $n = 0$ **then** $swap\ (s2m\ t)$

          else case t **of**

              leaf $x \Rightarrow$ **leaf** x

          $\mid$ **node** $x_1\ x_2 \Rightarrow$ **node** $(g\ (n-1)\ x_1)\ (g\ (n-1)\ x_2))$

Resulting stream-processing program:

$swap\_deep\_strm \overset{\text{def}}{\equiv}$

let $swap$ =

  fix $(f, t, \textbf{mcase } t \textbf{ of mleaf } x \Rightarrow \textbf{ write leaf}; \textbf{ write } x$

                    $\mid$ **mnode** $x_1\ x_2 \Rightarrow$ **write node**; $f\ ();\ f\ ())$ **in**

    $\lambda n.\textbf{fix } (g, t,$

        if $n = 0$ **then** $swap\ (s2m\ t)$

        else case read$()$ **of**

            leaf $\Rightarrow$ **let** $x =$ **read**$()$ **in write leaf**; **write** x

      $\mid$ **node** $\Rightarrow$ **write node**; $g\ (n-1)\ ();\ g\ (n-1)\ ())$

Fig. 2. A program which swaps children of nodes whose depth is more than n

We overcome the above-mentioned problems by developing an algorithm which, given any simply-typed tree-processing program (without the access order restriction), automatically inserts buffering primitives. The resulting program is guaranteed to be well-typed under our previous ordered-linear type system [7], so that the program can be further transformed into an equivalent stream-processing program using our previous framework [7].

For example, the program $swap\_deep'$ in Figure 2, which is ill-typed in the type system in [7], is translated into the program $swap\_deep$ in Figure 2 using the algorithm presented in this paper. As $swap\_deep$ is well-typed in the type system of [7], it can be translated into a stream-processing program $swap\_deep\_strm$.

The rest of the paper is organized as follows. In Section 2, we briefly review our previous framework [7]. Section 3 presents non-deterministic rules for inserting buffering primitives and proves the soundness of the rules. Then, we present a deterministic algorithm for inserting buffering primitives. We discuss related work in Section 6, and conclude in Section 7.

2   Language and Type System for Tree-Processing

This section gives an overview of our previous framework for generation of stream-processing programs [7]. The source language is a call-by-value λ-calculus extended with binary trees. The framework can easily be extended to deal with XML [6].

2.1   Language

Figure 3 gives the syntax of the tree-processing language. The operational semantics is summarized in the full version [14].

The meta-variables x and i range over the sets of variables and integers respectively. The first line of M gives standard constructs for the λ-calculus. **fix** (f, x, M) is a function that takes an argument to x and evaluates M. The whole function is referred to by f in M. We write $\lambda x.M$ for **fix** (f, x, M) when f is not free in M. We write **let** $x = M_1$ **in** M_2 for $(\lambda x.M_2)\ M_1$. Especially, if M_2 contains no free occurrence of x, we write $M_1; M_2$ for it.

The next line gives two kinds of tree constructors. **leaf** and **node** are constructors for *non-buffered trees*, which are intended to be represented in the stream format, and can be accessed only in a restricted manner. **mleaf** and **mnode** are constructors for *buffered trees*, which are stored in memory and can be accessed in an arbitrary manner.

The third line gives primitives for changing tree representations: The primitive *s2m* converts non-buffered trees to buffered trees, and *m2s* converts buffered trees to non-buffered trees. For a technical reason, we also have a construct **letbuf** $x = M_1$ **in** M_2, which is operationally the same as $(\lambda x.M_2)M_1$.

The last two lines of the definition of terms give destructors for the two versions of trees.

Terms, values and evaluation contexts:

$$M \text{ (terms)} ::= i \mid \textbf{fix } (f, x, M) \mid x \mid M_1\ M_2 \mid M_1 + M_2$$
$$\mid \textbf{leaf } M \mid \textbf{node } M_1\ M_2 \mid \textbf{mleaf } M \mid \textbf{mnode } M_1\ M_2$$
$$\mid s2m \mid m2s \mid \textbf{letbuf } x = M_1 \textbf{ in } M_2$$
$$\mid \textbf{case } y \textbf{ of leaf } x \Rightarrow M_1 \mid \textbf{node } x_1\ x_2 \Rightarrow M_2$$
$$\mid \textbf{mcase } y \textbf{ of mleaf } x \Rightarrow M_1 \mid \textbf{mnode } x_1\ x_2 \Rightarrow M_2$$
$$\tau \text{ (types)}\quad ::= \textbf{Int} \mid \textbf{Tree}^d \mid \tau_1 \rightarrow \tau_2$$
$$d \text{ (uses)}\quad ::= 1 \mid \omega \mid +$$

Fig. 3. The syntax of the tree-processing language and types

2.2 Type System

As mentioned in Section 1, we use an ordered linear type system to ensure that input trees are accessed in the appropriate order (i.e., the left-to-right, depth-first order).

The syntax of types is given in Figure 3. **Int** is the type of integers and $\tau_1 \to \tau_2$ is the type of functions from τ_1 to τ_2. We have three kinds of tree types. **Tree**$^\omega$ is the type of buffered trees. **Tree**^{1} and **Tree**$^+$ are the types of input trees and output trees respectively.

A type judgment of our type system is $\Gamma \mid \Delta \vdash M : \tau$. Here, Γ is a usual type environment, which is a mapping from a finite set of variables to types. We, however, impose a restriction that the codomain of Γ does not contain **Tree**^{1} or **Tree**$^+$. Δ is an *ordered linear type environment*, which is a sequence of bindings $x_1 : \textbf{Tree}^1, \ldots, x_n : \textbf{Tree}^1$ where $x_1 \cdots x_n$ are different from each other. That environment specifies not only that $x_1, \ldots, x_n$ are bound to input trees, but also that each of $x_1, \ldots, x_n$ must be accessed exactly once in this order and that each of the subtrees bound to $x_1, \ldots, x_n$ must be accessed in the left-to-right, depth-first order.

Figure 4 gives key typing rules. For the full rules, see the full version [14].

$$\frac{\Gamma \mid \Delta \vdash M : \textbf{Int}}{\Gamma \mid \Delta \vdash \textbf{leaf } M : \textbf{Tree}^+} \quad \text{(T-LEAF)}$$

$$\frac{\Gamma \mid \Delta_1 \vdash M_1 : \textbf{Tree}^+ \qquad \Gamma \mid \Delta_2 \vdash M_2 : \textbf{Tree}^+}{\Gamma \mid \Delta_1, \Delta_2 \vdash \textbf{node } M_1\ M_2 : \textbf{Tree}^+} \quad \text{(T-NODE)}$$

$$\frac{\Gamma \mid \Delta \vdash M : \textbf{Int}}{\Gamma \mid \Delta \vdash \textbf{mleaf } M : \textbf{Tree}^\omega} \quad \text{(T-MLEAF)}$$

$$\frac{\Gamma \mid \Delta_1 \vdash M_1 : \textbf{Tree}^\omega \qquad \Gamma \mid \Delta_2 \vdash M_2 : \textbf{Tree}^\omega}{\Gamma \mid \Delta_1, \Delta_2 \vdash \textbf{mnode } M_1\ M_2 : \textbf{Tree}^\omega} \quad \text{(T-MNODE)}$$

$$\frac{\begin{array}{c} \Gamma, x : \textbf{Int} \mid \Delta \vdash M_1 : \tau \\ \Gamma \mid x_1 : \textbf{Tree}^1, x_2 : \textbf{Tree}^1, \Delta \vdash M_2 : \tau \end{array}}{\Gamma \mid y : \textbf{Tree}^1, \Delta \vdash \textbf{case } y \textbf{ of leaf } x \Rightarrow M_1 \mid \textbf{node } x_1\ x_2 \Rightarrow M_2 : \tau} \quad \text{(T-CASE)}$$

$$\frac{\begin{array}{c} \Gamma, y : \textbf{Tree}^\omega, x : \textbf{Int} \mid \Delta \vdash M_1 : \tau \\ \Gamma, y : \textbf{Tree}^\omega, x_1 : \textbf{Tree}^\omega, x_2 : \textbf{Tree}^\omega \mid \Delta \vdash M_2 : \tau \end{array}}{\Gamma, y : \textbf{Tree}^\omega \mid \Delta \vdash \textbf{mcase } y \textbf{ of mleaf } x \Rightarrow M_1 \mid \textbf{mnode } x_1\ x_2 \Rightarrow M_2 : \tau} \quad \text{(T-MCASE)}$$

Fig. 4. A part of typing rules of $\Gamma \mid \Delta \vdash M : \tau$

2.3 Translation Algorithm

If a program is well-typed in the type system presented above, the program can be translated into an equivalent stream-processing program using a straight-forward algorithm. Figure 5 shows the highlight of the algorithm $\mathcal{A}$, which

$$\mathcal{A}(\textbf{leaf } M) = \textbf{write}(\textbf{leaf}); \textbf{write}(\mathcal{A}(M))$$
$$\mathcal{A}(\textbf{node } M_1 \ M_2) = \textbf{write}(\textbf{node}); \mathcal{A}(M_1); \mathcal{A}(M_2)$$
$$\mathcal{A}(\textbf{case } y \textbf{ of leaf } x \Rightarrow M_1 \mid \textbf{node } x_1 \ x_2 \Rightarrow M_2) =$$
$$\textbf{case read}() \textbf{ of leaf} \Rightarrow \textbf{let } x = \textbf{read}() \textbf{ in } \mathcal{A}(M_1)$$
$$\mid \textbf{node} \Rightarrow [()/x_1, ()/x_2]\mathcal{A}(M_2)$$

Fig. 5. Translation algorithm

converts tree constructors into stream output operations, and tree destructors into stream input operations. For other term constructors, $\mathcal{A}$ simply works as a homomorphism; For example, $\mathcal{A}(M_1 + M_2) = \mathcal{A}(M_1) + \mathcal{A}(M_2)$. The program *swap_deep_strm* in Figure 2 is obtained from *swap_deep* by using $\mathcal{A}$.

The definition of stream-processing language and a proof of the correctness of the algorithm are given in our previous paper [7].

3 Non-deterministic Specification for Automatic Insertion of Buffering Primitives

Now we discuss a method for automatically inserting *s2m* and *m2s*. Let us write $\Gamma \vdash_{\lambda \to} M : \tau$ for the type judgment for the usual *simply-typed* λ-calculus (see the full version [14]). The goal is to transform any program M such that $\emptyset \vdash_{\lambda \to} M : \textbf{Tree} \to \textbf{Tree}$ into an equivalent program M' such that $\emptyset \mid \emptyset \vdash M' : \textbf{Tree}^1 \to \textbf{Tree}^+$, by inserting *s2m* and *m2s* into M.

We first define correct transformations in a declarative and non-deterministic manner. We introduce a new judgment $\Gamma \mid \Delta \vdash M \rightsquigarrow M' : \tau$. The judgment means that (1) M and M' are equivalent if we ignore the representation of trees, and (2) $\Gamma \mid \Delta \vdash M' : \tau$ holds.

Definition 1. $\Gamma \mid \Delta \vdash M \rightsquigarrow M' : \tau$ *is the least relation that satisfies the rules in Figure 6.*

For example, the rule TR-STREAMTOMEM says that we can transform M under the assumption that x is an input tree by first inserting the conversion $s2m(x)$, and then transforming M under the assumption that x is a buffered tree.

Note that the rules are non-deterministic in the sense that there may be more than one valid transformations for each source program M. We present an algorithm that choose one from possible translations.

The following theorem guarantees the soundness of the judgment.

Theorem 1 (Soundness of $\Gamma \mid \Delta \vdash M \rightsquigarrow M' : \tau$). *If $\Gamma \mid \Delta \vdash M \rightsquigarrow M' : \tau$ holds, then $\Gamma \mid \Delta \vdash M' : \tau$ and $M \equiv erase(M')$.*

Here, $erase(M')$ is the term obtained by removing *s2m* and *m2s*, and replacing constructors and destructors for buffered trees with those for non-buffered trees. The first property of the lemma means that the result of the translation is well-typed (so that our previous framework can be applied to generate a

$$\Gamma \mid \emptyset \vdash i \rightsquigarrow i : \textbf{Int} \tag{TR-INT}$$

$$\frac{\Gamma \mid \Delta_1 \vdash M_1 \rightsquigarrow M_1' : \textbf{Int} \qquad \Gamma \mid \Delta_2 \vdash M_2 \rightsquigarrow M_2' : \textbf{Int}}{\Gamma \mid \Delta_1, \Delta_2 \vdash M_1 + M_2 \rightsquigarrow M_1' + M_2' : \textbf{Int}} \tag{TR-PLUS}$$

$$\Gamma, x : \tau \mid \emptyset \vdash x \rightsquigarrow x : \tau \tag{TR-VAR1}$$

$$\Gamma \mid x : \textbf{Tree}^1 \vdash x \rightsquigarrow x : \textbf{Tree}^1 \tag{TR-VAR2}$$

$$\frac{f : \tau_1 \rightarrow \tau_2, \Gamma, x : \tau_1 \mid \emptyset \vdash M \rightsquigarrow M' : \tau_2}{\Gamma \mid \emptyset \vdash \textbf{fix } (f, x, M) \rightsquigarrow \textbf{fix } (f, x, M') : \tau_1 \rightarrow \tau_2} \tag{TR-FIX1}$$

$$\frac{f : \textbf{Tree}^1 \rightarrow \tau, \Gamma \mid x : \textbf{Tree}^1 \vdash M \rightsquigarrow M' : \tau}{\Gamma \mid \emptyset \vdash \textbf{fix } (f, x, M) \rightsquigarrow \textbf{fix } (f, x, M') : \textbf{Tree}^1 \rightarrow \tau} \tag{TR-FIX2}$$

$$\frac{\Gamma \mid \Delta_1 \vdash M_1 \rightsquigarrow M_1' : \tau' \rightarrow \tau \qquad \Gamma \mid \Delta_2 \vdash M_2 \rightsquigarrow M_2' : \tau'}{\Gamma \mid \Delta_1, \Delta_2 \vdash M_1 \ M_2 \rightsquigarrow M_1' \ M_2' : \tau} \tag{TR-APP}$$

$$\frac{\Gamma \mid \Delta \vdash M \rightsquigarrow M' : \textbf{Int}}{\Gamma \mid \Delta \vdash \textbf{leaf } M \rightsquigarrow \textbf{leaf } M' : \textbf{Tree}^+} \tag{TR-LEAF1}$$

$$\frac{\Gamma \mid \Delta \vdash M \rightsquigarrow M' : \textbf{Int}}{\Gamma \mid \Delta \vdash \textbf{leaf } M \rightsquigarrow \textbf{mleaf } M' : \textbf{Tree}^\omega} \tag{TR-LEAF2}$$

$$\frac{\Gamma \mid \Delta_1 \vdash M_1 \rightsquigarrow M_1' : \textbf{Tree}^+ \qquad \Gamma \mid \Delta_2 \vdash M_2 \rightsquigarrow M_2' : \textbf{Tree}^+}{\Gamma \mid \Delta_1, \Delta_2 \vdash \textbf{node } M_1 \ M_2 \rightsquigarrow \textbf{node } M_1' \ M_2' : \textbf{Tree}^+} \tag{TR-NODE1}$$

$$\frac{\Gamma \mid \Delta_1 \vdash M_1 \rightsquigarrow M_1' : \textbf{Tree}^\omega \qquad \Gamma \mid \Delta_2 \vdash M_2 \rightsquigarrow M_2' : \textbf{Tree}^\omega}{\Gamma \mid \Delta_1, \Delta_2 \vdash \textbf{node } M_1 \ M_2 \rightsquigarrow \textbf{mnode } M_1' \ M_2' : \textbf{Tree}^\omega} \tag{TR-NODE2}$$

$$\frac{\Gamma, x : \textbf{Int} \mid \Delta \vdash M_1 \rightsquigarrow M_1' : \tau \qquad \Gamma \mid x_1 : \textbf{Tree}^1, x_2 : \textbf{Tree}^1, \Delta \vdash M_2 \rightsquigarrow M_2' : \tau}{\begin{array}{c} \Gamma \mid y : \textbf{Tree}^1, \Delta \vdash \textbf{case } y \textbf{ of leaf } x \Rightarrow M_1 \mid \textbf{node } x_1 \ x_2 \Rightarrow M_2 \\ \rightsquigarrow \textbf{case } y \textbf{ of leaf } x \Rightarrow M_1' \mid \textbf{node } x_1 \ x_2 \Rightarrow M_2' : \tau \end{array}} \tag{TR-CASE1}$$

$$\frac{\begin{array}{c} \Gamma, y : \textbf{Tree}^\omega, x : \textbf{Int} \mid \Delta \vdash M_1 \rightsquigarrow M_1' : \tau \\ \Gamma, y : \textbf{Tree}^\omega, x_1 : \textbf{Tree}^\omega, x_2 : \textbf{Tree}^\omega \mid \Delta \vdash M_2 \rightsquigarrow M_2' : \tau \end{array}}{\begin{array}{c} \Gamma, y : \textbf{Tree}^\omega \mid \Delta \vdash \textbf{case } y \textbf{ of leaf } x \Rightarrow M_1 \mid \textbf{node } x_1 \ x_2 \Rightarrow M_2 \\ \rightsquigarrow \textbf{mcase } y \textbf{ of mleaf } x \Rightarrow M_1' \mid \textbf{mnode } x_1 \ x_2 \Rightarrow M_2' : \tau \end{array}} \tag{TR-CASE2}$$

$$\frac{\Gamma, x : \textbf{Tree}^\omega \mid \Delta \vdash M \rightsquigarrow M' : \tau}{\Gamma \mid x : \textbf{Tree}^1, \Delta \vdash M \rightsquigarrow \textbf{letbuf } x = s2m(x) \textbf{ in } M' : \tau} \tag{TR-STREAMTOMEM}$$

$$\frac{\Gamma \mid \Delta \vdash M \rightsquigarrow M' : \textbf{Tree}^\omega}{\Gamma \mid \Delta \vdash M \rightsquigarrow m2s(M') : \textbf{Tree}^+} \tag{TR-MEMTOSTREAM}$$

Fig. 6. Rules for the judgment $\Gamma \mid \Delta \vdash M \rightsquigarrow M' : \tau$

stream-processing program). The second property states that the semantics of the program is preserved by the transformation.

The following lemma guarantees that there is at least one valid transformation for any simply-typed program.

Lemma 1. *If* $\Gamma' \vdash_{\lambda\to} M : \tau$ *then there exist* Γ, Δ, M' *and* τ' *such that* $\Gamma \mid \Delta \vdash M \rightsquigarrow M' : \tau'$ *and* $\Gamma' = eraseuse(\Gamma \cup \Delta)$ *and* $\tau = eraseuse(\tau')$.

Here, $eraseuse(\cdot)$ removes uses $(+, 1, \omega)$ from types.

We can easily check that the relation $\Gamma \mid \Delta \vdash M \rightsquigarrow M' : \tau$ contains a transformation that is optimal (in the sense that the resulting program copies as few trees as possible to memory) among those preserving typing and the structure of the source program. To formally state that property, let us write $M \rightsquigarrow M'$ if M' is obtained from M by inserting **letbuf** $x = s2m(x)$ **in** and $m2s$ and/or replacing some occurrences of **leaf**, **node**, and **case** with **mleaf**, **mnode**, and **mcase**. The following theorem states that *any* transformation that performs only such replacement and preserves types can be obtained by the transformation rules in Section 3, so that an optimal transformation can also be obtained.

Theorem 2 (Completeness of $\Gamma \mid \Delta \vdash M \rightsquigarrow M' : \tau$**).** *If* $\Gamma \vdash_{\lambda\to} M :$ **Tree** $\to$ **Tree** *and* $\Gamma \mid \emptyset \vdash M' :$ **Tree**$^1 \to$ **Tree**$^+$ *and* $M \rightsquigarrow M'$, *then* $\Gamma \mid \emptyset \vdash M \rightsquigarrow M' :$ **Tree**$^1 \to$ **Tree**$^+$.

Note that if we allow more aggressive transformation, we may obtain a more efficient program. For example, consider the program

$$\text{let } copy\_tree = \textbf{fix}(f, t, \textbf{case } t \textbf{ of leaf } x \Rightarrow \textbf{leaf } x$$
$$| \textbf{ node } x_1 \; x_2 \Rightarrow \textbf{node } (f \; x_1) \; (f \; x_2)) \textbf{ in}$$
$$\lambda t.\textbf{case } t \textbf{ of leaf } x \Rightarrow \textbf{leaf } x$$
$$| \textbf{ node } x_1 \; x_2 \Rightarrow \textbf{node } (\textbf{node } (copy\_tree \; x_1) \; (copy\_tree \; x_1)) \; (copy\_tree \; x_2).$$

If we allow code duplication, we would have the following program:

$$\text{let } copy\_tree\_s = \textbf{fix}(f, t, \textbf{case } t \textbf{ of leaf } x \Rightarrow \textbf{leaf } x$$
$$| \textbf{ node } x_1 \; x_2 \Rightarrow \textbf{node } (f \; x_1) \; (f \; x_2)) \textbf{ in}$$
$$\text{let } copy\_tree\_m = \textbf{fix}(f, t, \textbf{mcase } t \textbf{ of mleaf } x \Rightarrow \textbf{leaf } x$$
$$| \textbf{ mnode } x_1 \; x_2 \Rightarrow \textbf{node } (f \; x_1) \; (f \; x_2)) \textbf{ in}$$
$$\lambda t.\textbf{case } t \textbf{ of leaf } x \Rightarrow \textbf{leaf } x$$
$$| \textbf{ node } x_1 \; x_2 \Rightarrow$$
$$\textbf{node } (\textbf{letbuf } x_1 = s2m(x_1) \textbf{ in node } (copy\_tree\_m \; x_1) \; (copy\_tree\_m \; x_1))$$
$$(copy\_tree\_s \; x_2).$$

The program above does not buffer x_2, while any programs derived by $\Gamma \mid \Delta \vdash M \rightsquigarrow M' : \tau$ buffers x_2 because f must have type **Tree**$^\omega \to$ **Tree**$^+$. It is one of our future work to deal with such transformation.

4 Automatic Insertion Algorithm

The transformation rules presented in the previous section are non-deterministic in the sense that there may be more than one possible M' and τ that satisfy $\Gamma \mid \Delta \vdash M \leadsto M' : \tau$. We next present an algorithm for choosing one among those possibilities.

The algorithm consists of two sub-algorithms $\mathcal{I}$ and $\mathcal{P}$. Given a program of type **Tree** $\rightarrow$ **Tree**, $\mathcal{I}$ inserts $s2m$ and generates an intermediate program of type **Tree**^{1} $\rightarrow$ **Tree**$^\omega$. $\mathcal{P}$ takes the intermediate program as an input, inserts $m2s$, and generates a program of type **Tree**^{1} $\rightarrow$ **Tree**$^+$.

We focus on the algorithm $\mathcal{I}$ below, since $\mathcal{P}$ is fairly straightforward. $\mathcal{P}$ is briefly discussed at the end of this section.

4.1 Algorithm $\mathcal{I}$

We first give an overview of the algorithm $\mathcal{I}$. We shall introduce a new form of transformation judgment $\Theta \vdash M \leadsto M' : \tau$. Θ, called a *semi-ordered type environment*, is a combination of a type environment Γ and Δ. The rules for $\Theta \vdash M \leadsto M' : \tau$ is more deterministic than $\Gamma \mid \Delta \vdash M \leadsto M' : \tau$. In fact, there is only one transformation rule for each syntactic form of M. Using the new transformation rules, we can construct an algorithm $\mathcal{I}_1$, which, given Θ, M, and τ that may contain use variables to denote unknown uses, outputs M' and C, where C is a set of constraints on the use variables such that $\theta\Theta \vdash M \leadsto \theta M' : \theta\tau$ holds if the substitution θ satisfies C. Using $\mathcal{I}_1$, the algorithm $\mathcal{I}$ works as follows.

$$\mathcal{I}(M) = \text{let } (M', C) = \mathcal{I}_1(\emptyset, M, \textbf{Tree}^1 \rightarrow \textbf{Tree}^\omega) \text{ in}$$
$$\text{let } \theta = solve(C) \text{ in } \theta M'$$

Now let us look at the construction of $\mathcal{I}_1$ more closely. We construct $\mathcal{I}_1$ in three steps. First, we introduce a judgment $\Theta \vdash_I M \leadsto M' : \tau$ by combining Γ and Δ of $\Gamma \mid \Delta \vdash M \leadsto M' : \tau$. Then, we obtain $\Theta \vdash M \leadsto M' : \tau$ by deriving syntax-directed rules from $\Theta \vdash_I M \leadsto M' : \tau$. Finally, we derive $\mathcal{I}_1$ from the rules for $\Theta \vdash M \leadsto M' : \tau$.

We first define semi-ordered type environments. The semi-ordered type environment is necessary since at the time of running $\mathcal{I}_1$, we cannot tell which variable should be put into an ordered linear type environment Δ and which should be put into an ordinary type environment Γ.

Definition 2. *The use of a type τ, written $|\tau|$, is defined by:*

$$|\textbf{Int}| = \omega \qquad |\tau_1 \rightarrow \tau_2| = \omega \qquad |\textbf{Tree}^d| = d$$

Below, we use the total order $\geq$ on uses, defined by $\omega \geq 1$.

Definition 3 (Semi-ordered type environment). *A* semi-ordered type environment, *represented by Θ, is a sequence $x_1 : \tau_1, \ldots, x_n : \tau_n$ where each x_i is distinct from each other and $|\tau_i| \geq |\tau_j|$ whenever $i \leq j$. We write $x >_\Theta y$ if x occurs before y in Θ.*

$$coerce^{\Theta \Rightarrow \Theta}(M) = M$$

$$coerce^{(\Theta_1, x:\mathbf{Tree}^1, \Theta_2) \Rightarrow (\Theta_1, x:\mathbf{Tree}^\omega, \Theta_2')}(M) = (\mathbf{letbuf}\ x = s2m(x)\ \mathbf{in}\ coerce^{\Theta_2 \Rightarrow \Theta_2'}(M))$$

Fig. 7. Definition of $coerce^{\Theta \Rightarrow \Theta'}()$

In the definition of $\Theta \vdash M \rightsquigarrow M' : \tau$, we use two predicates, $\Theta_1 \succeq \Theta_2$ and $merge(\Theta, \Theta_1, \Theta_2)$. $\Theta_1 \succeq \Theta_2$ means that Θ_1 is obtained by replacing some of **Tree**^{1} in Θ_2 with **Tree**$^\omega$.

Definition 4. *We write $\tau_1 \succeq \tau_2$ when either $\tau_1 = \tau_2$ or $\tau_1 = $ **Tree**$^\omega$ and $\tau_2 = $ **Tree**^{1}. The relation is pointwise extended to that on semi-ordered environment; $x_1 : \tau_1, \ldots, x_n : \tau_n \succeq x_1 : \tau_1', \ldots, x_n : \tau_n'$ iff $\tau_i \succeq \tau_i'$ for every $i \in \{1, \ldots, n\}$.*

Intuitively, $merge(\Theta, \Theta_1, \Theta_2)$ defined below means that if variables can be accessed according to Θ, then they can be first accessed according to Θ_1 and then according to Θ_2. For example, if $\Theta = x : \mathbf{Tree}^\omega, y : \mathbf{Tree}^1, z : \mathbf{Tree}^1$, then $merge(\Theta, y : \mathbf{Tree}^1, (x : \mathbf{Tree}^\omega, z : \mathbf{Tree}^1))$ holds, but $merge(\Theta, z : \mathbf{Tree}^1, (x : \mathbf{Tree}^\omega, y : \mathbf{Tree}^1))$ does not, since the latter violates the condition that y should be read first.

Definition 5 (Merge of semi-ordered type environments). *Θ is a merge of Θ_1 and Θ_2, represented by $merge(\Theta, \Theta_1, \Theta_2)$, if and only if the following properties are satisfied:*

(1) $dom(\Theta_1) \cup dom(\Theta_2) \subseteq dom(\Theta)$ and $\Theta_1(x) = \Theta(x)$ for all $x \in dom(\Theta_1)$ and $\Theta_2(y) = \Theta(y)$ for all $y \in dom(\Theta_2)$
(2) $x >_{\Theta_1} y \implies x >_\Theta y$ and $x >_{\Theta_2} y \implies x >_\Theta y$
(3) $x \in dom(\Theta) \backslash (dom(\Theta_1) \cup dom(\Theta_2)) \implies |\Theta(x)| \geq \omega$
(4) $x \in dom(\Theta_1) \cap dom(\Theta_2) \implies |\Theta(x)| \geq \omega$
(5) If $y \in dom(\Theta_1)$, $x \in dom(\Theta_2)$, and $x >_\Theta y$, then $|\Theta(x)| \geq \omega$.

$$\frac{\tau = \Theta(x) \qquad \forall y \in dom(\Theta) \backslash \{x\}.|\Theta(y)| \geq \omega}{\Theta \vdash_I x \rightsquigarrow x : \tau} \quad (\text{Tr-Var'})$$

$$\frac{f : \tau_1 \rightarrow \tau_2, \Theta, x : \tau_1 \vdash_I M \rightsquigarrow M' : \tau_2 \qquad \forall y \in dom(\Theta).|\Theta(y)| \geq \omega}{\Theta \vdash_I \mathbf{fix}\ (f, x, M) \rightsquigarrow \mathbf{fix}\ (f, x, M') : \tau_1 \rightarrow \tau_2} \quad (\text{Tr-Fix'})$$

$$\frac{\Theta_1 \vdash_I M_1 \rightsquigarrow M_1' : \mathbf{Tree}^\omega \qquad \Theta_2 \vdash_I M_2 \rightsquigarrow M_2' : \mathbf{Tree}^\omega \qquad merge(\Theta, \Theta_1, \Theta_2)}{\Theta \vdash_I \mathbf{node}\ M_1\ M_2 \rightsquigarrow \mathbf{mnode}\ M_1'\ M_2' : \mathbf{Tree}^\omega}$$
$$(\text{Tr-Node'})$$

$$\frac{\Theta' \vdash_I M \rightsquigarrow M' : \tau \qquad \Theta' \succeq \Theta}{\Theta \vdash_I M \rightsquigarrow coerce^{\Theta \Rightarrow \Theta'}(M') : \tau} \quad (\text{Tr-StreamToMem'})$$

Fig. 8. A part of rules for $\Theta \vdash_I M \rightsquigarrow M' : \tau$

By the well-formedness condition of semi-ordered type environments, Θ_1 and Θ_2 can be decomposed into Γ_1, Δ_1 and Γ_2, Δ_2, where Γ_i is a sequence of bindings on types of use ω and Δ_i is a linear type environment. Thus, the conditions of $merge(\Theta, \Theta_1, \Theta_2)$ above essentially mean that Θ is of the form $\Gamma, \Delta_1, \Delta_2$ where Γ is obtained by merging Γ_1 and Γ_2 and adding extra bindings on types of use ω.

Figure 8 shows a part of rules for $\Theta \vdash_I M \rightsquigarrow M' : \tau$. The definition of $coerce^{\Theta \Rightarrow \Theta'}(M)$, which is used in the rule TR-STREAMTOMEM', is given in Figure 7. It inserts $s2m$ for each x such that $\Theta(x) = \mathbf{Tree}^1$ and $\Theta'(x) = \mathbf{Tree}^\omega$. Note that $coerce^{\Theta \Rightarrow \Theta'}(\cdot)$ is an operation on terms, so that it is reduced in the program transformation phase (when Θ and Θ' have been completely determined), not when the program is executed.

Next, we introduce a judgment $\Theta \vdash M \rightsquigarrow M' : \tau$.

Definition 6. *The relation $\Theta \vdash M \rightsquigarrow M' : \tau$ is the least relation closed under the rules in Figure 9.*

The rules in Figure 9 are syntax-directed version of the rules in Figure 8. For example, TR-SD-NODE corresponds to applications of the rule TR-STREAMTOMEM', followed by an application of TR-NODE'.

The following theorems describe soundness and completeness of $\Theta \vdash M \rightsquigarrow M' : \tau$ with respect to $\Gamma \mid \Delta \vdash M \rightsquigarrow M' : \tau$:

Theorem 3 (Soundness of $\Theta \vdash M \rightsquigarrow M' : \tau$). *If $\Theta \vdash M \rightsquigarrow M' : \tau$ holds, then there exist Γ and Δ that satisfy $\Gamma \mid \Delta \vdash M \rightsquigarrow M' : \tau$ and $\Theta = \Gamma, \Delta$.*

Theorem 4 (Completeness of $\Theta \vdash M \rightsquigarrow M' : \tau$). *Suppose that $\Gamma \mid \Delta \vdash M \rightsquigarrow M' : \tau$ is derived without using TR-LEAF1, TR-NODE1 and TR-MEMTOSTREAM. Then, $\Gamma, \Delta \vdash M \rightsquigarrow M' : \tau$.*

Based on the rules in Figure 9, we construct $\mathcal{I}_1$ in Figure 10 that takes Θ, M and τ as input and returns the result of translation M' and constraints C. C consists of inequalities between uses and equalities between types. It is obtained by reading the rules in Figure 9 in a bottom-up manner. In Figure 10, $rename(\Theta)$ returns a pair of the type environment obtained by replacing the uses variables occurs in Θ with fresh use variables, and a set of constraints for the renamed type environment being well-formed (i.e.,$|\Theta(x_i)| \geq |\Theta(x_j)|$ for any $x_i >_\Theta x_j$.) By abuse of notations, we write $\Theta_1 \succeq \Theta_2$ and $merge(\Theta, \Theta_1, \Theta_2)$ for the constraints on uses required for $\Theta_1 \succeq \Theta_2$ and $merge(\Theta, \Theta_1, \Theta_2)$ to hold respectively. The function $typeof(N)$ returns the simple type of N.[1]

The following theorem states soundness of $\mathcal{I}_1$.

Theorem 5. *Suppose $\mathcal{I}_1(\Theta, M, \tau) = M', C$. If θ is a solution of C then $\theta\Theta \vdash M \rightsquigarrow \theta M' : \theta\tau$ holds.*

---

[1] Here, we assume that the type reconstruction algorithm for $\emptyset \vdash_{\lambda\rightarrow} M : \mathbf{Tree} \rightarrow \mathbf{Tree}$ is applied, and that the type of each subterm has been already determined. The variables whose types are not uniquely determined are not accessed, so we can safely assume that $typeof()$ returns $\mathbf{Int}$ for those variables.

$$\frac{\forall y \in dom(\Theta')\backslash\{x\}.\ |\Theta'(y)| \geq \omega \qquad \Theta' \succeq \Theta \qquad \tau = \Theta'(x)}{\Theta \vdash x \rightsquigarrow coerce^{\Theta \Rightarrow \Theta'}(x) : \tau} \ (\text{Tr-SD-Var})$$

$$\frac{\forall x \in dom(\Theta').\ |\Theta'(x)| \geq \omega \qquad \Theta' \succeq \Theta}{\Theta \vdash i \rightsquigarrow coerce^{\Theta \Rightarrow \Theta'}(i) : \mathbf{Int}} \ (\text{Tr-SD-Int})$$

$$\frac{\Theta_1' \vdash M_1 \rightsquigarrow M_1' : \mathbf{Int} \qquad \Theta_2' \vdash M_2 \rightsquigarrow M_2' : \mathbf{Int}}{\Theta \vdash M_1 + M_2 \rightsquigarrow coerce^{\Theta_1 \Rightarrow \Theta_1'}(M_1') + coerce^{\Theta_2 \Rightarrow \Theta_2'}(M_2') : \mathbf{Int}} \ (\text{Tr-SD-Plus})$$

$$\frac{\begin{array}{c} f : \tau_1 \rightarrow \tau_2, \Theta', x : \tau_1 \vdash M \rightsquigarrow M' : \tau_2 \\ f : \tau_1 \rightarrow \tau_2, \Theta', x : \tau_1 \succeq f : \tau_1 \rightarrow \tau_2, \Theta, x : \tau_1' \qquad \forall y \in dom(\Theta).\ |\Theta(y)| \geq \omega \end{array}}{\Theta \vdash \mathbf{fix}\ (f, x, M) \rightsquigarrow \mathbf{fix}\ (f, x, coerce^{(f:\tau_1 \rightarrow \tau_2, \Theta, x:\tau_1) \Rightarrow (f:\tau_1 \rightarrow \tau_2, \Theta', x:\tau_1')}(M')) : \tau_1 \rightarrow \tau_2} \ (\text{Tr-SD-Fix})$$

$$\frac{\Theta_1' \vdash M_1 \rightsquigarrow M_1' : \tau_1 \rightarrow \tau_2 \qquad \Theta_2' \vdash M_2 \rightsquigarrow M_2' : \tau_1}{\Theta \vdash M_1\ M_2 \rightsquigarrow coerce^{\Theta_1 \Rightarrow \Theta_1'}(M_1')\ coerce^{\Theta_2 \Rightarrow \Theta_2'}(M_2') : \tau_2} \ (\text{Tr-SD-App})$$

$$\frac{\Theta' \vdash M \rightsquigarrow M' : \mathbf{Int} \qquad \Theta' \succeq \Theta}{\Theta \vdash \mathbf{leaf}\ M \rightsquigarrow \mathbf{mleaf}\ coerce^{\Theta \Rightarrow \Theta'}(M') : \mathbf{Tree}^\omega} \ (\text{Tr-SD-Leaf})$$

$$\frac{\Theta_1' \vdash M_1 \rightsquigarrow M_1' : \mathbf{Tree}^\omega \qquad \Theta_2' \vdash M_2 \rightsquigarrow M_2' : \mathbf{Tree}^\omega}{\Theta \vdash \mathbf{node}\ M_1\ M_2 \rightsquigarrow \mathbf{mnode}\ coerce^{\Theta_1 \Rightarrow \Theta_1'}(M_1')\ coerce^{\Theta_2 \Rightarrow \Theta_2'}(M_2') : \mathbf{Tree}^\omega} \ (\text{Tr-SD-Node})$$

$$\frac{\begin{array}{c} \Theta_1' \vdash y \rightsquigarrow y' : \mathbf{Tree}^d \qquad \Theta_2' \vdash M_1 \rightsquigarrow M_1' : \tau \qquad \Theta_3' \vdash M_2 \rightsquigarrow M_2' : \tau \\ \Theta_1' \succeq \Theta_1 \qquad \Theta_2' \succeq x : \mathbf{Int}, \Theta_{2L}, \Theta_{2R} \qquad \Theta_3' \succeq \Theta_{2L}, x_1 : \mathbf{Tree}^d, x_2 : \mathbf{Tree}^d, \Theta_{2R} \\ merge(\Theta, \Theta_1, (\Theta_{2L}, \Theta_{2R})) \qquad M_1'' = coerce^{(\Theta_{2L}, \Theta_{2R}) \Rightarrow (\Theta_2' \backslash \{x:\mathbf{Int}\})}(M_1') \\ M_2'' = coerce^{(\Theta_{2L}, x_1:\mathbf{Tree}^d, x_2:\mathbf{Tree}^d, \Theta_{2R}) \Rightarrow \Theta_3'}(M_2') \end{array}}{\Theta \vdash \begin{array}{l} \mathbf{case}\ y\ \mathbf{of} \\ \quad \mathbf{leaf}\ x \Rightarrow M_1 \\ \quad |\ \mathbf{node}\ x_1\ x_2 \Rightarrow M_2 \end{array} \rightsquigarrow \begin{array}{l} \mathbf{case}\ y\ \mathbf{of} \\ \quad \mathbf{leaf}\ x \Rightarrow M_1'' \\ \quad |\ \mathbf{node}\ x_1\ x_2 \Rightarrow M_2'' \end{array} : \tau} \ (\text{Tr-SD-Case})$$

Fig. 9. Typing rules for the judgment $\Theta \vdash M \rightsquigarrow M' : \tau$

Unfortunately, the converse of Theorem 5 does not hold. For example, consider the program $M = ((f\ x) + 1) + (f\ z)$. M can be transformed to both $M_1' = ((f\ x) + \mathbf{letbuf}\ y = s2m(y)\ \mathbf{in}\ 1) + (f\ z)$ and $M_2' = (f\ x) + (\mathbf{letbuf}\ y = s2m(y)\ \mathbf{in}\ 1 + (f\ z))$ under the semi-ordered environment $\Theta = f : \mathbf{Tree}^1 \rightarrow \mathbf{Int}, x : \mathbf{Tree}^1, y : \mathbf{Tree}^1, z : \mathbf{Tree}^1$ by the transformation rules in Figure 9. Only the latter derivation can, however, be derived by algorithm $\mathcal{I}_1$. This is because $\mathcal{I}_1(M_1 + M_2)$ divides the semi-ordered environment Θ into Θ_1

$$
\begin{aligned}
\mathcal{I}_1(\Theta, x, \tau) \quad &= \quad M, C \\
&where \quad \Theta', C_0 = rename(\Theta) \\
&\qquad C = \{|\Theta'(y)| \geq \omega | y \in Dom(\Theta')\backslash\{x\}\} \cup \Theta' \succeq \Theta \\
&\qquad\qquad \cup \{\tau = \Theta'(x)\} \cup C_0 \\
&\qquad M = coerce^{\Theta \to \Theta'}(x)
\end{aligned}
$$

$$
\begin{aligned}
\mathcal{I}_1(\Theta, \mathbf{fix}\ (f, x, M), \tau_1 \to \tau_2) \quad &= \quad M', C \\
&where \quad \Theta'' = f : \tau_1 \to \tau_2, \Theta', x : \tau_1' \\
&\qquad = rename(f : \tau_1 \to \tau_2, \Theta, x : \tau_1) \\
&\qquad C_1 = well\_formed(\Theta'') \quad C_3 = \mathcal{I}_1(\Theta'', M, \tau') \\
&\qquad C_2 = \Theta'' \succeq \Theta' \quad C_0 = \{|\Theta(y)| \geq \omega | y \in Dom(\Theta)\} \\
&\qquad C = C_0 \cup C_1 \cup C_2 \cup C_3 \\
&\qquad M' = \mathbf{fix}\ (f, x, coerce^{\Theta' \to \Theta''}(M))
\end{aligned}
$$

$$
\begin{aligned}
\mathcal{I}_1(\Theta, M_1\ M_2, \tau_2) \quad &= \quad M, C \\
&where \quad \Theta_1 = \Theta|_{\mathbf{FV}(M_1)} \quad \Theta_2 = \Theta|_{\mathbf{FV}(M_2)} \\
&\qquad \Theta_1' = rename(\Theta_1) \quad \Theta_2' = rename(\Theta_2) \\
&\qquad C_0 = well\_formed(\Theta_1') \quad C_1 = well\_formed(\Theta_2') \\
&\qquad \tau_1 = typeof(M_2) \quad M_1', C_2 = \mathcal{I}_1(\Theta_1', M_1, \tau_1 \to \tau_2) \\
&\qquad M_2', C_3 = \mathcal{I}_1(\Theta_2', M_2, \tau_1) \quad C_4 = \Theta_1' \succeq \Theta_1 \\
&\qquad C_5 = \Theta_2' \succeq \Theta_2 \quad C_6 = merge(\Theta, \Theta_1, \Theta_2) \\
&\qquad M_1'' = coerce^{\Theta_1 \to \Theta_1'}(M_1') \\
&\qquad M_2'' = coerce^{\Theta_2 \to \Theta_2'}(M_2') \\
&\qquad C = C_0 \cup \cdots \cup C_6
\end{aligned}
$$

$$
\begin{aligned}
\mathcal{I}_1(\Theta, \mathbf{node}\ M_1\ M_2, \mathbf{Tree}^d) \quad &= \quad M, C \\
&where \quad \Theta_1 = \Theta|_{\mathbf{FV}(M_1)} \quad \Theta_2 = \Theta|_{\mathbf{FV}(M_2)} \\
&\qquad \Theta_1' = rename(\Theta_1) \quad \Theta_2' = rename(\Theta_2) \\
&\qquad C_0 = well\_formed(\Theta_1') \quad C_1 = well\_formed(\Theta_2') \\
&\qquad M_1', C_2 = \mathcal{I}_1(\Theta_1', M_1, \mathbf{Tree}^\omega) \\
&\qquad M_2', C_3 = \mathcal{I}_1(\Theta_2', M_2, \mathbf{Tree}^\omega) \\
&\qquad C_4 = \Theta_1' \succeq \Theta_1 \quad C_5 = \Theta_2' \succeq \Theta_2 \\
&\qquad C_6 = merge(\Theta, \Theta_1, \Theta_2) \\
&\qquad M_1'' = coerce^{\Theta_1 \to \Theta_1'}(M_1') \\
&\qquad M_2'' = coerce^{\Theta_2 \to \Theta_2'}(M_2') \\
&\qquad M = \mathbf{mnode}\ M_1''\ M_2'' \\
&\qquad C = C_0 \cup \cdots \cup C_6 \cup \{d \geq \omega\}
\end{aligned}
$$

Fig. 10. A part of the automatic insertion algorithm. $typeof(M)$ returns the type of M inferred by the type reconstruction algorithm for $\Gamma \vdash_{\lambda \to} M : \tau$.

and Θ_2 in a fixed way (see Figure 10). This is not a problem from the viewpoint of the optimality of the transformation result: for any term M' obtained from M by using the rules in Figure 9, algorithm $\mathcal{I}_1$ generates a term M'' that is as efficient as M'. In the above example, M_1' is as efficient as M_2' ($s2m(y)$ in both terms can be replaced by *skip_tree*. See Section 5.), so that producing only M_1' is sufficient.

Let $(M'', C) = \mathcal{I}_1(M)$. The constraints C can be reduced to a set of constraints on uses of the form $\{u_1 \geq d_1, \ldots, u_n \geq d_n\}$, where $u_1, \ldots, u_n$ are distinct use variables and $d_1, \ldots, d_n$ are expressions contructed from use variables, constants, and the operation $max(d, d')$ that takes an upper-bound of two uses d and d'. Since $d_1, \ldots, d_n$ are monotonic on $u_1, \ldots, u_n$, we can apply the standard algorithm [13] to obtain the least solution of C. The output of algorithm $\mathcal{I}$ is the term obtained by substituting the least solution for the use variables in M'' and reducing *coerce*.

4.2   Algorithm $\mathcal{P}$

We design $\mathcal{P}$ in a way similar to $\mathcal{I}$. We first introduce a judgment $\Gamma \vdash M \rightsquigarrow M' : \tau$ in a syntax-directed manner. Figure 11 shows a part of the rules for $\Gamma \vdash M \rightsquigarrow M' : \tau$. In the figure, $\tau_1 \succeq_{\mathcal{P}} \tau_2$ is the least reflexive transitive binary relation that satisfies $\mathbf{Tree}^+ \succeq_{\mathcal{P}} \mathbf{Tree}^\omega$. Γ is not ordered since $\mathcal{I}$ already guarantees that variables of type $\mathbf{Tree}^1$ are accessed in the correct order.

$$coerce\_out^{\mathbf{Tree}^\omega \Rightarrow \mathbf{Tree}^+}(M) = m2s(M)$$
$$coerce\_out^{\tau \Rightarrow \tau}(M) = M$$

$$\frac{\Gamma, f : \tau_1 \rightarrow \tau_2, x : \tau_1 \vdash M \rightsquigarrow M' : \tau_2' \qquad \tau_2 \succeq_{\mathcal{P}} \tau_2'}{\Gamma \vdash \mathbf{fix}\ (f, x, M) \rightsquigarrow \mathbf{fix}\ (f, x, coerce\_out^{\tau_2' \Rightarrow \tau_2}(M')) : \tau_1 \rightarrow \tau_2}\ \text{(TO-Fix)}$$

$$\frac{\Gamma \vdash M \rightsquigarrow M' : \mathbf{Int}}{\Gamma \vdash \mathbf{mleaf}\ M \rightsquigarrow \mathbf{leaf}^d\ M' : \mathbf{Tree}^d}\ \text{(TO-Leaf)}$$

$$\frac{\begin{array}{cc} \Gamma \vdash M_1 \rightsquigarrow M_1' : \mathbf{Tree}^{d_1} & \Gamma \vdash M_2 \rightsquigarrow M_2' : \mathbf{Tree}^{d_2} \\ \mathbf{Tree}^d \succeq_{\mathcal{P}} \mathbf{Tree}^{d_1} & \mathbf{Tree}^d \succeq_{\mathcal{P}} \mathbf{Tree}^{d_2} \\ M_1'' = coerce\_out^{\mathbf{Tree}^{d_1} \Rightarrow \mathbf{Tree}^d}(M_1) & M_2'' = coerce\_out^{\mathbf{Tree}^{d_2} \Rightarrow \mathbf{Tree}^d}(M_2) \end{array}}{\Gamma \vdash \mathbf{mnode}\ M_1\ M_2 \rightsquigarrow \mathbf{node}^d\ M_1''\ M_2'' : \mathbf{Tree}^d}$$
$$\text{(TO-Node)}$$

$$\frac{\begin{array}{cc} \Gamma \vdash M \rightsquigarrow M' : \mathbf{Tree}^d & \Gamma, x : \mathbf{Int} \vdash M_1 \rightsquigarrow M_1' : \tau_1 \\ \multicolumn{2}{c}{\Gamma, x_1 : \mathbf{Tree}^d, x_2 : \mathbf{Tree}^d \vdash M_2 \rightsquigarrow M_2' : \tau_2} \\ \multicolumn{2}{c}{\tau \succeq_{\mathcal{P}} \tau_1 \qquad \tau \succeq_{\mathcal{P}} \tau_2} \end{array}}{\Gamma \vdash \begin{array}{l} \mathbf{case}^d\ M\ \mathbf{of} \\ \quad \mathbf{leaf}^d\ x \Rightarrow M_1 \\ \mid \mathbf{node}^d\ x_1\ x_2 \Rightarrow M_2 \end{array} \rightsquigarrow \begin{array}{l} \mathbf{case}^d\ M'\ \mathbf{of} \\ \quad \mathbf{leaf}^d\ x \Rightarrow coerce\_out^{\tau_1 \Rightarrow \tau}(M_1) \\ \mid \mathbf{node}^d\ x_1\ x_2 \Rightarrow coerce\_out^{\tau_2 \Rightarrow \tau}(M_2) \end{array} : \tau}$$
$$\text{(TO-Case)}$$

Fig. 11. A part of declarative definition of the algorithm that inserts $m2s$

Based on $\Gamma \vdash M \rightsquigarrow M' : \tau$, we construct a sub-algorithm $\mathcal{P}_1$ that takes Γ, M and τ, and returns M' and C where C is a set of constraints on the use variables such that $\theta\Gamma \vdash M \rightsquigarrow \theta M' : \theta\tau$ if the substitution θ satisfies C.

By combining $\mathcal{I}$ and $\mathcal{P}$, we have an algorithm that transform any program M such that $\emptyset \vdash M : \textbf{Tree} \to \textbf{Tree}$ into M' such that $\emptyset \mid \emptyset \vdash M' : \textbf{Tree}^1 \to \textbf{Tree}^+$. For the definition of $\mathcal{P}$, see the full version [14].

5   Post-processing to Eliminate Redundant Buffering

Our algorithm presented so far inserts *s2m* and *m2s*, which copy trees from the input stream to memory, and from the memory to the output stream. Therefore, for example, the identity function $\lambda x.x$ of type $=\textbf{Tree} \to \textbf{Tree}$ is transformed into $\lambda x.\textbf{letbuf}\ x = s2m(x)\ \textbf{in}\ m2s(x)$, which contains redundant buffering. We apply the following transformation rules in the post-processing phase to eliminate such redundant buffering, before applying our previous framework [7].

$$\textbf{letbuf}\ x = s2m(x)\ \textbf{in}\ m2s(x) \Longrightarrow copy\_tree(x)$$
$$\textbf{letbuf}\ x = s2m(x)\ \textbf{in}\ M \Longrightarrow skip\_tree(x); M \quad \text{if } x \notin \textbf{FV}(M)$$

Here, $copy\_tree(x)$ copies a tree from the input stream to the output stream without buffering the tree, and $skip\_tree(x)$ simply ignores a tree in the input stream. For example, the program $\lambda x.\textbf{letbuf}\ x = s2m(x)\ \textbf{in}\ m2s(x)$ is replaced by $\lambda x.copy\_tree(x)$.

6   Related Work

Nakano and Nishimura [8, 9, 10, 11] proposed a method for translating tree-processing programs to stream-processing programs using attribute grammars or attribute tree transducers [2]. In their method, programmers write XML processing as an attribute grammar or an attributed tree transducer. Then, those are composed with parsing and unparsing ones by using composition methods such as descriptional composition [3] and translated to a grammar that directly deals with streams. An advantage of our method is that we can deal with source programs that involve side-effects (e.g. programs that print the value of every leaf) while that seems difficult in their method based on attribute grammars (since the evaluation order is important for side effects). We also believe that our correctness proof is simpler than theirs. Comparison of the efficiency of programs generated by our method and those generated by their method is left for future work.

7   Conclusion

We have proposed a method for automatically inserting buffering primitives into tree-processing programs; by combining it with our previous framework, any simply-typed tree-processing program can automatically be transformed into an equivalent stream-processing program. We have already implemented a prototype system to automatically insert buffering primitives. We plan to extend it to implement a generator for XML stream-processing programs.

Acknowledgement

We thank members of "Programming Language Principles" group at University of Tokyo. We are also grateful to anonymous reviewers for their comments.

References

1. T. Bray, J. Paoli, C.M.Sperberg-McQueen, and E. Maler. Extensible markup language (XML) 1.0 (second edition). Technical report, World Wide Web Consortium, Oct. 2000. http://www.w3.org/TR/REC-xml.
2. Z. Fülöp. On attributed tree transducers. In *Acta Cybernetica*, volume 5, pages 261–280, 1981.
3. H. Ganzinger and R. Giegerich. Attribute coupled grammars. In *Proceedings of the ACM SIGPLAN '84 Symposium on Compiler Construction*, 1984.
4. H. Hosoya and B. C. Pierce. XDuce: A typed XML processing language. *ACM Transactions on Internet Technology (TOIT)*, 3(2):117–148, 2003.
5. H. Hosoya, J. Vouillon, and B. C. Pierce. Regular expression types for XML. In *Proceedings of the International Conference on Functional Programming (ICFP)*, pages 11–22, Sept. 2000.
6. K. Kodama. Derivation of XML stream processor based on ordered linear type. Master's thesis, Tokyo Institute of Technology, Mar. 2005.
7. K. Kodama, K. Suenaga, and N. Kobayashi. Translation of tree-processing programs into stream-processing programs based on ordered linear type. In *Programming Languages and Systems: Second Asian Symposium, APLAS 2004*, pages 41–56, Nov. 2004.
8. K. Nakano. Composing stack-attributed tree transducers. Technical Report METR-2004-01, Department of Mathematical Informatics, University of Tokyo, Japan, 2004.
9. K. Nakano. An implementation scheme for XML transformation languages through derivation of stream processors. In *Programming Languages and Systems: Second Asian Symposium, APLAS 2004*, pages 74–90, Nov. 2004.
10. K. Nakano and S. Nishimura. Deriving event-based document transformers from tree-based specifications. In M. van den Brand and D. Parigot, editors, *Electronic Notes in Theoretical Computer Science*, volume 44. Elsevier Science Publishers, 2001.
11. S. Nishimura and K. Nakano. XML stream transformer generation through program composition and dependency analysis. *Science of Computer Programming*, 54:257–290, Aug. 2004.
12. J. Polakow. *Ordered linear logic and applications*. PhD thesis, Carnegie Mellon University, June 2001. Available as Technical Report CMU-CS-01-152.
13. J. Rehof and T. Mogensen. Tractable constraints in finite semilattices. *Science of Computer Programming*, 35(2):191–221, 1999.

14. K. Suenaga, N. Kobayashi, and A. Yonezawa.   Extension of type-based approach to generation of stream-processing programs by automatic insertion of buffering primitives. Full paper. Available from `http://www.yl.is.s.u-tokyo.ac.jp/~kohei/doc/paper/lopstr05-full.pdf`.

15. V.Benzaken, G.Castagna, and A.Frisch. CDuce: An XML-centric general-purpose language. In *Proceedings of the ACM International Conference on Functional Programming*, 2003.

16. W3C. *Document Object Model (DOM) Level 1 Specification*, Oct. 1998.

Non-leftmost Unfolding in Partial Evaluation of Logic Programs with Impure Predicates

Elvira Albert[1], Germán Puebla[2], and John P. Gallagher[3]

[1] School of Computer Science, Complutense U. of Madrid
`elvira@sip.ucm.es`
[2] School of Computer Science, Technical U. of Madrid
`german@fi.upm.es`
[3] Department of Computer Science, University of Roskilde
`jpg@ruc.dk`

Abstract. Partial evaluation of logic programs which contain *impure* predicates poses non-trivial challenges. Impure predicates include those which produce side-effects, raise errors (or exceptions), and those whose truth value varies according to the degree of instantiation of arguments[1]. In particular, non-leftmost unfolding steps can produce incorrect results since the independence of the computation rule no longer holds in the presence of impure predicates. Existing proposals allow non-leftmost unfolding steps, but at the cost of accuracy: bindings and failure are not propagated backwards to predicates which are potentially impure. In this work we propose a partial evaluation scheme which substantially reduces the situations in which such backpropagation has to be avoided. With this aim, our partial evaluator takes into account the information about purity of predicates expressed in terms of *assertions*. This allows some optimizations which are not feasible using existing partial evaluation techniques. We argue that our proposal goes beyond existing ones in that it is a) accurate, since the classification of pure vs impure is done at the level of atoms instead of predicates, b) extensible, as the information about purity can be added to programs using assertions without having to modify the partial evaluator itself, and c) automatic, since (backwards) analysis can be used to automatically infer the required assertions. Our approach has been implemented in the context of `CiaoPP`, the abstract interpretation-based preprocessor of the `Ciao` logic programming system.

1 Introduction and Motivation

For logic programs without impure predicates, non-leftmost unfolding is sound thanks to the independence of the computation rule (see for example [13]).[2] Unfortunately, non-leftmost unfolding poses several problems in the context of *full* Prolog programs with *impure* predicates, where such independence does not hold anymore. For instance, `ground/1` is an *impure* predicate since, under LD resolution, the goal `ground(X),X=a` fails whereas `X=a,ground(X)` succeeds with

---

[1] The term "partial deduction" is often used when referring to partial evaluation of pure logic programs [7]; hence we do not use it in this context.

[2] However, non-deterministic unfolding of nonleftmost atoms can degrade efficiency.

P.M. Hill (Ed.): LOPSTR 2005, LNCS 3901, pp. 115–132, 2006.

```
:- module(main_prog,[main/2],[]).
:- use_module(comp,[long_comp/2],[]).
:- entry main(X,a).

main(X,Y)     :- problem(X,Y), q(X).

problem(a,Y):- ground(Y),long_comp(c,Y).
problem(b,Y):- ground(Y),long_comp(d,Y).

q(a).
```

Fig. 1. Motivating Example

computed answer X/a. Those executions are not equivalent and, thus, the independence of the computation rule does no longer hold. As a result, given the goal $\leftarrow$ ground(X),X=a, if we allow the non-leftmost unfolding step which binds the variable X in the call to ground(X), the goal will succeed at specialization time, whereas the initial goal fails in LD resolution at run-time. The above problem was early detected [16] and it is known as the problem of *backpropagation of bindings*. Also *backpropagation of failure* is problematic in the presence of impure predicates. For instance, $\leftarrow$ write(hello),fail behaves differently from $\leftarrow$ fail.

However, it is well-known that *non-leftmost* unfolding is essential in partial evaluation in some cases for the satisfactory propagation of static information (see, e.g., [8]). Informally, given a program P and a goal $\leftarrow A_1, \ldots, A_n$, it can happen that the leftmost atom A_1 cannot be selected for unfolding due to several circumstances. Among others, if A_1 is an atom for a predicate defined in P (thus the code is available to the partial evaluator) it can happen that i) unfolding A_1 endangers termination (for example, A_1 may homeomorphically embed [11] some selected atom in its sequence of covering ancestors), or ii) the atom A_1 unifies with several clause heads (deterministic unfolding rules do not unfold non-deterministically for atoms other than the initial query). If A_1 is an atom for an external predicate whose code is not present nor available to the partial evaluator, it can happen that A_1 is not sufficiently instantiated so as to be executed at this moment.

Example 1. Our motivating example is the Ciao program in Fig. 1, which uses the impure (predefined) predicate ground/1. Predicate long_comp/2 is external to the user module comp. Consider a deterministic unfolding rule and the entry declaration in Fig 1. The unfolding rule performs an initial step and derives the goal problem(X,a),q(X). Then, it cannot select the leftmost atom problem(X,a) because its execution performs a non deterministic step.

In this situation, different decisions can be taken. a) We can stop unfolding at this point. However, in general, it may be profitable to unfold atoms other than the leftmost. Interesting computation rules are able to detect the above circumstances and "jump over" the problematic atom in order to proceed with the specialization of another atom (in this case q(X)). We can then decide to b) unfold q(X) but avoiding backpropagating bindings or failure onto problem(X,a). And the final possibility c) is to unfold q(X) while allowing backpropagation onto `problem(X,a)`. However, this will require that some additional requirements hold on the atom(s) to the left of the selected one. Our main aim in this work is to identify and characterize the conditions under which the possibility c) above is applicable and build a partial evaluation system which can effectively prove such conditions in order to perform backpropagation of bindings and failure as much as possible.

There are several solutions in the literature (see, e.g.,[1, 2, 8, 9, 10]) which allow unfolding non-leftmost atoms by avoiding the backpropagation of bindings and failure, i.e., in the spirit of possibility b). Basically, the common idea is to represent explicitly the bindings by using unification [10] or residual case expressions [1] rather than backpropagating them (and thus applying them onto leftmost atoms). For our example, by using unification, we can unfold `q(X)` and obtain the resultant `main(X,a):-problem(X,a),X=a`. This guarantees that the resulting program is correct, but it definitely introduces some inaccuracy, since bindings (and failure) generated during unfolding of non-leftmost atoms are hidden from atoms to the left of the selected one. The relevant point to note is that preventing backpropagation, by using one of the existing methods, can be a bad idea for at least the following reasons:

1. *Backpropagation of bindings and failure can lead to an early detection of failure*, which may result in important speedups. For instance, if we allow backpropagating the binding `X=a` to the left atom, we get rid of the whole (failing) computation for `problem(b,a)` in the residual program.
2. *Backpropagation of bindings can make the profitability criterion for the leftmost atom to hold*, which may result in more aggressive unfolding. In the example, by backpropagating, we obtain the atom `problem(a,a)` which allows a deterministic computation rule to proceed to its unfolding.
3. *Backpropagation of bindings may allow improved indexing* by further instantiating arguments in clause heads. This is often good from a performance point of view (see, e.g., [17]). In our example, we will obtain the clause head `main(a,a)` with more indexing than `main(X,a)`.

The bottom line is that backpropagation should be avoided only when it is really necessary since interesting specializations can no longer be achieved when it is disabled.

The remaining of the paper is organized as follows. The next section provides an overview of our partial evaluation scheme. Section 3 recalls some preliminary notions. In Sect. 4 we formalize the notion of purity at the level of atoms. Section 5 presents the soundness conditions which allow safe backpropagation of bindings and failure. In Sect. 6, we propose a partial evaluation scheme based on purity assertions which are automatically inferred by backwards analysis. We conclude in Sect. 7.

2   An Overview of Our Partial Evaluation Scheme

Automatically figuring out when bindings and/or failure can be safely backpropagated onto an atom whose execution potentially reaches an impure predicate

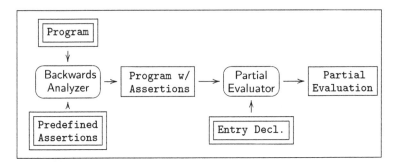

Fig. 2. Partial Evaluation based on Assertions and Backwards Analysis

has been considered a difficult challenge and, to our knowledge, there is no accurate, satisfactory solution. Existing methods [8] are based on simple reachability analysis. As soon as an impure predicate p/n can be reached from a predicate q/m, also q/m is considered impure and backpropagation onto any atom A for q/m is not allowed. Unfortunately, this notion of impurity quickly expands from a predicate to all predicates which use it. For example, the fact that there is a call to an impure predicate within **problem/2** will avoid backpropagating the binding for X and thus achieving the above three enumerated effects.

Figure 2 illustrates our partial evaluation scheme which is made up of three main components. First, we propose to use *assertions* which establish the conditions under which atoms (i.e., calls) for potentially impure predicates become pure. The classification of pure vs impure is thus done at the level of atoms instead of predicates, which will give us more precise results. We start from a set of **Predefined Assertions** provided by the underlying system for predefined predicates. Second, the role of **Backwards Analyzer** is to automatically infer, from the predefined assertions, sufficient conditions under which atoms are pure. The result is specified by extending the program, resulting in **Program with Assertions**. Notice that this is a goal-independent process which can be started in our system regardless of whether PE is performed or not. Third, and independently from the backwards analysis process, the user can decide to partially evaluate the program. To do so, an initial call has to be provided by means of an **Entry Declaration**. A Partial Evaluator is executed from such program and entry with the only consideration that, whenever a non-leftmost unfolding step needs to be performed, it will take into account the information available in the generated assertions. In our example, we will show that it is able to detect that, in the context described by our entry, all calls to **problem/2** are pure since the second argument is always ground. This allows us to backpropagate the binding for X and obtain the fact "**main(a,a).**" as partially evaluated program which achieves the three benefits enumerated above.

3 Background

We assume some basic knowledge on the terminology of logic programming. See for example [13] for details. Very briefly, an *atom A* is a syntactic construction of the form $p(t_1, \ldots, t_n)$, where p/n, with $n \geq 0$, is a predicate symbol and $t_1, \ldots, t_n$ are terms. The function *pred* applied to atom A, i.e., $pred(A)$, returns the predicate symbol p/n for A. Most real-life Prolog programs use predicates which are not defined in the program (module) being developed. Thus, predicates are classified into *internal* and *external*. Internal procedures are defined in the current program (module) and we assume that its code is available to the partial evaluator, whereas external predicates are not present. Examples of external predicates include the traditional "built-in" (predefined) predicates, such as constraints, basic input/output facilities (e.g., **open**). We will also consider as external predicates those defined in a different module, procedures written in another language, etc.

A *clause* is of the form $H \leftarrow B$ where its head H is an atom and its body B is a conjunction of atoms. A *program* is a finite set of clauses. A *goal* (or query) is a conjunction of atoms. The concept of *computation rule* is used to select an atom within a goal for its evaluation. The operational semantics of programs is based on derivations. Consider a program P and a goal G of the form $\leftarrow A_1, \ldots, A_R, \ldots, A_k$. Let $\mathcal{R}$ be a computation rule such that $\mathcal{R}(G) = A_R$. Let $C = H \leftarrow B_1, \ldots, B_m$ be a renamed apart clause in program P. Then $\theta(A_1, \ldots, A_{R-1}, B_1, \ldots, B_m, A_{R+1}, \ldots, A_k)$ is *derived* from G and C via $\mathcal{R}$ where $\theta = mgu(A_R, H)$. An *SLD derivation* for $P \cup \{G\}$ consists of a possibly infinite sequence $G = G_0, G_1, G_2, \ldots$ of goals, a sequence $C_1, C_2, \ldots$ of properly renamed apart clauses of P, and a sequence $\theta_1, \theta_2, \ldots$ of mgus such that each G_{i+1} is derived from G_i and C_{i+1} using θ_{i+1}. A derivation step can be non-deterministic when A_R unifies with several clauses in P, giving rise to several possible SLD derivations for a given goal. Such SLD derivations can be organized in *SLD trees*. A finite derivation $G = G_0, G_1, G_2, \ldots, G_n$ is called *successful* if G_n is empty. In that case $\theta = \theta_1 \theta_2 \ldots \theta_n$ is called the computed answer for goal G. Such a derivation is called *failed* if it is not possible to perform a derivation step with G_n. We will also allow *incomplete* derivations in which, though possible, no further resolution step is performed. We refer to SLD resolution restricted to the case of leftmost computation rule as LD resolution.

Partial Evaluation (PE) [4, 12] is a program transformation technique which specializes a program w.r.t. part of its known input data. Hence it is sometimes also known as program specialization. Informally, given an input program and a set of atoms, the PE algorithm applies an *unfolding rule* in order to compute finite (possibly incomplete) SLD trees for these atoms. This process returns a set of *resultants* (or residual rules), i.e., a residual program, associated to the root-to-leaf derivations of these trees. Formally, an unfolding rule computes a set of finite SLD derivations $D_1, \ldots, D_n$ (i.e., a possibly incomplete SLD tree) of the form $D_i = A, \ldots, G_i$ with computed answer substitution θ_i for $i = 1, \ldots, n$ whose associated *resultants* (or residual rules) are $\theta_i(A) \leftarrow G_i$. Note that in contrast to PE of pure programs, in the presence of impure predicates, failing derivations cannot be blindly eliminated from the set of resultants, since this may not preserve the behaviour of the program w.r.t. side-effects. Each unfolding step during partial evaluation can be conceptually divided into two steps. First, given a goal $\leftarrow A_1, \ldots, A_R, \ldots, A_k$ the computation rule determines the selected atom A_R. Second, it must be decided whether unfolding (or evaluation) of A_R is *profitable*. It must be noted that the unfolding process requires the introduction of this profitability test in order to guarantee that unfolding terminates. Also, unfolding usually continues as long as some evidence is found that further unfolding will improve the quality of the resultant program.

3.1   Leftmost Unfolding with Impure and External Predicates

The trivial computation rule which always returns the leftmost atom in a goal is interesting in that it avoids several correctness and efficiency issues in the context of PE of full Prolog programs. Such issues are discussed in depth throughout this paper. When a (leftmost) atom A_R is selected during PE, with $pred(A_R)$ = p/n being an external predicate, it may not be possible to unfold A_R for several reasons. First, we may not have the code defining p/n and, even if we have it, unfolding A_R may introduce in the residual program calls to predicates which are private to the module where p/n is defined. Also, it can be the case that the execution of atoms for (external) predicates produces other outcomes such as side-effects, errors, and exceptions. Note that this precludes the evaluation of such atoms to be performed at PE time, since those effects need to be performed at run-time. In spite of this, if the executable code for the external predicate p/n is available, and under certain conditions, it can be possible to fully evaluate A_R at specialization time. The notion of *evaluable* atom [14] captures the requirements which allow the *leftmost* execution of external predicates at PE time. Informally, an atom is evaluable if its execution satisfies four conditions: 1) it universally terminates, 2) it does not produce side-effects, 3) it does not issue errors and 4) it is sufficiently instantiated. We use eval(E) to denote that the expression E is evaluable.

4   From Impure Predicates to Impure Atoms

Existing techniques for PE allow the unfolding of non-leftmost atoms by combining a classification of predicates into pure and impure with techniques for avoiding backpropagation of binding and failure in the case of impure predicates. In order to classify predicates as pure or impure, existing methods [8] are based on simple reachability analysis.

Our work improves on existing techniques by 1) providing a finer-grained notion of impurity, which rather than being defined at the level of *predicates*, is defined at the level of individual *atoms*, and 2) splitting the notion of purity into its constituent properties: binding-sensitivity, errors and side effects. Defining purity at the level of atoms is of interest since it is often the case that some atoms for a predicate are pure whereas others are impure. As an example, the atom $var(X)$ is impure (binding sensitive), whereas the atom $var(f(X))$ is not (it is no longer binding sensitive). As will be seen later, this allows *reducing* substantially the situations in which backpropagation has to be avoided.

4.1   Binding-Sensitivity

A *binding-sensitive* predicate is characterized by having a different success or failure behaviour under leftmost execution if bindings are backpropagated onto it. Examples of binding-sensitive predicates are `atom/1`, `number/1`, `ground/1`, `var/1`, `nonvar/1`, etc.

Definition 1 (binding insensitive atom). *An atom A is* binding insensitive, *denoted* $\mathsf{bind\_ins}(A)$, *if $\forall$ sequence of distinct variables $\langle X_1, \ldots, X_k \rangle$ s.t. $X_i \in vars(A)$, $i = 1, \ldots, k$ and $\forall$ sequence of terms $\langle t_1, \ldots, t_k \rangle$, the goal $\leftarrow (X_1 = t_1, \ldots, X_k = t_k, A)$ succeeds in LD resolution with computed answer σ iff the goal $\leftarrow (A, X_1 = t_1, \ldots, X_k = t_k)$ also succeeds in LD resolution with computed answer σ.*

Let us note that in the definition above we are only concerned with successful derivations, which we aim to preserve. However, we are not in principle concerned about preserving infinite failure. For example, $\leftarrow (A, X = t)$ and $\leftarrow (X = t, A)$ might have the same set of answers but a different termination behaviour. In particular, the former might have an infinite derivation under LD resolution while the second may finitely fail.

If an atom contains no variables, binding insensitivity trivially holds. This is quite useful in practice, since it may allow considering a good number of atoms as binding insensitive without the need of sophisticated analyses.

4.2   Side-Effects

Predicates p/n for which $\leftarrow A, fail$ and $\leftarrow fail$, with $pred(A) = p/n$, are not equivalent in LD resolution are termed as *"side-effects"* in [16]. Typical examples of predicates with side-effects are `write/1` and `assert/1`.

Definition 2 (side-effect-free atom). *An atom A is* side-effect free, *denoted* $\mathsf{sideff\_free}(A)$, *if the run-time behaviour of $\leftarrow A, fail$ is equivalent to that of $\leftarrow fail$.*

Since side-effects have to be preserved in the residual program, we have to avoid any kind of backpropagation which can anticipate failure and, therefore, hide an existing side-effect.

4.3   Run-Time Errors

There are some predicates whose call patterns are expected to be of a certain type and/or instantiation state. If an atom A does not correspond to the intended call pattern, the execution of A will issue some *run-time errors*. Since we consider such run-time errors as part of the behaviour of a program, we will require that the partial evaluation process produces a residual program whose behaviour w.r.t. run-time errors is identical to that of the original program, i.e., run-time errors must not be introduced to, nor removed from, the program.

For instance, the predefined predicate `is/2` requires its second argument to be an arithmetic expression. If that is detected not to be the case at run-time, an error is issued. Clearly, backpropagation is dangerous in the context of atoms which may issue run-time errors, since it can anticipate the failure of a call to the left of `is/2` (thus omitting the error), or it can make the call to `is/2` not to issue an error (if there is some free variable in the second argument which gets instantiated to an arithmetic expression after backpropagation).

Definition 3 (error-free atom). *An atom A is* error-free *if the execution of A does not issue any error. We write* error_free(*A*) *where A is error-free.*

Somewhat surprisingly this condition for PE corresponds to that used in [6] for computing safe call patterns. Unfortunately, the way in which errors are issued can be implementation dependent. Some systems may write error messages and continue execution, others may write error messages and make the execution of the atom fail, others may halt the execution, others may raise exceptions, etc. Though errors are often handled using side-effects, we will make a distinction between side-effects and errors for two reasons. First, side-effects can be an expected outcome of the execution, whereas run-time errors should not occur in successful executions. Second, it is often the case that a predicate which contains side-effects produces them unconditionally for all (or most of) atoms for that predicate. However, predicates which can generate run-time errors can be guaranteed not to issue errors when certain preconditions about the call are satisfied, i.e., when the atom is well-moded and well-typed. A practical implication of the above distinction is that simple reachability analysis will be used for propagating side-effect freeness at the level of predicates, whereas a more refined, atom-based classification will be used in the case of error-freeness.

5   Soundness Conditions for Backpropagation

Given the definitions of binding insensitive, side-effect free, and error free atoms, we proceed to define aggregate properties which summarize the effect of such individual properties. These properties will allow us to define the soundness conditions under which backpropagation of bindings and failure is correct.

5.1   Backpropagation of Failure

The next definition formalizes the concept of *observable-free* atom which is required in order to determine whether backpropagation of *failure* is permitted.

Definition 4 (observable-free atom). *An atom A is* observable-free, *denoted* observable_free(*A*), *if* error_free(*A*) $\wedge$ sideff_free(*A*).

Intuitively, if an atom A is not observable-free, then $\leftarrow A, fail$ may behave differently from $\leftarrow fail$ and thus backpropagation onto A has to be avoided. The notion of *observable-safe step* characterizes the derivation steps for which backpropagation of failure is not problematic.

Definition 5 (observable-safe derivation step). *Let P be a program, let* $G =\leftarrow A_1, \ldots, A_n$ *be a goal and let* $\mathcal{R}$ *be a computation rule s.t.* $\mathcal{R}(G) = A_R$. *Let C be a renamed apart clause in P s.t. the head of C unifies with* A_R. *We say that the derivation step for G and C via* $\mathcal{R}$ *is* observable-safe *if* observable_free(A_1) $\wedge$ $\ldots \wedge$ observable_free(A_{R-1}).

The notion of observable-safe derivation step can be incorporated in a PE system in a straightforward way. More concretely, the computation rule used within the unfolding rule can be defined in such a way that tries to select first those atoms whose evaluation gives rise to observable-safe steps. Clearly, sometimes there will be no such possibility and it will be forced to either select an atom whose evaluation performs a non observable-safe step or stop unfolding. In each case, the partial evaluator will treat failing derivations as follows. 1) If all steps are observable-safe, then the failing derivation does not need to be taken into account for code generation, as it is done in traditional PE. 2) In contrast, if it contains one or more steps which are not observable-safe, then if the final goal in the derivation is of the form $\leftarrow A_1, \ldots, A_R, \ldots, A_n$, the partial evaluator has to produce a resultant associated to it of the form $\theta(A) \leftarrow A_1, \ldots, A_{R-1}, fail$, where $fail/0$ is a predefined predicate which finitely fails. Note that all atoms to the right of A_R, i.e., $A_{R+1}, \ldots, A_n$ can be safely be removed from the resultant.

5.2   Backpropagation of Bindings

The notion of *pure* atom is necessary in order to ensure that backpropagation of bindings does not change the runtime behaviour of the original program.

Definition 6 (pure atom). *An atom A is pure, denoted* pure(A), *if* observable_free(A) $\wedge$ bind_ins(A).

The notion of *backpropagation-safe* derivation step characterizes the derivation steps in which backpropagation of bindings (and failure) can be safely performed.

Definition 7 (backpropagation-safe derivation step). *With the same conditions as Definition 5, we say that the derivation step for G and C via $\mathcal{R}$ is* backpropagation-safe *if* pure$(A_1) \wedge \ldots \wedge$ pure(A_{R-1}).

We say that a computation rule $\mathcal{R}$ is *backpropagation-safe* if it always selects atoms in such a way that the derivation step is backpropagation-safe. It is easy to incorporate the idea of backpropagation-safe in a PE system. Note that by definition, leftmost unfolding is always backpropagation-safe. Thus, one simple but very inaccurate policy is to restrict ourselves to leftmost unfolding in the presence of impure predicates. If we would like to use a computation rule which is not always backpropagation-safe, then backpropagation has to be avoided in those steps which are possibly unsafe by using one of the existing proposals (e.g.,[1, 2, 8, 9, 10]).

5.3   Sound Derivations

Finally, we introduce the concept of *sound step* which requires that the selected atom is either user-defined or can be executed (or both), as well as the step be backpropagation-safe. We first present the notion of *evaluable* atom which provides the conditions under which an atom can be executed at specialization time. In order to provide a precise definition in the context of external predicates, we need to introduce first the notion of terminating atom.

Definition 8 (terminating atom). *An atom A is called terminating, denoted* termin(A), *if the LD tree for $\leftarrow A$ is finite. We write* termin(A) *where A is terminating.*

The definition above is equivalent to *universal termination*, i.e., the search for all solutions to the atom can be performed in finite time. Note that this condition is not necessary for internal predicates since the unfolding rule incorporates mechanisms for ensuring their termination. If the code of the external predicate was available, we could simply unfold the predicate using the same mechanisms as for internal ones.

Definition 9 (evaluable atom). *An atom A is* evaluable, *denoted* eval(A), *if* pure(A) $\wedge$ termin(A).

The notion of evaluable atoms can be extended in a natural way to boolean expressions composed of conjunction and disjunctions of atoms.

Definition 10 (sound derivation step). *With the same conditions as Definition 5, we say that the derivation step for G and C via $\mathcal{R}$ is* sound *if*
$$\text{pure}(A_1) \wedge \ldots \wedge \text{pure}(A_{R-1})$$
$$pred(A_R) \text{ is defined in } P \ \vee \ \text{eval}(A_R)$$

It is important to note that if A_R is an atom for a predicate defined in program P, then no further condition is required on the selected atom itself. As a result, leftmost unfolding of user-defined predicates is always sound, even if the program contains impure predicates. Also, even if the predicate is user-defined, our implementation will fully execute the atom, rather than unfold it, if eval(A_R) can be guaranteed to hold. This produces important speedups in the PE process.

Our next theorem states that even in the presence of impure predicates, the independence of the computation rule still holds as long as we restrict ourselves to computation rules which are backpropagation-safe.

Theorem 1 (independence of the computation rule). *Let P be program and G a goal. Let $\mathcal{R}$ be a backpropagation-safe computation rule. There is a successful LD derivation for G with c.a. σ iff there is a successful SLD derivation for G via $\mathcal{R}$ with c.a. σ' s.t. $\sigma(G)$ is a variant of $\sigma'(G)$.*

The above theorem extends the classical result in logic programming theory for pure programs to impure programs but only for those cases where the computation rule, though it can potentially choose a non-leftmost atom, it will never "jump over" a possibly impure atom.

Also, in the context of impure predicates we are interested in preserving the *observables* which are generated during the execution of the program.

Definition 11 (observables). *Let P be a program and a G be a goal. Let D be a LD derivation for $P \cup \{G\}$. We define the sequence of* observables *of the derivation D, denoted $\mathcal{O}(D)$, as the sequence of side-effects and errors which occur in D.*

Our unfolding process has to preserve observables both for successful and failing derivations, since otherwise observables would be eliminated from the program.

Theorem 2 (preservation of observables). *Let P be program and G a goal. Let $\mathcal{R}$ be a backpropagation-safe computation rule. There is an LD derivation D for G with $\mathcal{O}(D) \neq \emptyset$ iff there is a SLD derivation D' for G via $\mathcal{R}$ s.t. $\mathcal{O}(D') = \mathcal{O}(D)$.*

Our safety conditions for non-leftmost unfolding preserve computed answers, but has the well-known implication that an infinite failure can be transformed into a finite failure. However, in our framework this will only happen for predicates which do not have side-effects, since non-leftmost unfolding is only allowed in the presence of pure atoms. Nevertheless, our framework can be easily extended to preserve also infinite failure by including termination as an additional property that non-leftmost unfolding has to take into account, i.e. this implies requiring that all atoms to the left of the selected atom should be evaluable and not only pure.

6 Partial Evaluation with Purity Assertions

Though Definition 10 provides conditions under which backpropagation does not need to be hidden, it cannot be used as the basis for an effective PE mechanism, since in general it is not possible to determine at specialization time whether a derivation step is backpropagation-safe or not. In this section, we propose a PE scheme which takes into account purity conditions stated by means of *assertions*. We use the assertion language of CiaoPP [15] to provide the concrete syntax of several kinds of assertions. The assertions include *sufficient conditions* (*SC*) which are *decidable* and under which atoms for a predicate are pure. Thus, they can be used as an effective method to guarantee that certain non-leftmost derivation steps are backpropagation-safe.

Example 2. In Figure 3, we present sufficient conditions for a few predefined predicates (builtins) in Ciao which guarantee that the atoms for the corresponding predicates satisfy the purity properties discussed in the previous section, where *arithexp(X)* stands for X being an arithmetic expression which should be ground at the time of its evaluation, *struct(X)* succeeds iff X is bound to a functor with arity strictly greater than zero, and *nnegint(X)* succeeds iff X is bound

		observable-free		
		pure		
		eval		
predicate	sideff_free	error_free	bind_ins	termin
var(X)	true	true	nonvar(X)	true
nonvar(X)	true	true	nonvar(X)	true
write(X)	false	true	ground(X)	true
assert(X)	false	false	ground(X)	true
A <= B	true	arithexp(A)∧arithexp(B)	true	true
A >= B	true	arithexp(A)∧arithexp(B)	true	true
ground(X)	true	true	ground(X)	true
A = B	true	true	true	true
append(A,B,C)	true	true	true	list(A)∨list(C)
functor(A,B,C)	true	nonvar(A)∨(atom(B)∧nnegint(C))	true	true
arg(A,B,C)	true	nnegint(A)∧struct(B)	true	true
open(A,B,C)	false	false	ground(C)	true

Fig. 3. Purity conditions for some predefined predicates

to a non-negative integer. For example, unification is pure and evaluable in all circumstances. The library predicate append/3 is pure but only evaluable if either the first or third argument is bound to a list skeleton. The library predicate open/3 requires its third argument to be a variable. Thus, backpropagation in this case can introduce errors which would not appear in LD resolution.

Since we consider modular programs, in the following definitions, we have to indicate always the module in which the predicate is defined. We say that the execution of an atom A with $Pred(A) = p/n$ on a logic programming system Sys (by Sys we mean a Prolog implementation, e.g., Ciao or Sicstus) in which the module M (where the predicate p/n is defined), together with all modules transitively used by M, have been loaded *trivially succeeds*, denoted by triv_suc(Sys, M, A), when the execution of A terminates and succeeds only once with the empty computed answer, that is, it performs no bindings.

Definition 12 (binding insensitive assertion). *Let p/n be a predicate defined in module M. The assertion* :- trust comp p(X1,...,Xn):SC+bind_ins. *is a correct binding insensitive assertion for predicate p/n in a logic programming system Sys if, $\forall A$ s.t. $A = \theta(p(X_1, \ldots, X_n))$,*

1. eval($\theta(SC)$), *and*
2. triv_suc($Sys, M, \theta(SC)$) $\Rightarrow$ bind_ins(A).

The fourth column in Fig. 3 shows the sufficient conditions (SC in Def. 12) stated in several binding insensitive assertions for the predicates in the first column ($p(X_1, ..., X_n)$ in Def. 12). For instance, ground(X) is a sufficient condition for bind_ins(write(X)) to hold.

Given a set of assertions AS and an atom A, we use bind_ins(A, AS) to denote that there exists an assertion :- trust comp p(X1,...,Xn) : SC + bind_ins in AS s.t. $A = \theta(p(X_1, \ldots, X_n))$ and triv_suc($Sys, M, \theta(SC)$).

Definition 13 (error-free assertion). *Let p/n be a predicate defined in module M. The assertion* ":- trust comp p(X1,...,Xn) : SC + error_free." *is a correct error-free assertion for predicate p/n if, $\forall A$ s.t. $A = \theta(p(X_1, \ldots, X_n))$,*

1. eval($\theta(SC)$), *and*
2. triv_suc($Sys, M, \theta(SC)$) $\Rightarrow$ error_free(A).

It should be noted that some builtin predicates can behave in a different way on different systems. In particular, certain calls can fail in a system and issue an error in a different one.

The third column in Fig. 3 illustrates some sufficient conditions for error-freeness for a few predefined predicates. For instance, the SC for predicate A>=B states that both arguments should be arithmetic expressions. This guarantees error free calls to predicate >=/2.

Given a set of assertions AS and an atom A, we use error_free(A, AS) to denote that there exists an assertion :- trust comp p(X1,...,Xn) : SC + error_free in AS s.t. $A = \theta(p(X_1, \ldots, X_n))$ and triv_suc($Sys, M, \theta(SC)$).

Definition 14 (side-effect free assertion). *Let p/n be an external predicate defined in module M. The assertion* `:- trust comp p(X1,...,Xn)+sideff_free.` *is a correct* side-effect free assertion *for predicate p/n if, $\forall \theta$, the execution of $\theta(p(X_1, ..., X_n))$ does not produce any side effect, i.e.,* sideff_free(A).

The second column in Fig. 3 shows which predicates are side-effect free. In contrast to the two previous assertions, side-effect assertions are unconditional, i.e., their SC always takes the value true. For brevity, both in the text and in the implementation we omit the SC from them. Let us note that the set of side-effect free atoms is included in the set of error-free atoms, i.e., if A is not a side-effect free atom, then the execution of $\leftarrow A, fail$ is not equivalent to $\leftarrow fail$ and, thus, A is also not side-effect free. Nevertheless, we differentiate side-effects and errors both for conceptual clarity and also because a simple reachability analyses can be used to infer side-effects while errors are more accurately dealt by context-sensitive analyzers.

Given a set of assertions AS and an atom A, we use sideff_free(A, AS) to denote that there exists an assertion `:- trust comp p(X1,...,Xn) + sideff_free` in AS s.t. $A = \theta(p(X_1, ..., X_n))$.

Example 3. The following assertions are predefined in `Ciao` for predicate `>=/2`:

```
:- trust comp A >= B : (arithexp(A),arithexp(B)) + error_free.
:- trust comp A >= B + sideff_free.
:- trust comp A >= B + bind_ins.
```

An important thing to note is that rather than using the overall eval assertions (see [14]), we prefer to have separate assertions for each of the different properties required for an atom to be evaluable. However, users can write eval assertions directly if they prefer so. There are several reasons for this. On one hand, it will allow weakening the conditions required for different purposes. For example, binding insensitivity is not required for avoiding backpropagation of failure. Also, eval assertions include termination which is not required for ensuring correctness w.r.t. computed answers (see Sect. 4) nor termination of internal predicates. Second, it will allow us the use of different analyses for inferring each of these properties (e.g., a simple reachability analysis is sufficient for unconditional side-effects while more elaborated analysis tools are needed for error and binding sensitivity). Finally, having separate properties will allow reusing such assertions for other purposes different from partial evaluation. For instance, side-effect and error free assertions are also interesting for other purposes (e.g., for program verification, for automatic parallelization) and are frequently required by programmers separately.

6.1 Automatic Inference of Purity Assertions

In the case of leftmost unfolding, eval assertions [14] can be used in order to determine whether evaluation of atoms for external predicates can be fully done at specialization time or not. Such eval assertions (or assertions for their constituent properties) should be present whenever possible for all library (including builtin) predicates. Though the presence of such assertions is not required, as the lack of assertions is interpreted as the predicate not being evaluable under any circumstances, the more eval assertions are present for external predicates, the more profitable partial evaluation will be. Ideally, eval assertions can be provided by the system developers and the user does not need to add any eval assertion.

If non-leftmost unfolding is allowed, an important distinction is that pure assertions are of interest not only for external predicates but also for internal, i.e., user-defined predicates. As already mentioned, the lack of pure assertions must be interpreted as the predicate not being pure, since impure atoms can be reached from them. Thus, for non-leftmost unfolding to be able to "jump over" internal predicates, it is required that such pure assertions are available not only for external predicates, but also for predicates internal to the module. Such assertions can be manually added by the user or, much more interestingly, as our system does, by *backwards* analysis [3,5,6]. Indeed, we believe that manual introduction of assertions about purity of goals is too much of a burden for the user. Therefore, accurate non-leftmost unfolding becomes a realistic possibility only thanks to the availability of analysis.

Using a simple reachability analysis for error-free and binding-insensitivity assertions would result in very imprecise results, as in other existing approaches. Thus, we would like to perform a context-sensitive analysis which would allow us to determine that some particular contexts guarantee the purity of atoms. The main difficulty with this context-sensitive approach to purity analysis is that it is rather difficult to find out which are the contexts of interest which may appear during a particular PE process. One possibility would be to use a set of representative initial contexts, but this is rather difficult to do, especially for domains with an infinite number of abstract values.

A much more promising approach is based on backwards analysis [3,5,6] of logic programs. This kind of analysis has been successfully applied in termination analysis and inference of call patterns which are guaranteed not to produce any runtime error. We propose a novel application of backwards analysis for automatically inferring binding-insensitive, error-free and side-effect free assertions which are useful for improving the accuracy of partial evaluation, as it has been discussed throughout the paper. In our implementation, we rely on the backwards analysis technique of [3]. In this approach, the user first identifies a number of properties that are required to hold at body atoms at specific program points. A meta-program is then automatically constructed, which captures the dependencies between initial goals and the specified program points. For our specific application, we need to observe the occurrences of *all* predicates since the lack of purity assertions must be interpreted as the atom not being pure. Therefore, all program points are subject of analysis. Standard abstract interpretation techniques are applied to the meta-program; from the results of the analysis, conditions on initial goals can be derived which guarantee that all the given properties hold whenever the specified program points are reached. In our particular application, we infer the conditions under which calls to all predicates are pure. The details on how the meta-program is constructed are outside the scope of this paper (see [3]). We simply show by means of an example the kind of information it infers.

Example 4. Consider the purity conditions for predicate `ground/1` in Fig 3 and the program in Fig. 1. Predicate `long_comp/2` is externally defined in module `comp` along with these predefined assertions:

```
:- trust comp long_comp(X,Y) : true + error_free.
:- trust comp long_comp(X,Y) + sideff_free.
:- trust comp long_comp(X,Y) : ground(Y) + bind_ins.
```

For simplicity we consider in this example a simple domain with elements `ground` and `nonground`. Note that our framework can be extended to reason about many other properties like `arithexp`, `list`, etc. by using an abstract domain which captures such information. In particular, we need to include the definitions for the properties we want to capture.

Backwards analysis of the running example and the available assertions (for `long_comp/2` and `ground/1`), infers the following assertions for `problem/2`:

```
:- trust comp problem(X,Y) : true + error_free.
:- trust comp problem(X,Y) + sideff_free.
:- trust comp problem(X,Y) : ground(Y) + bind_ins.
```

The last assertion indicates that calls performed to `problem(X,Y)` with the second argument being ground are binding insensitive. This allows our specializer to "jump over" the call to problem and backpropagate bindings, which will in turn trigger further unfolding.

6.2   Combining Assertions with Partial Evaluation

We now provide an extension of the definition of safe derivation which takes into account the purity conditions in our assertions. We use $\mathsf{pure}(A, AS)$ to denote $\mathsf{bind\_ins}(A, AS) \wedge \mathsf{error\_free}(A, AS) \wedge \mathsf{sideff\_free}(A, AS)$.

Definition 15 (backpropagation-safe derivation step w.r.t. assertions).
Let AS be a correct set of assertions. Let P be a program, let $G = \leftarrow A_1, \ldots, A_n$ be a goal and let $\mathcal{R}$ be a computation rule s.t $\mathcal{R}(G) = A_R$. Let C be a renamed apart clause in P s.t. the head of C unifies with A_R. We say that the derivation step for G and C via $\mathcal{R}$ is backpropagation-safe *w.r.t. AS if $\mathsf{pure}(A_1, AS) \wedge \ldots \wedge \mathsf{pure}(A_{R-1}, AS)$.*

In order to integrate the above notion in an unfolding rule, the same ideas sketched in Sect. 5.3 apply here. We also give the corresponding definition for sound derivation based on purity assertions.

Definition 16 (sound derivation step w.r.t. assertions). *With the same conditions as Definition 7, we say that the derivation step for G and C via $\mathcal{R}$ is sound w.r.t. AS if*

$$\mathsf{pure}(A_1, AS) \wedge \ldots \wedge \mathsf{pure}(A_{R-1}, AS)$$
$$pred(A_R) \text{ is defined in } P \ \vee \ \mathsf{eval}(A_R, AS)$$

An important difference between the above definition w.r.t Definition 10 is that the former is *effective* since the sufficient conditions provided by assertions can effectively be used at specialization time in order to determine that certain atoms are pure. This in turn will allow performing backpropagation of bindings and failure for non-leftmost unfolding steps under circumstances where existing techniques would need to resort to not backpropagating.

Similar theorems to Theorem 1 and Theorem 2 can be enunciated which guarantee the correctness of derivation steps performed using a computation rule which is backpropagation-safe with respect to a set of correct purity assertions.

Example 5. Consider a deterministic unfolding rule which only performs sound derivation steps. In our running example, it performs an initial step and derives the goal `problem(X,a),q(X)`. Now, it cannot select the atom `problem(X,a)` because its execution performs a non-deterministic step. Fortunately, the assertions inferred for `problem(X,Y)` in Ex. 4 allow us to jump over this atom and specialize first `q(X)`. In particular, the first two assertions, since their SC is `true`, guarantee that there is no problem related to errors or side-effects. From the last assertion, we know that the above call is binding insensitive, since the condition "`ground(a)`" trivially succeeds. If atom `q(X)` is evaluated first, then variable X gets instantiated to a. Now, the unfolding rule already can select the deterministic atom `problem(a,a)` and obtain the fact " `main(a,a).`" as partially evaluated program. The interesting point to note is that, without the help of assertions, the derivation is stopped when the atom `problem(X,a)` is selected because any call to `problem` is considered potentially dangerous since its execution reaches a binding sensitive predicate. The equivalent specialized rule in this case is: "`main(X,a):-problem(X,a),q(X).`" A detailed explanation on the improvements achieved by our specialized program is provided in the three points enumerated in Sect. 1.

7   Conclusions

We have presented a practical partial evaluation scheme for full Prolog programs with impure predicates. As it is well known, impure features pose non-trivial challenges in the context of non-leftmost unfolding in partial evaluation. Existing (more conservative) approaches avoid backpropagating bindings and failure in the presence of such problematic predicates at the cost of accuracy. However, under certain conditions, calls to apparently impure predicates in reality are pure and thus backpropagation can be safely performed onto them. Our proposal is more accurate in that the partial evaluator takes into account purity conditions (stated by means of assertions) in order to decide whether backpropagation during non-leftmost unfolding is safe. Thanks to the use of backwards analysis, correct and precise sufficient conditions can be automatically inferred for all predicates from a set of predefined assertions available in the system. Our approach has been successfully integrated in the context of `CiaoPP`, the analysis/specialization preprocessor of the `Ciao` logic programming system, in which we have available a full assertion language and a number of analyzers. As for future work, we plan to exploit our automatically inferred assertions for purity in an abstract partial evaluation framework, where we can prove that certain backpropagations are safe using a combination of sharing analysis with refined notions of independence.

Acknowledgments

This work was funded in part by the Information Society Technologies programme of the European Commission, Future and Emerging Technologies under the FP5 IST-2001-38059 *ASAP* and FP6 IST-15905 *MOBIUS* projects and by the Spanish Ministry of Science and Education under the TIC 2002-0055 *CUBICO* project. Part of this work was performed during a research stay of Elvira Albert and Germán Puebla at University of Roskilde supported by respective grants from the Secretaría de Estado de Educación y Universidades, Spanish Ministry of Science and Education. J. Gallagher's research is supported in part by the IT-University of Copenhagen.

References

1. E. Albert, M. Hanus, and G. Vidal. A practical partial evaluation scheme for multiparadigm declarative languages. *Journal of Functional and Logic Programming*, 2002(1), 2002.
2. S. Etalle, M. Gabbrielli, and E. Marchiori. A Transformation System for CLP with Dynamic Scheduling and CCP. In *Proc. of the ACM Sigplan PEPM'97*, pages 137–150. ACM Press, 1997.
3. J. Gallagher. A Program Transformation for Backwards Analysis of Logic Programs. In Proc. of *LOPSTR 2003*, LNCS 3018, p. 92–105. Springer-Verlag, 2004.
4. J.P. Gallagher. Tutorial on specialisation of logic programs. In *Proceedings of PEPM'93, the ACM Sigplan Symposium on Partial Evaluation and Semantics-Based Program Manipulation*, pages 88–98. ACM Press, 1993.
5. Jacob M. Howe, Andy King, and Lunjin Lu. Analysing Logic Programs by Reasoning Backwards. *Program Development in Computational Logic*, LNCS, pages 380–393. Springer-Verlag, May 2004.
6. A. King and L. Lu. A Backward Analysis for Constraint Logic Programs. *Theory and Practice of Logic Programming*, 2(4–5):32, July 2002.
7. J. Komorowski. An Introduction to Partial Deduction. In A. Pettorossi, editor, *Meta Programming in Logic, Proceedings of META'92*, volume 649 of *LNCS*, pages 49–69. Springer-Verlag, 1992.
8. M. Leuschel and M. Bruynooghe. Logic program specialisation through partial deduction: Control issues. *Theory and Practice of Logic Programming*, 2(4 & 5): 461–515, July & September 2002.
9. M. Leuschel, J. Jørgensen, W. Vanhoof, and M. Bruynooghe. Offline specialisation in prolog using a hand-written compiler generator. *TPLP*, 4(1–2):139 – 191, 2004.
10. Michael Leuschel. Partial evaluation of the "real thing". In *Proc. of LOPSTR'94 and META'94*, LNCS 883, pages 122–137. Springer-Verlag, 1994.
11. Michael Leuschel. On the power of homeomorphic embedding for online termination. Proc. of SAS'98, LNCS 1503, pages 230–245, 1998. Springer-Verlag.
12. J. W. Lloyd and J. C. Shepherdson. Partial evaluation in logic programming. *The Journal of Logic Programming*, 11:217–242, 1991.

13. J.W. Lloyd. *Foundations of Logic Programming*. Springer, second, extended edition, 1987.
14. G. Puebla, E. Albert, and M. Hermenegildo. Efficient Local Unfolding with Ancestor Stacks for Full Prolog. In Proc. of *LOPSTR'04*, number 3573 in LNCS, pages 149–165. Springer-Verlag, June 2005.
15. G. Puebla, F. Bueno, and M. Hermenegildo. An Assertion Language for Constraint Logic Programs. In *Analysis and Visualization Tools for Constraint Programming*, pages 23–61. Springer LNCS 1870, 2000.
16. D. Sahlin. Mixtus: An automatic partial evaluator for full Prolog. *New Generation Computing*, 12(1):7–51, 1993.
17. R. Venken and B. Demoen. A partial evaluation system for prolog: some practical considerations. *New Generation Computing*, 6:279–290, 1988.

A Transformational Semantics of Static Embedded Implications of Normal Logic Programs

Edelmira Pasarella[1], Fernando Orejas[1], Elvira Pino[1], and Marisa Navarro[2]

[1] Dpto de L.S.I., Universitat Politècnica de Catalunya,
Campus Nord, Edifici Omega, Jordi Girona 1-3, 08034 Barcelona, Spain
{edelmira, orejas, pino}@lsi.upc.edu
[2] Dpto de L.S.I., Universidad del País Vasco,
Paseo Manuel de Lardizabal, 1, Apdo 649, 20080 San Sebastián, Spain
marisa@si.ehu.es

Abstract. There are mainly two approaches for structuring logic programs. The first one is based on defining some notion of program unit or module and on providing a number of composition operators. The second approach consists in enriching logic programming with a mechanism of abstraction and scoping rules that are frequently found, for instance, in procedural programming. More precisely, this approach has been advocated by Miller and others using implications embedded in the goals of the given program as a structuring mechanism. However, as Giordano, Martelli and Rossi pointed out, we can associate two different visibility rules (static and dynamic) to this kind of structuring mechanism where, obviously, the semantics of the given program depends on the chosen rule.

In this paper we consider normal constraint logic programs (with constructive negation á la Drabent as operational semantics) extended with embedded implications with a static visibility rule. This class of programs combines the expressive power of normal programs with the capability to organize and to enhance dinamically their sets of clauses. In particular, first, we introduce an operational semantics based on constructive negation for this class of programs, taking into account the static visibility rule. Then, we present an alternative semantics in terms of a transformation of the given structured program into a flat one. Finally, we prove the adequacy of this transformation by showing that it preserves the computed answers of the given program. Obviously, this transformation semantics can be used as the basis for an implementation of this structuring mechanism.

1   Introduction

There are mainly two approaches (see [5] for a survey) for structuring logic programs. The first one is based on defining some notion of program unit or module and on providing a number of composition operators. Basically, this approach is oriented towards programming-in-the-large and is called explicit modularity. The second approach consists in enriching logic programming with a mechanism of abstraction and scoping rules that are frequently found, for instance, in procedural programming. Hence, this approach seems to be suitable for programming-in-the-small in a structured way. It is usually called implicit modularity. More precisely, this approach has been advocated by Miller and others using implications embedded in the goals of the given program as a

P.M. Hill (Ed.): LOPSTR 2005, LNCS 3901, pp. 133–146, 2006.
© Springer-Verlag Berlin Heidelberg 2006

structuring mechanism. However, as Giordano, Martelli and Rossi [9] pointed out, we can associate two different visibility rules (static and dynamic) to this kind of structuring mechanism where, obviously, the semantics of the given program depends on the chosen rule.

As far as we know, Gabbay and Reyle [7, 8] presented the first approach proposing to extend Prolog with what is known as hypothetical or embedded implication. Later, Miller [15] introduced the idea of using this class of programs for structuring logic programs. Miller used Harrop formulas [17] which are different from the ones we consider herein. In particular, we do not consider disjunctive goals and goals in which explicit quantifiers occur.

Since embedded implication can be seen as a structuring device for logic programs, one can actually define two classes of logic languages depending on the scoping rule used for accessing predicate definitions [9]. The dynamic and static (also called lexical) schemes are two well-known schemes in procedural programming. In adapting them to logic programming, the language presented by Miller follows the dynamic approach.

In the dynamic scheme, both implications, clausal implication and embedded implication, are interpreted as intuitionistic implications. So, the operational semantics is given by the deduction theorem

$$\frac{P \cup Q \vdash_d G}{P \vdash_d Q \supset G}$$

The intuitive idea is that, given a program P, to prove the query $Q \supset G$ it is necessary to load Q and proceed the inference process with $P \cup Q$. Once G succeeds or fails, Q must be discarded. From a software engineering point of view, Miller's proposal allows us to organize collections of program units without the need of explicit composition operations. A main result of Miller's approach is that the proof-theoretic semantics for this kind of programs can be given in terms of intuitionistic logic.

Giordano, Martelli and Rossi [9] proposed a variation of Miller's approach. In particular, they showed that the clausal and the embedded implications can be interpreted in different ways. Moreover, in [5] a general inference rule is given to explain the interpretation of embedded implication:

$$\frac{P^* \cup Q \vdash_s G}{P \vdash_s Q \supset G}$$

where $P^* = \{a : a \text{ is atomic and } P \vdash_s a\}$.

This rule corresponds nicely to the intuition of static scoping. It does not consider all possible derivations from $P \cup Q$, as in the case of the dynamic approach. To prove the goal $Q \supset G$, the definitions in Q are activated but P cannot use them. Therefore, the behavior that we have described above is similar to the process of activating a block in a procedural language with static scope. In [1] this matter is addressed and some considerations for implementing both static and dynamic languages are discussed. The algebraic semantics proposed in [9] is basically the one proposed by Miller but extended to be able to interpret the clausal implication in a classical way. Considering classical and intuitionistic implications together rises some problems because the new semantics fits neither in classical logic nor in intuitionistic logic. This has been addressed in [2, 12] where a complete logic (extending classical first order logic with the intuitionistic implication) is presented as the underlying logic of such static programming language. The example below, borrowed from [5], illustrates the difference between the two languages mentioned above.

Example 1. Let $P = \{p \leftarrow q\}$. To prove $P \vdash_d \{q\} \supset p$ we have to see if $P \cup \{q\} \vdash_d p$ and this holds if $P \cup \{q\} \vdash_d q$ which is a tautology. However, in the static case, $P \vdash_s \{q\} \supset p$ holds if $P^* \cup \{q\} \vdash_s p$, but $P^* = \emptyset$.

In this example it is clear that, by using the dynamic scope rule, an initial sequent is obtained, while by using the static scope rule there is no rule to apply. Therefore, the query succeeds only in the dynamic approach. There are more characterizations of implicit modularity. For instance, in [16] a language is proposed in which embedded implications override those definitions provided by the external context but this approach is beyond this paper.

As far as we know most of the attempts for extending normal logic programming with embedded implication have been done by considering negation as finite failure, sometimes with some additional restrictions, such as stratification. Gabbay [7], McCarty [13, 14], Bonner and McCarty [4], and Giordano and Olivetti [11] have worked in this direction. The rule for combining dynamic logic programs with finite failure is the following

$$\frac{P \cup Q \vdash_d \neg p}{P \vdash_d Q \supset \neg p}$$

and the sequent $P \cup Q \vdash_d \neg p$ is considered an initial sequent when for each clause $p \leftarrow \overline{G}$ there exists a finitely failed tree of $\overline{G}$ with respect to $P \cup Q$. When considering static normal programs, the intuitive idea behind the derivation rules is that only the positive knowledge inferred from outermost blocks and the last activated definitions must be considered. In particular, the rule for combining static logic programs with finite failure is the following

$$\frac{P^* \cup Q \vdash_s \neg p}{P \vdash_s Q \supset \neg p}$$

and the sequent $P^* \cup Q \vdash_s \neg p$ is considered an initial sequent when for each clause $p \leftarrow \overline{G}$ there exists a finitely failed tree of $\overline{G}$ with respect to $P^* \cup Q$. Let us consider the following propositional normal logic programs and the derivations in both dynamic and static approaches:

Example 2. Let $P = \{t \leftarrow q\} \quad Q = \{q; p \leftarrow \neg t\}$

	Dynamic	Static
	$P \nvdash_d Q \supset p$	$P \vdash_s Q \supset p$
	$P \vdash_d Q \supset \neg p$	$P \nvdash_s Q \supset \neg p$

Note that, for readability, we do not use the comma symbol (,) to separate clauses in set of clauses. Instead, we use the semicolon symbol (;).

In [19] we studied the extension of normal logic programs, with constructive negation, with embedded implications with dynamic visibility. In particular, we used a kind of complex Beth models to provide an algebraic semantics, obtaining soundness and completeness results. Now, in this paper, we consider the same kind of programs, but with static scoping. However, we follow a more pragmatic approach. Instead of developing a new framework to define the declarative semantics of this class of programs, we show how these programs can be transformed into standard normal programs. Moreover, we prove that this translation is sound and complete with respect to the operational semantics of the extended programs. In addition, it must be pointed out that this transformation is easy to implement, which means that we can easily build this kind of extension on top of a standard logic programming language. This approach has been used in [18] to deal with positive propositional static programs. Indeed, herein we actually extend that work. This approach has also been used in [3] to translate modal logic programs with embedded implication into Horn programs.

This paper is organized as follows. In the following section we present some basic notions and terminology. Section 3 introduces an operational semantics for the class of static normal logic programs with embedded implications based on SLDFA resolution [6]. Section 4 presents the transformation semantics and, finally, in Section 5, we prove the soundness and completeness of the transformation.

2   Preliminaries

A *countable signature* Σ consists of a pair of sets (FS_Σ, PS_Σ) of function and predicate symbols, respectively, with some associated arity. Terms, atoms or first-order formulas built by using functions and/or predicates from Σ and, also, variables from a fixed countable set X of variable symbols are called Σ-terms, Σ-atoms and Σ-formulas, respectively. Predicate symbols, atoms and literals are denoted by $p, q, \ldots$, by a, b and by the character ℓ, respectively. A formula whose subterms are variables is called a *flat* formula. Considering a first-order logic formula φ, $\varphi^\forall$ and $\varphi^\exists$ are the universal and existential closure of φ, respectively. The logical constants are respectively denoted by $\underline{t}$ and $\underline{f}$. The set of variables appearing in a term t (resp. formula φ) is denoted $var(t)$ (resp. $var(\varphi)$) and $FV(\varphi)$ denotes the set of free variables occurring in φ. Programs are denoted P and Q. In general, subscripts and superscripts will be used if needed and a bar is used to denote (finite) sequences of objects.

An *extended Σ-literal*, denoted G, is either a normal Σ-literal, b or $\neg b$, where b is a Σ-atom; or a Σ-*expression* of the form $Q \supset G'$ where Q is a Σ-program and G' is an extended Σ-literal. An *extended Σ-goal* is either the logical constant $\underline{t}$ or a sequence of extended Σ-literals. *Normal logic program with embedded implications* over a signature Σ are finite sets of clauses

$$a \leftarrow G_1, \ldots, G_k, k \geq 0$$

being a a Σ-atom and $G_1, \ldots, G_k$ an extended Σ-goal (also written as $(G_1, \ldots, G_k)$ if needed for readability). We denote with C_Σ (resp. G_Σ) and $C_\Sigma^\supset$ (resp. $G_\Sigma^\supset$) to the sets of all the normal Σ-clauses (resp. Σ-goals) and all the normal Σ-clauses (resp. Σ-goals) in which embedded implication occurs.

We consider that any Σ-program is written following the structure of constraint normal Σ-programs, with flat head. That is, any clause

$$p(t_1,\ldots,t_n) \leftarrow G_1,\ldots,G_k, k \geq 0$$

is written as the constrained clause

$$p(x_1,\ldots,x_n) \leftarrow G_1,\ldots,G_k \square x_1 = t_1,\ldots,x_n = t_n, k \geq 0$$

Moreover, we suppose that the identical tuple $x_1,\ldots,x_n$ of *fresh variables* occurs in all clauses (in a program) with predicate p in its heads. Also, just to simplify, clauses of the form $a \leftarrow \underline{t} \square \underline{t}$ are written as a.

Free variables in a clause are assumed to be implicitly quantified universally. This means that the scope of a variable is the clause where it is defined. For example, the clause $p(x) \leftarrow \{q(x)\} \supset r(x)$ is interpreted as $\forall x(p(x) \leftarrow \{\forall y q(y)\} \supset r(x))$ and the clause $p \leftarrow \{q(y)\} \supset r(y)$ as $p \leftarrow \exists y(\{\forall z q(z)\} \supset r(y))$.

The *set of definitions of a predicate p* is established with respect to a given program P as follows:

$$Def(P,p) \equiv \{p(\bar{x}) \leftarrow \overline{G}\square c \in P\}$$

Constraints occurring in programs are *equality Σ-constraints*, that is, arbitrary first-order Σ-formulas in which the only relational symbol occurring in atoms is the equality (formulas composing equality atoms with the connectives $\neg, \wedge, \vee, \rightarrow$, and the quantifiers $\forall, \exists$. Constraints are denoted by using the letters c and d (possibly with sub or super-scripts). We will handle constraints in a logical way, using logical consequence of the *free equality theory, FET_Σ*. A constraint c is *satisfiable* (resp. *unsatisfiable*) if, and only if, $FET_\Sigma \models c^\exists$ (resp. $FET_\Sigma \models \neg(c^\exists)$); a constraint d is *less general* than c if, and only if, $FET_\Sigma \models (d \rightarrow c)^\forall$. For the sake of simplicity in what follows we drop the prefix $\Sigma-$ when referring to programs, clauses, etc.

To finish this section we slightly remind SLDFA-resolution. This approach to constructive negation is based on computing *failed answers* of goals of the form $\neg \bar{\ell} \square c$ with respect to a normal program P. To do it, Drabent proposes a nondeterministic method useful for our purposes. The idea is to construct an SLDFA-finitely failed tree starting with an (prefailed) SLDFA-derivation tree with root $\leftarrow \bar{\ell} \square c$. Let us call this tree T. The method proceeds by choosing a finite set of nodes of T, called cross-section of T, such that every successful or infinite branch intersects with this set. Next step is to instantiate T by a constraint c' such that $c \wedge c'$ is satisfiable and $FV(c') \cup FV(T) \subseteq FV(\bar{\ell} \square c)$. That is, for each node $\leftarrow \bar{\ell} \square d$ in T, if $d \wedge c'$ is satisfiable, to change it into $\leftarrow \bar{\ell} \square d \wedge c'$ otherwise, to prune the subtree whose root is $\leftarrow \bar{\ell} \square d$. Whenever the instantiated (prefailed) tree is finite and has no successful branches it becomes into an SLDFA-finitely failed tree. Thus, to transform T into an SLDFA-finitely failed tree it is enough to choose a cross-section and "find" an adequate constraint c' such that after instantiating T, the subtrees whose roots are in the selected cross-section have been pruned. In particular, considering a (prefailed) tree of $\leftarrow a \square c$, to prune all the nodes in a cross-section $\{\leftarrow \bar{\ell}_1 \square d_1,\ldots,\leftarrow \bar{\ell}_m \square d_m\}$, the tree must be instantiated with a constraint c' such that

$FET_\Sigma \models (c' \rightarrow \neg d_1 \wedge \ldots \wedge \neg d_m)^\forall$. A most general c' satisfying this is (equivalent to) $\neg d_1 \wedge \ldots \wedge \neg d_m$. Hence, if $c \wedge \neg d_1 \wedge \ldots \wedge \neg d_m$ is satisfiable, the tree becomes into an SLDFA-tree and, therefore $c \wedge \neg d_1 \wedge \ldots \wedge \neg d_m$ is a failed answer of $\leftarrow a \Box c$ with respect to the considered program.

3   Operational Semantics

In this section, we propose an operational semantics which can be seen as a combination of the operational semantics defined in [9] and SLDFA resolution [6]. This semantics is obviously quite close to the one defined in [19] for normal logic programs with embedded implications when using dynamic scoping. The semantics is presented in terms of a derivation relation over sequents of the form $S \vdash_s \overline{G} \Box c$, where S is a stack of programs and $\overline{G} \Box c$ is a goal. Here below we present a definition of stack.

Definition 1. *(Stack of programs) Given the programs $P_1, \ldots, P_k$, $k > 0$, a stack of programs S_k is a sequence $\langle \emptyset, P_1, \ldots, P_k \rangle$ written as $P_1 | \ldots | P_k$. A stack of programs increases/decreases following a LIFO strategy, assuming that the last added program is P_k. The length of S_k is k.*

For technical reasons we assume that every stack includes the empty program at the bottom. The basic idea is quite simple. If we want to solve a positive goal $p(\overline{x}) \Box c$, given the stack of programs $P_1 | \ldots | P_k$, we can choose a rule from one of the programs in the stack P_i, $p(\overline{x}) \leftarrow \overline{G} \Box d$, and then solve all the goals in the rule using the stack $P_1 | \ldots | P_i$. If we want to solve a negative goal $\neg p(\overline{x}) \Box c$, given the stack of programs $P_1 | \ldots | P_k$, then for every rule $p(\overline{x}) \leftarrow \overline{G} \Box d$ in P_i (for any i), we have to prove that some subset of the goals in $\overline{G} \Box c \wedge d$ can be refuted in the stack $P_1 | \ldots | P_i$. Obviously, an implication goal $P \supset G \Box c$ can be solved in the stack $P_1 | \ldots | P_k$ if $G \Box c$ can be solved in the stack $P_1 | \ldots | P_k | P$ and $\neg (P \supset G) \Box c$ can be solved in the stack $P_1 | \ldots | P_k$ if $\neg G \Box c$ can be solved in the stack $P_1 | \ldots | P_k | P$. It may be noted that this semantics follows the intuition of static visibility, i.e. for solving a goal in a rule of a given program unit, we can only use rules from more external program units.

Our semantics is given by the following mutually recursive definitions.

Definition 2. *Let S be a stack of programs and $\overline{G} \Box c$ a goal. $S \vdash_s \overline{G} \Box c$ can be proved with computed answer c' if and only if, there exists a finite sequence of applications of the derivation relation $\rightsquigarrow$ of the form $S \vdash_s \overline{G} \Box c \rightsquigarrow \ldots \rightsquigarrow S \vdash_s \Box c'$, $FET_\Sigma \models c'^\exists$ and $FET_\Sigma \models (c' \rightarrow c)^\forall$.*

Definition 3. *The derivation relation $\rightsquigarrow$ over sequents is defined as follows:*

1. *$P_1 | \ldots | P_k \vdash_s \overline{G}_1, p(\overline{x}), \overline{G}_2 \Box c \rightsquigarrow P_1 | \ldots | P_k \vdash_s \overline{G}_1, \overline{G}_2 \Box c'$ if there exists $i \in \{1, \ldots, k\}$ such that there exists a (renamed apart) clause $p(\overline{x}) \leftarrow \overline{G} \Box d \in Def(P_i, p)$ and $P_1 | \ldots | P_i \vdash_s \overline{G} \Box c \wedge d$ can be proved with computed answer c'.*
2. *$P_1 | \ldots | P_k \vdash_s \overline{G}_1, \neg p(\overline{x}), \overline{G}_2 \Box c \rightsquigarrow P_1 | \ldots | P_k \vdash_s \overline{G}_1, \overline{G}_2 \Box c'$ if, and only if, the following two conditions hold:*
   (a) For every $i \in \{1, \ldots, k\}$ there exists a satisfiable constraint c^i, $FET_\Sigma \models (c^i \rightarrow c)^\forall$ such that for every (renamed apart) clause $p(\overline{x}) \leftarrow G_1^i, \ldots, G_{m_i}^i \Box d^i \in$

Def(P_i, p) *there exists* $J_i \subseteq \{1, \ldots, m_i\}$ *such that* $\forall j \in J_i : P_1|\ldots|P_i \vdash_s \neg G^i_j \square d^i$
can be proved with computed answer d^i_j *and* $FET_\Sigma \models (c^i \rightarrow \neg d^i \vee \bigvee_{j \in J_i} d^i_j)^\forall$.
This means that $P_1|\ldots|P_i \vdash_s \neg p(\bar{x})\square c \rightsquigarrow P_1|\ldots|P_i \vdash_s \square c^i$.
  (b) $FET_\Sigma \models (c' \rightarrow \bigwedge^k_{i=1} c^i)^\forall$.
3. $P_1|\ldots|P_{k-1} \vdash_s \overline{G}_1, P_k \supset G, \overline{G}_2\square c \rightsquigarrow P_1|\ldots|P_{k-1} \vdash_s \overline{G}_1, \overline{G}_2\square c'$ *if* $P_1|\ldots|P_k \vdash_s G\square c$ *can*
be proved with computed answer c'.
4. $P_1|\ldots|P_{k-1} \vdash_s \overline{G}_1, \neg(P_k \supset G), \overline{G}_2\square c \rightsquigarrow P_1|\ldots|P_{k-1} \vdash_s \overline{G}_1, \overline{G}_2\square c'$ *if* $P_1|\ldots$
$|P_k \vdash_s \neg G\square c$ *can be proved with computed answer* c'.

Each item in this definition is called a derivation step.

We assume that whenever an expression of the form $\neg\neg a\square c$ occurs in the right-hand side of a sequent, it denotes $a\square c$. Next we give the intuition behind our operational semantics.

In the rest of this section we present some examples to show how the operational semantics works. Mainly derivation steps 3.2 and 3.3 will be illustrated.

Example 3. Let $P = \{p(x) \leftarrow \square x = a\}$ and $Q = \{p(x) \leftarrow \square x = b\}$. The derivation $P \vdash_s$
$Q \supset \neg p(x) \rightsquigarrow P \vdash_s \square x \neq a \wedge x \neq b$ is justified because the following subderivations:

- $P|Q \vdash_s \neg p(x) \rightsquigarrow P|Q \vdash_s \square x \neq b$.
- $P \vdash_s \neg p(x) \rightsquigarrow P \vdash_s \square x \neq a$

The following example adapts the one presented in [6].

Example 4. Let $P = \{r \leftarrow Q_1 \supset \neg p(x), Q_2 \supset \neg q(x)\}$, $Q_1 = \{p(x) \leftarrow p(x); p(x) \leftarrow \square x = a\}$ and $Q_2 = \{q(x) \leftarrow q(x)\square x = a; q(x) \leftarrow \neg s(x); s(x) \leftarrow \square x = a\}$. The derivation $P \vdash_s$
$\neg r \rightsquigarrow P \vdash_s \square t$ does exist because, considering the clause defining r in P and condition
(a) in Definition 3.2, we have that $P \vdash_s \neg(Q_1 \supset \neg p(x))$ can be proved with computed
answer $x = a$, $P \vdash_s \neg(Q_2 \supset \neg q(x))$ can be proved with computed answer $x \neq a$ and
$FET_\Sigma \models (\underline{t} \rightarrow x = a \vee x \neq a)^\forall$.

The following example shows a failed derivation.

Example 5. Let $P = \{p(x) \leftarrow \square x = a\}$ and $Q = \{p(x) \leftarrow \neg r(x); r(x) \leftarrow \square x = a\}$ Starting
a derivation from the sequent $P \vdash_s Q \supset \neg p(x)$ we can not obtain a computed answer. The
reason is that $P|Q \vdash_s r(x) \rightsquigarrow P|Q \vdash_s \square x = a$, therefore $P|Q \vdash_s \neg p(x) \rightsquigarrow P|Q \vdash_s \square x = a$
and $P \vdash_s \neg p(x) \rightsquigarrow P \vdash_s \square x \neq a$. Hence, condition (b) in Definition 3.2 does not hold
because there is not a satisfiable constraint less general than $x = a \wedge x \neq a$.

4   A Transformational Semantics

In this section we define the semantics of extended programs in terms of a translation
into the class of (standard) normal programs. This approach has several advantages. On
one hand, we can (indirectly) provide a declarative semantics of extended programs,
without having to use a more complex logic (see, e.g. [10] where a modal logic is
used). In particular, it is enough to consider the declarative semantics of the translated
program. On the other hand, this transformational semantics is easy to implement. This

means that we can easily build this kind of extension on top of a standard logic programming language.

The idea underlying this translation is quite simple. On one hand, we rename all the predicates inside the implications to new fresh names. In addition, we add rules of the form $p_i(x) \leftarrow p_j(x)$ where p_i and p_j are the names for the same predicate p in the program units P_i and P_j, respectively, and where P_j includes P_i.

Hereafter we assume that programs are defined over the signature $\Sigma = < FS, PS >$. In the following definitions PS' is a set of "fresh" predicates, that is, $PS \cap PS' = \emptyset$.

Definition 4. *Let P be a program. Then, a renaming for predicates with respect to P is a substitution of the form $\sigma : PS \cup PS' \rightarrow PS \cup PS'$, such that for all $p \in PS \cup PS'$*

$$\sigma(p) = \begin{cases} gen(p) & \text{if } Def(P,p) \neq \emptyset \\ p & \text{otherwise} \end{cases} \tag{1}$$

where $gen : PS \cup PS' \rightarrow PS'$ is a function such that whenever it is applied returns a new predicate symbol in PS' never used before. This definition is extended in order to apply a renaming to goals, clauses and programs as follows $\sigma(p(\bar{x})) = \sigma(p)(\bar{x})$, $\sigma(\neg p(\bar{x})) = \neg\sigma(p)(\bar{x})$, $\sigma(P \supset G) = \sigma(P) \supset \sigma(G)$, $\sigma((G_1, \ldots, G_m)) = (\sigma(G_1), \ldots, \sigma(G_m))$, $\sigma(p(\bar{x}) \leftarrow \bar{G} \Box c) = \sigma(p)(\bar{x}) \leftarrow \sigma(\bar{G}) \Box c$, and $\sigma(\{C_1, \ldots, C_n\}) = \{\sigma(C_1), \ldots, \sigma(C_n)\}$.

Notice that the function *gen* is a generator of "fresh" predicate symbols. Also, one can compose $\sigma_1 \sigma_2 \ldots \sigma_k(p)$ even though each σ_i, for $i \in \{1, \ldots, k\}$, is not necessarily defined with respect to the same program. Moreover, the definition of *gen* ensures that a never used before predicate symbol will be obtained each time.

For the sake of simplicity we adopt the variable substitution notation. This means we denote $\sigma(p)$ as $p\sigma$ and similarly for goals, clauses and programs. Also, we denote the composition of renamings $\sigma_1 \ldots \sigma_i$ as $\bar{\sigma}_i$.

Definition 5. *The translation function $\mathbb{T} : \mathcal{P}(C_{\Sigma'}^{\supset}) \rightarrow \mathcal{P}(C_{\Sigma'})$, where $\Sigma' = < FS, PS \cup PS' >$ is defined in terms of the functions $\mathbb{T}_\kappa : C_{\Sigma'}^{\supset} \rightarrow \mathcal{P}(C_{\Sigma'})$ and $\mathbb{T}_\gamma : G_{\Sigma'}^{\supset} \rightarrow G_{\Sigma'} \times \mathcal{P}(C_{\Sigma'})$ as follows. For every program P,*

$$\mathbb{T}(P) = \emptyset \quad \text{if } P = \emptyset$$
$$\mathbb{T}(P) = \cup_{i=1}^{n} \mathbb{T}_\kappa(C_i) \quad \text{if } P = \{C_1, \ldots, C_n\}$$

such that

1. *$\mathbb{T}_\kappa(p(\bar{x}) \leftarrow \bar{G} \Box c) = \{p(\bar{x}) \leftarrow \bar{G}' \Box c\} \cup P'$ where $\mathbb{T}_\gamma(\bar{G}) = \langle \bar{G}', P' \rangle$*
2. *If $G = \underline{t}$ then $\mathbb{T}_\gamma(G) = \langle \underline{t}, \emptyset \rangle$*
3. *If $G = p(\bar{x})$ then $\mathbb{T}_\gamma(G) = \langle p(\bar{x}), \emptyset \rangle$*
4. *If $G = \neg p(\bar{x})$ then $\mathbb{T}_\gamma(G) = \langle \neg p(\bar{x}), \emptyset \rangle$*
5. *If $G = Q \supset G_0$ then $\mathbb{T}_\gamma(G) = \langle G', \mathbb{T}(Q\sigma_G) \cup Q' \cup ext(\sigma_G) \rangle$ where*
   (a) *σ_G is a renaming w.r.t. Q*
   (b) *$\mathbb{T}_\gamma(G_0 \sigma_G) = \langle G', Q' \rangle$*
   (c) *$ext(\sigma_G) = \{p\sigma_G(\bar{x}) \leftarrow p(\bar{x}) \mid \sigma_G(p) \neq p \wedge Def(Q,p) \neq \emptyset\}$*

6. *For all extended goals G, G' occurring in P, if $G \neq G'$ then for each p in PS either*
   $\sigma_G(p) \neq \sigma_{G'}(p)$ *or* $\sigma_G(p) = \sigma_{G'}(p) = p$

This definition is extended to $\overline{G} = (G_1, \ldots, G_m)$ as follows
$\mathbb{T}_\gamma(\overline{G}) = \langle (G'_1, \ldots, G'_m), \cup_{i=1}^m P'_i \rangle$ *where for each i in $\{1, \ldots, m\}$ $\mathbb{T}_\gamma(G_i) = \langle G'_i, P'_i \rangle$.*

Notice that the set $ext(\sigma)$ links renamed predicates with their "old" names in such a way that the visibility through innermost to outermost program is preserved. The following example illustrates how the translation algorithm works.

Example 6. Let $P = \{p(x) \leftarrow \Box x = a; q \leftarrow \{p(x) \leftarrow \Box x = b\} \supset \neg p(x)\}$. The translation of P is the following:

1. $\mathbb{T}(P) = \mathbb{T}_\kappa(p(x) \leftarrow \Box x = a) \cup \mathbb{T}_\kappa(q \leftarrow \{p(x) \leftarrow \Box x = b\} \supset \neg p(x))$
2. $\mathbb{T}_\kappa(p(x) \leftarrow \Box x = a) = \{p(x) \leftarrow \Box x = a\}$
3. $\mathbb{T}_\kappa(q \leftarrow \{p(x) \leftarrow \Box x = b\} \supset \neg p(x)) = \{q \leftarrow G'\} \cup P'$
   where $\mathbb{T}_\gamma(\{p(x) \leftarrow \Box x = b\} \supset \neg p(x)) = \langle G', P' \rangle$
   Now, let us see how to obtain $\mathbb{T}_\gamma(\{p(x) \leftarrow \Box x = b\} \supset \neg p(x))$. In this case, we have to use Definition 5.5. On one hand, it is necessary a renaming w.r.t. the program $\{p(x) \leftarrow \Box x = b\}$. Let σ be such a renaming. Therefore, $\sigma(\neg p(x)) \equiv \neg p\sigma(x)$ and $\sigma(\{p(x) \leftarrow \Box x = b\}) = \{p\sigma(x) \leftarrow \Box x = b\}$. On the other hand, using Definition 5.4, $\mathbb{T}_\gamma(\neg p\sigma(x)) = \langle \neg p\sigma(x), \emptyset \rangle$, $ext(\sigma) = \{p\sigma(x) \leftarrow p(x)\}$ and $\mathbb{T}(\{p\sigma(x) \leftarrow \Box x = b\}) = \{p\sigma(x) \leftarrow \Box x = b\}$. So, we obtain $\mathbb{T}_\gamma(\{p(x) \leftarrow \Box x = b\} \supset \neg p(x)) = \langle \neg p\sigma(x), \{p\sigma(x) \leftarrow \Box x = b; p\sigma(x) \leftarrow p(x)\} \rangle$ and, consequently, we have that

$$\mathbb{T}(P) = \{p(x) \leftarrow \Box x = a; \ q \leftarrow \neg p\sigma(x); \ p\sigma(x) \leftarrow \Box x = b; \ p\sigma(x) \leftarrow p(x)\}.$$

Since derivation steps are defined in terms of sequents in which stacks of programs occur, it is necessary to extend the function $\mathbb{T}$.

Definition 6. *Let S and $S_k = P_1 | \ldots | P_k$, $k \geq 1$, be the set of all the possible sequences of programs and a sequence of programs, respectively. Then, $\hat{\mathbb{T}} : S \to \mathcal{P}(C_{\Sigma'})$ is inductively defined, as follows:*

1. $\hat{\mathbb{T}}(P_1) = \mathbb{T}(P_1)$
2. $\hat{\mathbb{T}}(S_{k-1} | P_k) = \hat{\mathbb{T}}(S_{k-1}) \cup \mathbb{T}(P_k \overline{\sigma}_k) \cup ext(\sigma_k)$ *where σ_1 is the identity renaming and σ_k, $k > 1$, is a renaming with respect to $P_k \overline{\sigma}_{k-1}$.*

The following example illustrates how $\hat{\mathbb{T}}$ works.

Example 7. Let $P_1 = \{p \leftarrow q\}$ and $P_2 = \{s; \ p \leftarrow \neg t; \ p \leftarrow s\}$
$\hat{\mathbb{T}}(P_1 | P_2) = \hat{\mathbb{T}}(P_1) \cup \mathbb{T}(P_2 \sigma_1 \sigma_2) \cup ext(\sigma_2)$ where σ_2 is a renaming with respect to $P_2 \sigma_1$. From Definition 6 is easy to see that

$$\hat{\mathbb{T}}(P_1 | P_2) = \{p \leftarrow q\} \cup \{s\sigma_2; p\sigma_2 \leftarrow \neg t; p\sigma_2 \leftarrow s\sigma_2\} \cup \{s\sigma_2 \leftarrow s; p\sigma_2 \leftarrow p\}.$$

5   Soundness and Completeness

In this section we prove the soundness and completeness of the transformational semantics defined in previous section. We begin with the completeness theorem.

Theorem 1. *Let $S_k = P_1|\ldots|P_k$, $k \geq 1$ and $\overline{G}$ be a stack of programs and a goal, respectively. Then, If $S_k \vdash_s \overline{G} \square c$ can be proved with computed answer c', then there exist $c_1,\ldots,c_m$ SLDFA-computed answers of $\leftarrow \overline{G} \square c$ with respect to $\hat{\mathbb{T}}(S_k) \cup P'$ and $FET_\Sigma \models (c' \rightarrow c_1 \vee \ldots \vee c_m)^\forall$, where $\mathbb{T}_\gamma(\overline{G}\overline{\sigma}_k) = \langle \overline{G}', P' \rangle$.*

Proof. We proceed by induction on the number of derivation steps, n which is the sum of the number of derivation steps in the main derivation and the number of derivation steps in each subderivation. The theorem trivially holds when $n = 0$. Assume the theorem holds for a number of derivation steps $\leq n$. Let us prove for $n+1$. We proceed by case analysis on $\overline{G}$.

1. $\overline{G} = p(\overline{x})$. Thus, there exists $i \in \{1,\ldots,k\}$ such that there exists a (renamed apart) clause $p(\overline{x}) \leftarrow \overline{G}^i \square d^i \in Def(P_i, p)$ and $S_i \vdash_s \overline{G}^i \square c \wedge d^i$ can be proved with computed answer c'. By the induction hypothesis there exist $c_1,\ldots,c_{m_i}$ SLDFA-computed answers of $\leftarrow \overline{G}'^i \square c \wedge d^i$ with respect to $\hat{\mathbb{T}}(S_i) \cup P'_i$ and $FET_\Sigma \models (c' \rightarrow c_1 \vee \ldots \vee c_{m_i})^\forall$ where $\mathbb{T}_\gamma(\overline{G}^i \overline{\sigma}_i) = \langle \overline{G}'^i, P'_i \rangle$. Additionally, we have that for each clause $p(\overline{x}) \leftarrow \overline{G}^i \square d^i$ in $Def(P_i, p)$ there exists the corresponding translated clause in $\hat{\mathbb{T}}(S_k)$. That is, $p\overline{\sigma}_i(\overline{x}) \leftarrow \overline{G}'^i \square d^i$, where $\mathbb{T}_\gamma(\overline{G}^i \overline{\sigma}_i) = \langle \overline{G}'^i, P'_i \rangle$, $P'_i \subseteq \hat{\mathbb{T}}(S_k)$. Thus, since $\mathbb{T}_\gamma(p\overline{\sigma}_k(\overline{x})) = \langle p\overline{\sigma}_k(\overline{x}), \emptyset \rangle$ and using (if needed) those clauses in $ext(\sigma_j)$, for $j \in \{i+1,\ldots,k\}$, we can construct the following SLDFA-derivations of $\leftarrow p\overline{\sigma}_k(\overline{x}) \square c$ with respect to $\hat{\mathbb{T}}(S_k)$:
$$\leftarrow p\overline{\sigma}_k(\overline{x}) \square c; \overbrace{}^{k-i\ \text{steps}}; \leftarrow p\overline{\sigma}_i(\overline{x}) \square c; \leftarrow \overline{G}'^i \square c \wedge d^i; \ldots \leftarrow \square c_j$$ where $j \in \{1,\ldots,m_i\}$ and $FET_\Sigma \models (c' \rightarrow c_1 \vee \ldots \vee c_{m_i})^\forall$.

2. $\overline{G} = \neg p(\overline{x})$. Therefore $S_k \vdash_s \neg p(\overline{x}) \square c$ with computed answer c'. That is for every $i \in \{1,\ldots,k\}$ there exists a satisfiable constraint c^i, $FET_\Sigma \models (c^i \rightarrow c)^\forall$ such that for every (renamed apart) clause $p(\overline{x}) \leftarrow G^i_1,\ldots,G^i_{m_i} \square d^i \in Def(P_i, p)$ there exists $J_i \subseteq \{1,\ldots,m_i\}$ such that for each $j \in J_i : S_i \vdash_s \neg G^i_j \square d^i$ can be proved with computed answer d^i_j, $FET_\Sigma \models (c^i \rightarrow \neg d^i \vee \bigvee_{j \in J_i} d^i_j)^\forall$ and $FET_\Sigma \models (c' \rightarrow \bigwedge_{i=1}^k c^i)^\forall$. By the induction hypothesis, for every $i \in \{1,\ldots,k\}$, for each clause $p(\overline{x}) \leftarrow G^i_1,\ldots,G^i_{m_i} \square d^i$ in $Def(P_i, p)$ and for each $j \in J_i$ there exists an SLDFA finitely failed tree of $\leftarrow G'^i_j \square d^i$ with respect to $\hat{\mathbb{T}}(S_i) \cup P'^i_j \subseteq \hat{\mathbb{T}}(S_k)$ where $\mathbb{T}_\gamma(G^i_j \overline{\sigma}^i) = \langle G'^i_j, P'^i_j \rangle$. Additionally, there exists a clause $p\overline{\sigma}_i(\overline{x}) \leftarrow G'^i_1,\ldots,G'^i_{m_i} \square d^i$, where $\mathbb{T}_\gamma((G^i_1,\ldots,G^i_{m_i})\overline{\sigma}_i) = \langle (G'^i_1,\ldots,G'^i_{m_i}), \bigcup_{l=1}^{m_i} P'^i_l \rangle$ and $\bigcup_{l=1}^{m_i} P'^i_l \subseteq \hat{\mathbb{T}}(S_k)$. Now, using these clauses and (if needed) those ones in $ext(\sigma_l)$, for $l \in \{i+1,\ldots,k\}$, we can construct an SLDFA finitely failed tree of $\leftarrow p\overline{\sigma}_k(\overline{x}) \square c$ with respect $\hat{\mathbb{T}}(S_k)$ as follows. First, we construct the corresponding prefailed tree and then, we select any cross section of this tree and instantiate it by $\bigwedge_{i=1}^k c^i$ obtaining an SLDFA finitely failed tree of $\leftarrow p\overline{\sigma}_k(\overline{x}) \square c$ with respect $\hat{\mathbb{T}}(S_k)$. Hence, since $FET_\Sigma \models (c' \rightarrow \bigwedge_{i=1}^k c^i)^\forall$, there exists an SLDFA-derivation of $\leftarrow \neg p\overline{\sigma}_k(\overline{x}) \square c$ with respect to $\hat{\mathbb{T}}(S_k)$ with computed answer c'.

3. $\overline{G} = Q \supset G_Q$. Therefore, $S_k \vdash_s Q \supset G_Q \square c$ with computed answer c' and the number of derivation steps used in this derivation is $n+1$. Thus, $S_k|Q \vdash_s G_Q \square c$ can be proved with computed answer c' in a number of steps less or equal than n and by the induction hypothesis, there exist $c_1,\ldots,c_m$ SLDFA-computed answers of $\leftarrow G'_Q \square c$ with respect to $\hat{\mathbb{T}}(S_k|Q) \cup P'_Q$ and $FET_\Sigma \models (c' \rightarrow c_1 \vee \ldots \vee$

$c_m)^\forall$ where $\mathbb{T}_\gamma(G_Q\bar\sigma_k\sigma_Q) = \langle G'_Q, P'_Q\rangle$. By definition of $\hat{\mathbb{T}}$, $\hat{\mathbb{T}}(S_k|Q) = \hat{\mathbb{T}}(S_k) \cup \mathbb{T}(Q\bar\sigma_k\sigma_Q) \cup ext(\sigma_Q)$, and, by definition of $\mathbb{T}_\gamma$, $\mathbb{T}_\gamma((Q \supset G_Q)\bar\sigma_k) = \mathbb{T}_\gamma(Q\bar\sigma_k \supset G_Q\bar\sigma_k) = \langle G'_Q, P''\rangle$, where $P'' = \mathbb{T}(Q\bar\sigma_k\sigma_Q) \cup P'_Q \cup ext(\sigma_Q)$. Consequently, there exist $c_1,\ldots,c_m$ SLDFA-computed answers of $\leftarrow G'_Q\square c$ with respect to $\hat{\mathbb{T}}(S_k) \cup P''$ and $FET_\Sigma \models (c' \rightarrow c_1 \vee \ldots \vee c_m)^\forall$ where $\mathbb{T}_\gamma((Q \supset G_Q)\bar\sigma_k) = \langle G'_Q, P''\rangle$.

4. $\overline{G} = (G_1,\ldots,G_l)$. Therefore, for each $i \in \{1,\ldots,l\}$, $S_k \vdash_s G_i\square c$ can be proved with computed answer c'_i, $FET_\Sigma \models (c' \rightarrow c'_i)^\forall$ in a number of derivation steps less or equal than n. By the induction hypothesis, for every $i \in \{1,\ldots,l\}$, there exist $c^i_1,\ldots,c^i_{l_i}$ SLDFA-computed answers of $\leftarrow G'_i\square c$ with respect to $\hat{\mathbb{T}}(S_k) \cup P'_i$ where $\mathbb{T}_\gamma(G_i\bar\sigma_k) = \langle G'_i, P'_i\rangle$ and $FET_\Sigma \models (c'_i \rightarrow c^i_1 \vee \ldots \vee c^i_{l_i})^\forall$. Then, there exist $c_1,\ldots,c_m$ SLDFA-computed answers of $\leftarrow G'_1,\ldots,G'_l \square c$ with respect to $\hat{\mathbb{T}}(S_k) \cup \bigcup_{i=1}^l P'_i$. By definition of $\mathbb{T}_\gamma$, $\mathbb{T}_\gamma((G_1,\ldots,G_l)\bar\sigma_k) = \langle (G'_1,\ldots,G'_l), \bigcup_{i=1}^l P'_i\rangle$ and, additionally $FET_\Sigma \models (c' \rightarrow c^i_1 \vee \ldots \vee c^i_{l_i})^\forall$. Consequently, there exist $c_1,\ldots,c_m$ SLDFA-computed answers of $\leftarrow G'_1,\ldots,G'_l \square c$ with respect to $\hat{\mathbb{T}}(S_k) \cup \bigcup_{i=1}^l P'_i$ and $FET_\Sigma \models (c' \rightarrow c_1 \vee \ldots \vee c_m)^\forall$. ∎

In particular, when the sequence S_k is a simple program P and the goal is of the form $\ell\square c$ the next corollary is obtained:

Corollary 1. *Let P be a program and $\ell\square c$ a goal. If $P \vdash_s \ell\square c$ can be proved with computed answer c', then there exist $c_1,\ldots,c_m$ SLDFA-computed answers of $\ell\square c$ with respect to $\mathbb{T}(P)$, and $FET_\Sigma \models (c' \rightarrow c_1 \vee \ldots \vee c_m)^\forall$.*

This corollary establishes that given a program P, for each normal goal that can be (statically) proved from P there exists a successful SLDFA derivation with respect to the translated program $\mathbb{T}(P)$. This result can be directly generalized to goals of the form $\overline{\ell}\square c$. In the case of goals in which embedded implications occur it is necessary to prove the following corollary.

Corollary 2. *Let P and G be a program and a goal, respectively. If $P \vdash_s G\square c$ can be proved with computed answer c', then there exist $c_1,\ldots,c_m$ SLDFA-computed answers of $G'\square c$ with respect to P', where $\mathbb{T}_\gamma(P \supset G) = \langle G', P'\rangle$ and $FET_\Sigma \models (c' \rightarrow c_1 \vee \ldots \vee c_m)^\forall$.*

Proof. From the deduction theorem [12] and the Definition 1, we have that $P \vdash_s G$ implies $\emptyset \vdash_s (P \supset G)$. The proof follows from Definition 6.1 and Theorem 1. ∎

Next theorem establishes the soundness of the transformational semantics.

Theorem 2. *Let $S_k = P_1|\ldots|P_k$, $k \geq 1$ and $\overline{G}$ be a stack of programs and a goal, respectively. If $\mathbb{T}_\gamma(\overline{G}\bar\sigma_k) = \langle \overline{G}', P'\rangle$ and there exist $c_1,\ldots,c_m$ SLDFA-computed answers of $\leftarrow \overline{G}'\square c$ with respect to $\hat{\mathbb{T}}(S_k) \cup P'$, then $S_k \vdash_s \overline{G}\square c$ can be proved with computed answer c' and $FET_\Sigma \models (c' \rightarrow c_1 \vee \ldots \vee c_m)^\forall$.*

Proof. As in previous theorem, we proceed by induction on the number of SLDFA-derivation steps, n. The base step is when $n = 0$. In this case the theorem trivially holds.

Assume the theorem holds whenever the number of SLDFA-derivation steps is $\leq n$. Let us prove for $n + 1$. We proceed by case analysis on $\overline{G}$.

1. $\overline{G} = p(\overline{x})$. Therefore, $\mathbb{T}_\gamma(\overline{G}\overline{\sigma}_k) = \langle p\overline{\sigma}_k(\overline{x}), \emptyset \rangle$, where $Def(\hat{\mathbb{T}}(S_k), p\overline{\sigma}_k) \neq \emptyset$ and there exists $c_1, \ldots, c_m$ SLDFA-computed answers of $\leftarrow p\overline{\sigma}_k(\overline{x}) \square c$ with respect to $\hat{\mathbb{T}}(S_k)$ in $n+1$ derivations steps. Then, there exists a (renamed apart) clause $p\overline{\sigma}_k(\overline{x}) \leftarrow \overline{\ell}\square d \in Def(\hat{\mathbb{T}}(S_k), p\overline{\sigma}_k)$ such that $c \wedge d$ is a satisfiable constraint and thus the considered derivations are of the form:
$\leftarrow p\overline{\sigma}_k(\overline{x})\square c; \leftarrow \overline{\ell}\square c \wedge d; \ldots; \leftarrow \square c_l, l \in \{1, \ldots, m\}$
There are two cases:
   (a) There exists a (renamed apart) clause $p(\overline{x}) \leftarrow \overline{G}_p \square d \in Def(P_k, p)$ and $\mathbb{T}_\gamma(\overline{G}_p\overline{\sigma}_k) = \langle \overline{\ell}, P'_p \rangle$ and $P'_p \subseteq \hat{\mathbb{T}}(S_k)$. Hence, there exist $c_1, \ldots, c_m$ SLDFA-computed answers of $\leftarrow \overline{\ell}\square c \wedge d$ with respect to $\hat{\mathbb{T}}(S_k)$ in a number of derivations steps less or equal than n. Applying the induction hypothesis we obtain that $S_k \vdash_s \overline{G}_p \square c \wedge d$ can be proved with computed answer c'.
   (b) $Def(P_k, p) = \emptyset$ and there exists $i \in \{1, \ldots, k\}$, $i \neq k$ such that $p(\overline{x}) \leftarrow \overline{G}^i \square d \in Def(P_i, p)$ and $\mathbb{T}_\gamma(\overline{G}^i\overline{\sigma}_k) = \langle \overline{\ell}^i, P' \rangle$ and $P' \subseteq \hat{\mathbb{T}}(S_k)$. Then, considering those clauses in $ext(\sigma_j)$, $j \in \{i+1, \ldots, k\}$, the considered derivations are of the form:
$$\leftarrow p\overline{\sigma}_k(\overline{x})\square c; p\overline{\sigma}_{k-1}(\overline{x})\square c; \overbrace{}^{k-i \text{ steps}}; \leftarrow p\overline{\sigma}_i(\overline{x})\square c; \leftarrow \overline{\ell}^i \square c \wedge d; \ldots \leftarrow \square c_l, l \in \{1, \ldots, m\}$$
Hence, there exist $c_1, \ldots, c_m$ SLDFA-computed answers of $\leftarrow \overline{\ell}^i \square c \wedge d$ with respect to $\hat{\mathbb{T}}(S_i)$ in a number of derivations steps less or equal than n and by the induction hypothesis it follows that $S_i \vdash_s \overline{G}^i \square c \wedge d$ with computed answer c'.
Consequently, $S_k \vdash_s p(\overline{x})\square c$ can be proved with computed answer c' and $FET_\Sigma \models (c' \to c_1 \vee \ldots \vee c_m)^\forall$.

2. $\overline{G} = \neg p(\overline{x})$. Therefore, $\mathbb{T}_\gamma(\overline{G}\overline{\sigma}_k) = \langle \neg p\overline{\sigma}_k(\overline{x}), \emptyset \rangle$. Thus, there exists an SLDFA-finitely failed tree of $\leftarrow p\overline{\sigma}_k(\overline{x})\square c$ with respect to $\hat{\mathbb{T}}(S_k)$. Let c' the corresponding failed answer. This implies that for each $i \in \{1, \ldots, k\}$ and for all clause $p(\overline{x}) \leftarrow G^i_1, \ldots, G^i_{m_i} \square d^i$ in $Def(P_i, p)$, considering their corresponding translated clauses $p\overline{\sigma}_i(\overline{x}) \leftarrow \ell^i_1, \ldots, \ell^i_{m_i} \square d^i \in \hat{\mathbb{T}}(S_k)$, where $\mathbb{T}_\gamma((G^i_1, \ldots, G^i_{m_i})\overline{\sigma}_k) = \langle (\ell^i_1, \ldots, \ell^i_{m_i}), \bigcup^{m_i}_{l=1} P_l \rangle$, $\bigcup^{m_i}_{l=1} P_l \subseteq \hat{\mathbb{T}}(S_k)$ there exists $J_i \subseteq \{1, \ldots, m_i\}$ such that for each $j \in J_i$, there exists an SLDFA-finitely failed tree of $\leftarrow \ell^i_j \square d^i$ with respect to $\hat{\mathbb{T}}(S_k)$. Let d^i_j the corresponding failed answers, then there exists c^i such that $FET_\Sigma \models (c^i \to \neg d^i \vee \bigvee_{j \in J_i} d^i_j)^\forall$ and $FET_\Sigma \models (c' \to \bigwedge^k_{i=1} c^i)^\forall$. The constraint c^i is one of those constraints that can be used to instantiate the SLDFA-subtree whose root is $\leftarrow p\overline{\sigma}_i(\overline{x})\square c$. Besides, by the definition of failed answer and the by the induction hypothesis $S_k \vdash_s \neg G^i_j \square d^i$ can be proved with computed answers d^i_j. Therefore, $S_k \vdash_s \neg p(\overline{x})\square c$ can be proved with computed answer c'.

3. $\overline{G} = Q_1 \supset \ldots \supset Q_m \supset \ell$. Therefore, there exist $c_1, \ldots, c_m$ SLDFA-computed answers of $\leftarrow \ell\overline{\sigma}_{k+m}(\overline{x})\square c$ with respect to $\hat{\mathbb{T}}(S_k) \cup \bigcup^m_{i=1} Q'_i$ in $n+1$ derivations steps where $\mathbb{T}_\gamma(\overline{G}\overline{\sigma}_k) = \langle \ell\overline{\sigma}_{k+m}, \bigcup^m_{i=1} Q'_i \rangle$. Hence, there are two possibilities depending on the kind, either positive or negative, of the literal $\ell\overline{\sigma}_{k+m}$ and using similar arguments as in cases 1 and 2 of this proof, we obtain that $S_k|Q_1|\ldots|Q_m \vdash_s \ell\overline{\sigma}_{k+m}\square c$ can be proved with computed answer c' and $FET_\Sigma \models (c' \to c_1 \vee \ldots \vee c_m)^\forall$. Consequently, $S_k \vdash_s Q_1 \supset \ldots \supset Q_m \supset \ell\square c$ can be proved with computed answer c' and $FET_\Sigma \models (c' \to c_1 \vee \ldots \vee c_m)^\forall$.

4. $\overline{G} = (G_1, \ldots, G_l)$. Then, there exist $c_1, \ldots, c_m$ SLDFA-computed answers of $\leftarrow \ell_1\overline{\sigma}_{k+j_1}, \ldots, \ell_l\overline{\sigma}_{k+j_l}\square c$ with respect to $\hat{\mathbb{T}}(S_k) \cup \bigcup^l_{i=1} Q_i$ in $n+1$ derivations

steps, where $\hat{\mathbb{T}}((G_1,\ldots,G_l)\overline{\sigma}_k) = \hat{\mathbb{T}}((G_1\overline{\sigma}_k,\ldots,G_l\overline{\sigma}_k)) = \langle(\ell_1\overline{\sigma}_{k+j_1},\ldots,\ell_l\overline{\sigma}_{k+j_l}),\bigcup_{i=1}^{l} Q_i\rangle$. That is, for $i \in \{1,\ldots,l\}$ $\mathbb{T}_\gamma(G_i\overline{\sigma}_k) = \langle\ell_i\overline{\sigma}_{k+j_i},Q_i\rangle$ with $j_i \geq 0$. By definition of the SLDFA operational semantics, there exist $c_1^1,\ldots,c_{m_1}^1$ SLDFA-computed answers of $\leftarrow\ell_1\overline{\sigma}_{k+j_1}\Box c$ with respect to $\hat{\mathbb{T}}(S_k) \cup Q_1$ in a number of derivation steps less or equal than n. Thus, by induction hypothesis, $S_k \vdash_s G_1\Box c$ can be proved with computed answer d and $FET_\Sigma \models (d \rightarrow c_1^1 \vee \ldots \vee c_{m_1}^1)^\forall$. Additionally, there exist $d_1,\ldots,d_{m'}$ SLDFA-computed answers of $\leftarrow\ell_2\overline{\sigma}_{k+j_1},\ldots,\ell_l\overline{\sigma}_{k+j_l}\Box d$ with respect to $\hat{\mathbb{T}}(S_k) \cup \bigcup_{i=2}^{l} Q_i$ in a number of derivations steps less or equal than n, where for every $j \in \{1,\ldots,m'\}$ $FET_\Sigma \models (d_j \rightarrow c_1 \vee \ldots \vee c_m)^\forall$. Hence, by induction hypothesis, $S_k \vdash_s G_2,\ldots,G_l\Box d$ can be proved with computed answer c' and $FET_\Sigma \models (c' \rightarrow d_1 \vee \ldots \vee d_{m'})^\forall$. Consequently, $S_k \vdash_s G_1,\ldots,G_l\Box c$ can be proved with computed answer c' and $FET_\Sigma \models (c' \rightarrow c_1 \vee \ldots \vee c_m)^\forall$. ∎

Acknowledgements. This work has been supported by the CICYT project GRAMMARS (ref. TIN2004-07925-C03-01).

References

1. R. Arruabarrena and M. Navarro.: On extended logic language supporting program structuring. In *Proc. of the Joint Conference on Declarative Programming, APPIA-GULP-PRODE'96.* (1996) 191–203
2. R. Arruabarrena, P. Lucio, and M.Navarro, M.: A Strong Logic Programming View for Static Embedded Implications. In *Proc. of the Second International Conference on Foundations of Software Science and Computation Structures, FOSSACS'99.* LNCS **1578**, Springer (1999) 56–72
3. M. Baldoni, L. Giordano, and A. Martelli.: Translating a modal Language with embedded implication into Horn clause logic. In *Proc. of the 5th International Workshop on Extensions of Logic Programming*, LNCS **1050**, Springer (1996) 19–33
4. A. J. Bonner and L. T. McCarty.: Adding negation-as-failure to intuitionistic logic programming. In *Proc. of the North American Conference on Logic Programming, NACLP'90* (1990) 681–703
5. M. Bugliesi, E. Lamma, and Mello Paola.: Modularity in logic programming. Journal of Logic Programming 19/20 (1994) 443–502
6. W. Drabent.: What is a failure? An approach to constructive negation. Acta Informática **32** (1995) 27–59,
7. M. Gabbay.: N–PROLOG: An extension of Prolog with hypothetical implications II. Logical foundations and negation as failure. Journal of Logic Programming **1(4)** (1985) 251–283
8. M. Gabbay and U. Reyle.: N–PROLOG: An extension of Prolog with hypothetical implications. I. Journal of Logic Programming **1(4)** (1985) 319–355
9. L. Giordano, A. Martelli, and G. Rossi.: Extending Horn clause logic with implication goals. Theoretical Computer Science **95(1)** (1992) 43–74
10. L. Giordano and A. Martelli.: Structuring Logic Programs: A Modal Approach. Journal of Logic Programming **21** (1994) 59–94
11. L. Giordano and N. Olivetti.: Combining negation as failure and embedded implication in logic programs. Journal of Logic Programming **36** (1998) 91–147
12. P. Lucio.: Structured sequent calculi for combining intuitionistic and classical first-order logic. In *Proc. of the Third International Workshop on Frontiers of Combining Systems, FroCoS '00* LNAI **1794**, Springer (2000) 88–104

13. L.T. McCarty.: Clausal intuitionistic logic I. Fixed point semantics. Journal of Logic Programming **5** (1988) 1–31
14. L.T. McCarty.: Clausal intuitionistic logic II. Tableau proof procedures. Journal of Logic Programming **5** (1988) 93–132
15. D. Miller.: A logical analysis of modules in logic programming. Journal of Logic Programming **6(1-2)** (1989) 79–108
16. L. Monteiro and A. Porto.: A language for contextual logic programming. In *Logic Programming Languages: constraints, functions and objects*. MIT Press (1993) 115–147
17. G. Nadathur and D. Miller.: Higher–order logic programming. In *Handbook of Logic in Artificial Intelligence and Logic Programming*, Vol 5. Clarendon Press (1998) 499–590
18. M. Navarro.: From modular Horn programs to flat ones: a formal proof for the propositional case. In *Proc. of the Second International Symposium on Innovation in Information and Communication Technology, ISIICT2004* (2004) Technical Report UPV-EHU/ LSI/ TR 01-2004. http://www.sc.ehu.es/marisa.
19. F. Orejas, E. Pasarella, and E. Pino.: Semantics of normal logic programs with embeddded implications. In *Proc. of the 17th International Conference, ICLP 2001*, LNCS **2237**, Springer (2001) 255–268

Converting One Type-Based Abstract Domain to Another

John P. Gallagher[1], Germán Puebla[2], and Elvira Albert[3]

[1] Department of Computer Science, Univ. of Roskilde
jpg@ruc.dk
[2] School of Computer Science, Technical Univ. of Madrid
german@fi.upm.es
[3] School of Computer Science, Complutense Univ. of Madrid
elvira@sip.ucm.es

Abstract. The specific problem that motivates this paper is how to obtain abstract descriptions of the meanings of imported predicates (such as built-ins) that can be used when analysing a module of a logic program with respect to some abstract domain. We assume that abstract descriptions of the imported predicates are available in terms of some "standard" assertions. The first task is to define an abstract domain corresponding to the assertions for a given module and express the descriptions as objects in that domain. Following that they are automatically transformed into the analysis domain of interest. We develop a method which has been applied in order to generate call and success patterns from the CiaoPP assertions for built-ins, for any given regular type-based domain. In the paper we present the method as an instance of the more general problem of mapping elements of one abstract domain to another, with as little loss in precision as possible.

1 Motivation

When performing static analysis of a logic program, the source code for some parts of it may be inaccessible for some reason (the code might be in external modules, built-in system predicates, foreign-language libraries, and so on). In order to analyse such a program accurately, abstract descriptions of the behaviour of the missing code have to be supplied, otherwise some coarse over-approximation (or sometimes under-approximation) has to be used.

It can take considerable effort to specify the properties of built-ins and library predicates over a given abstract domain, and those properties need to be specified for each domain for which the calling code is to be analysed. Our intention is to specify once and for all the properties of library predicates, using a general and expressive abstract domain of descriptions; these specifications are then converted to another abstract domain when a particular analysis is to be performed.

The following general principles of abstract domain construction [1] are applied. Given two abstract interpretations of a concrete semantics, say $\mathcal{A}_1$ and

P.M. Hill (Ed.): LOPSTR 2005, LNCS 3901, pp. 147–162, 2006.

$\mathcal{A}_2$, with abstraction and concretisation functions α_1, γ_1, α_2 and γ_2 respectively, the aim is to translate descriptions in $\mathcal{A}_1$ to descriptions in $\mathcal{A}_2$. The best representative of an element $a_1 \in \mathcal{A}_1$ in $\mathcal{A}_2$ is $\alpha_2(\gamma_1(a_1))$. If we can implement a function equivalent to this we can just apply it to descriptions expressed using elements of $\mathcal{A}_1$ to obtain descriptions in $\mathcal{A}_2$. For the abstract domains that we consider, namely those based on regular types, we show that the function can be implemented by constructing the *reduced product domain* $\mathcal{A}_1 \star \mathcal{A}_2$, with concretisation function $\gamma_\star$. Our method can be presented as the computation, for a given element $a_1 \in \mathcal{A}_1$, of the corresponding element $a_\star \in \mathcal{A}_1 \star \mathcal{A}_2$, such that $\gamma_\star(a_\star) = \gamma_1(a_1)$, and then computing the most precise element a_2 in the domain of $\mathcal{A}_2$ such that $\gamma_\star(a_\star) \sqsubseteq \gamma_2(a_2)$. a_1 has an exact representative in $\mathcal{A}_1 \star \mathcal{A}_2$ but we cannot in general find an exact representative of $a_\star$ in $\mathcal{A}_2$. In our method, $\mathcal{A}_1$ is the general-purpose domain, while $\mathcal{A}_2$ is a particular analysis domain.

Assertions in CiaoPP. In the CiaoPP system [2] an assertion language is provided that allows properties of predicates to be stated in a flexible, general language. The properties of built-ins and many library predicates have been expressed in this assertion language. The question addressed in this work is how to use such information in an analysis over a (new) particular abstract domain. The method described in this paper allows us to take any given assertions about a module's imported predicates and translate them safely (and accurately) into the domain under consideration. We use domains based on regular types, realised as pre-interpretations [3], using a subset of the CiaoPP assertion language to explain the approach.

In the CiaoPP assertion language, approximations of the success set of a predicate can be specified, among many other aspects of computation. We do not enter into the notation for the assertions here; detailed examples can be seen in [2]. We can extract this information in the form of a set of abstract atoms of the form $p(d_1, \dots, d_n)$, for a predicate p/n, where $d_1, \dots, d_n$ are the names of abstract term descriptions defined within the CiaoPP system.

Example 1. The success of $length/2$ is described by $\{length(list, int)\}$. Here int is a primitive type and $list$ is defined by a set of regular type rules. If the analysis of interest concerns modes g (*ground*) and $nong$ (*non-ground*), then this description would be transformed automatically into $\{length(g, g), length(nong, g)\}$. In order to achieve this transformation we need to derive the information that a $list$ can be either ground or non-ground, while an int is ground.

An alternative approach (currently pursued in the CiaoPP system) is to define relationships between analysis domains in advance (a type lattice) [2]. For example, the fact that arithmetic expressions are ground can be pre-defined. Once that is done, an assertion, say, that the predicate $< /2$ succeeds with both arguments bound to arithmetic expressions can safely be translated into the modes domain as an assertion that both arguments are ground.

In contrast, the approach defined here allows arbitrary relationships to be derived automatically, for user-defined types as well as pre-defined ones. We focus here on transforming assertions about success of predicates, but the same approach can be followed for assertions on calls.

Related Work. The most closely related work is concerned with systematically constructing abstract domains from other domains [1, 4]. These principles have been applied in combining different abstractions from primitive operations in the ASTRÉE analyser (see e.g [5]). We make use of the reduced product in this paper, but domain construction is not our main aim, but rather to transfer information from one given domain to another given domain. Although the principles are well understood (see Section 2), we do not know of other work that applies them systematically to this problem.

Section 2 explains the general principles behind our solution. In Section 3 we review the kind of abstract domain that we deal with, namely, domains based on regular types and define a general solution for such domains. In Section 4 we describe how we construct a single set of regular types from the various different kinds of assertion in the CiaoPP assertion language, and thus define the standard domain. Section 5 presents the procedure for mapping descriptions in the standard domain into any given user-supplied domain based on regular types. The soundness and precision of the procedure are established by relating it to the general solution. Section 6 contains the results of some experiments in transforming CiaoPP assertions into various simple mode and type domains. Finally in Section 7 we present conclusions and future work.

2   General Characterisation of the Problem

We restrict our attention to abstract interpretations based on a Galois connection, which is given by a 4-tuple $\langle (\mathcal{D}, \sqsubseteq_{\mathcal{D}}), (\mathcal{A}, \sqsubseteq_{\mathcal{A}}), \alpha, \gamma \rangle$ where $(\mathcal{D}, \sqsubseteq_{\mathcal{D}})$ and $(\mathcal{A}, \sqsubseteq_{\mathcal{A}})$ are partially ordered sets, the concrete and abstract domain of interpretation respectively, and $\alpha : \mathcal{D} \to \mathcal{A}$ and $\gamma : \mathcal{A} \to \mathcal{D}$ are adjoined functions satisfying

$$\forall x \in \mathcal{D}, y \in \mathcal{A} : (\alpha(x) \sqsubseteq_{\mathcal{A}} y) \iff (x \sqsubseteq_{\mathcal{D}} \gamma(y)).$$

$\alpha(x)$ represents the best possible description of some concrete object x in the abstract domain $\mathcal{A}$, while $\gamma(y)$ represents the most imprecise element of the concrete domain $\mathcal{D}$ that is described by some abstract object y.

If $(\mathcal{D}, \sqsubseteq_{\mathcal{D}})$ and $(\mathcal{A}, \sqsubseteq_{\mathcal{A}})$ are complete lattices, then the functions α and γ determine each other; in particular we have $\alpha(x) = \sqcap \{y \mid x \sqsubseteq_{\mathcal{D}} \gamma(y)\}$, where $\sqcap$ is the meet operator in $(\mathcal{A}, \sqsubseteq_{\mathcal{A}})$.

Suppose $\langle (\mathcal{D}, \sqsubseteq_{\mathcal{D}}), (\mathcal{A}_1, \sqsubseteq_{\mathcal{A}_1}), \alpha_1, \gamma_1 \rangle$ and $\langle (\mathcal{D}, \sqsubseteq_{\mathcal{D}}), (\mathcal{A}_2, \sqsubseteq_{\mathcal{A}_2}), \alpha_2, \gamma_2 \rangle$ are two abstract interpretations with same concrete domain. Then given an element $a_1 \in \mathcal{A}_1$, we can compute the best representation in $\mathcal{A}_2$ of a_1 as $\alpha_2(\gamma_1(a_1))$.

In the applications considered in this paper, the domains are complete lattices. We are not provided explicitly with the abstraction function α. Therefore, the expression $\alpha_2(\gamma_1(a_1))$ mentioned above is rewritten as

$$\alpha_2(\gamma_1(a_1)) = \sqcap \{y \in \mathcal{A}_2 \mid \gamma_1(a_1) \sqsubseteq_{\mathcal{D}} \gamma_2(y)\}$$

This expression suggests that all elements y of the set $\mathcal{A}_2$ have to be enumerated, which is not practical in general. A practical algorithm for computing the required element of $\mathcal{A}_2$ is obtained in the remainder of the paper, for domains that are based on pre-interpretations.

3   Analysis Domains Based on Regular Types

As shown in [3], any set of regular types (a non-deterministic finite tree automaton) over a logic program's signature can be used to build a pre-interpretation, and hence an abstract interpretation of the program. In this section we summarise this family of abstract interpretations and some key properties.

A set of *regular types* is defined by a set of type symbols Q, a signature Σ, and a set of rules of the form $f(d_1, \ldots, d_n) \to d$, where $f/n \in \Sigma$ and $d, d_1, \ldots, d_n \in Q$. A set of regular type definitions can be seen as a finite tree automaton (FTA). For our purposes we regard the two notions as interchangeable, and speak of the states of an FTA as "types". (We assume that every state of an FTA is an accepting (or final) state.) Let Term_Σ be the set of terms constructible from the function symbols in Σ. Given a state (type) d, let $L(d) \subseteq \mathsf{Term}_\Sigma$ be the set of terms accepted by d; that is, for all $t \in L(d)$ there is a bottom-up derivation starting at t and ending at d. We can also think of $L(d)$ as standing for the terms of "type" d. Full details of these concepts can be found in the literature [6].

It is known [6] that an arbitrary FTA can be transformed to an equivalent *bottom-up deterministic* FTA (or DFTA). The defining condition of a DFTA is that there are no two rules with the same left hand side. An arbitrary FTA can also be *completed*, meaning that it is extended so that there exists a rule $f(d_1, \ldots, d_n) \to d$ for each choice of $f, d_1, \ldots, d_n$. (An extra state may need to be added to the FTA.) Let $\mathcal{Q}$ be the set of states of a complete DFTA. Thus $\{L(d) \mid d \in \mathcal{Q}\}$ is a disjoint partition of Term_Σ. That is, each $t \in \mathsf{Term}_\Sigma$ is accepted by exactly one state in a bottom-up derivation in a complete DFTA.

Example 2. Let $\Sigma = \{[\,]/0, [.|.]/2, a/0, s/1\}$. The following rules define a complete DFTA over Σ:

$$\{[\,] \to list, [list|list] \to list, [nonlist|list] \to list,$$
$$[list|nonlist] \to nonlist, [nonlist|nonlist] \to nonlist, a \to nonlist,$$
$$s(list) \to nonlist, s(nonlist) \to nonlist\}$$

The rules define two types *list* and *nonlist*. Each term in Term_Σ is accepted by one of these two. This induces a partition of Term_Σ into two disjoint sets, lists and non-lists. The above DFTA could be obtained by determinizing and completing the following FTA:

$$\{[\,] \to list, [dynamic|list] \to list, [\,] \to dynamic,$$
$$[dynamic|dynamic] \to dynamic, s(dynamic) \to dynamic, a \to dynamic\}$$

Note that the two types *list* and *dynamic* are not disjoint, in fact $L(list) \subset L(dynamic)$ in this case.

Representation of States in a Determinized FTA. Let Q be the set of states of an FTA. The textbook algorithm for determinization [6] constructs a DFTA whose set of states is some subset of 2^Q, say $\mathcal{Q}$. Let $\{d_1, \ldots, d_k\}$ be a state in $\mathcal{Q}$. The set of terms accepted by $\{d_1, \ldots, d_k\}$ in the determinized DFTA is exactly those terms that are accepted by all of $d_1, \ldots, d_k$ in the original FTA and by *no other state*. This is summarised formally as follows.

Property 1. $\{d_1, \ldots, d_k\} \in \mathcal{Q}$ iff $(L(d_1) \cap \ldots \cap L(d_k)) \setminus \bigcup\{L(d') \mid d' \in Q \setminus \{d_1, \ldots, d_k\}\}$ is nonempty.

Define $\mathsf{dettypes}(d, \mathcal{Q}) = \{d' \mid d' \in \mathcal{Q}, d \in d'\}$. Let $d \in Q$, and let $L_Q(d)$ represent the terms accepted by d in the original FTA. Let $\{d_1, \ldots, d_k\} \in \mathcal{Q}$ and let $L_{\mathcal{Q}}(\{d_1, \ldots, d_k\})$ be the set of terms accepted by $\{d_1, \ldots, d_k\}$ in the corresponding DFTA. Then we have $L_Q(d) = \cup\{L_{\mathcal{Q}}(d') \mid d' \in \mathsf{dettypes}(d, \mathcal{Q})\}$.

Intuitively, $\mathsf{dettypes}(d, \mathcal{Q})$ tells us the set of states in $\mathcal{Q}$ into which d is split during determinization. Thus, the use of sets of states from the original FTA to denote states in the DFTA gives us a convenient way of relating each state in the original FTA with the "equivalent" set of states in the corresponding DFTA.

Example 3. Let $Q = \{list, dynamic\}$ with transitions as defined in Example 2. The determinization algorithm yields states $\mathcal{Q} = \{\{list, dynamic\}, \{dynamic\}\}$ corresponding to *list* and *nonlist* respectively. Then $\mathsf{dettypes}(dynamic, \mathcal{Q}) = \{\{list, dynamic\}, \{dynamic\}\}$ and $\mathsf{dettypes}(list, \mathcal{Q}) = \{\{list, dynamic\}\}$. This shows that the type *list* in the original FTA corresponds to $\{list, dynamic\}$ in the DFTA, while the type *dynamic* is split into two disjoint types $\{list, dynamic\}$ (lists) and $\{dynamic\}$ (non-lists) in the DFTA.

Determinization of the Union of Two FTAs. Let $\langle Q_1, \Sigma, \Delta_1 \rangle$ and $\langle Q_2, \Sigma, \Delta_2 \rangle$ be FTAs based on the same signature and let $\langle Q_1 \cup Q_2, \Sigma, \Delta_1 \cup \Delta_2 \rangle$ be the union of the two automata. (Note, we can assume without loss of generality that Q_1 and Q_2 are disjoint.) Determinize all three automata; we will refer to the sets of states of the respective DFTAs as $\mathcal{Q}_1$, $\mathcal{Q}_2$ and $\mathcal{Q}_\star$.

3.1   Correspondence Between Pre-interpretations and DFTAs

A *pre-interpretation* J of a signature Σ is defined by a domain Q_J and a mapping I_J which maps each n-ary function symbol $f/n \in \Sigma$ to a function $Q_J^n \to Q_J$, denoted f_J.

It was shown in [3] that a complete DFTA is equivalent to a *pre-interpretation* of Σ. Thus when we speak of a pre-interpretation we could equally well refer to a completed DFTA and vice versa. Each rule $f(d_1, \ldots, d_n) \to d$ in the DFTA corresponds to an equation $f_J(d_1, \ldots, d_n) = d$ in the pre-interpretation J. The set of rules with the same function f/n on the left defines the function f_J onto which f/n is mapped by I_J. The DFTA is complete, hence the function f_J is total.

Example 4. The DFTA in Example 2 can be written as the pre-interpretation J with domain $\{list, nonlist\}$ and functions $[]_J, [.|.]_J, a_J, s_J$ defined by:

$$\{[]_J = list, [list|list]_J = list, [nonlist|list]_J = list, [list|nonlist]_J = nonlist,$$
$$[nonlist|nonlist]_J = nonlist, a_J = nonlist,$$
$$s_J(list) = nonlist, s_J(nonlist) = nonlist\}$$

3.2 Concrete and Abstract Domains of Interpretation

We take the concrete semantic domain of a logic program to be the set of its Herbrand interpretations [7] over an extended signature containing constants corresponding to variables, thus allowing information about term instantiation to be captured [11]. Note that models based on this semantics cannot capture certain properties directly, such as definite freeness. However the semantics provides a useful approximation of the computed answers. Let Σ be the signature of the language of the program, consisting of a set of ranked function and predicate symbols. Let Atom_Σ be the set of atoms of form $p(t_1, \ldots, t_n)$ where $p \in \Sigma$ is an n-ary predicate symbol and $t_1, \ldots, t_n \in \mathsf{Term}_\Sigma$. Atom_Σ is often called the Herbrand base of P. A Herbrand interpretation of P is a subset of Atom_Σ, representing the atoms interpreted as true. The lattice of Herbrand interpretations $\mathcal{D} = \langle 2^{\mathsf{Atom}_\Sigma}, \subseteq, \cup, \cap, \emptyset, \mathsf{Atom}_\Sigma \rangle$ is called the *concrete domain*.

From a Pre-Interpretation to an Abstract Domain. Let J be a pre-interpretation of Σ with domain Q_J. The set Atom_J is the set of expressions $p(d_1, \ldots, d_n)$ where $p \in \Sigma$ is an n-ary predicate symbol and $d_1, \ldots, d_n \in Q_J$. The lattice of interpretations over J, $\mathcal{A}_J = \langle 2^{\mathsf{Atom}_J}, \subseteq, \cup, \cap, \emptyset, \mathsf{Atom}_J \rangle$ is called the *abstract domain based on pre-interpretation J*. A Galois connection between $\mathcal{A}_J$ and $\mathcal{D}$ is given by the concretisation function $\gamma_J : 2^{\mathsf{Atom}_J} \to 2^{\mathsf{Atom}_\Sigma}$.

$$\gamma_J(S) = \bigcup \{\{p(t_1, \ldots, t_n) \mid t_i \in L(d_i), 1 \leq i \leq n\} \mid p(d_1, \ldots, d_n) \in S\}.$$

The expression $L(d_i)$ above refers to the subset of Term_Σ accepted by d_i (considered as the state of a DFTA), as mentioned above.

Although we are not concerned with the semantic function in the present work, we note that the least model $M_J[P]$ of a program P for a pre-interpretation J can be obtained by a fixpoint computation. $M_J[P]$ is an abstraction of the least Herbrand model $M[P]$, in the sense that $\gamma(M_J[P]) \supseteq M[P]$. So any FTA forms the basis for an abstraction of a program in which the meaning of a predicate p is abstracted by a set of domain atoms over the corresponding disjoint types.

Property 2. Let $\mathcal{A}_J$ be the abstract domain constructed from pre-interpretation J. Then each element of the abstract domain represents a unique element of the concrete domain; that is, for all $S_1, S_2 \in 2^{\mathsf{Atom}_J}$, $S_1 = S_2$ iff $\gamma_J(S_1) = \gamma_J(S_2)$. This holds because for all $d_1, d_2 \in Q_J$, $d_1 = d_2$ iff $L(d_1) \cap L(d_2) \neq \emptyset$.

Constructing a Product Domain. Suppose J_1 and J_2 are DFTAs obtained from FTAs $\langle Q_1, \Sigma, \Delta_1 \rangle$ and $\langle Q_2, \Sigma, \Delta_2 \rangle$ respectively.

Let $\mathcal{A}_1 = \langle 2^{\mathsf{Atom}_{J_1}}, \subseteq, \cup, \cap, \emptyset, \mathsf{Atom}_{J_1}\rangle$ and $\mathcal{A}_2 = \langle 2^{\mathsf{Atom}_{J_2}}, \subseteq, \cup, \cap, \emptyset, \mathsf{Atom}_{J_2}\rangle$ be the resulting abstract domains. We form a product domain $\mathcal{A}_\star = \langle 2^{\mathsf{Atom}_{J_\star}},$ $\subseteq, \cup, \cap, \emptyset, \mathsf{Atom}_{J_\star}\rangle$ where $J_\star$ is the DFTA of the union $\langle Q_1 \cup Q_2, \Sigma, \Delta_1 \cup \Delta_2\rangle$.

Claim. We claim that $\mathcal{A}_\star$ is the reduced cartesian product $\mathcal{A}_1 \star \mathcal{A}_2$ [1].

This claim is informally justified as follows. The reduced product of $\mathcal{A}_1$ and $\mathcal{A}_2$ is defined as the result of applying a reduction operator ρ [1] to the cartesian product of domains of $\mathcal{A}_1$ and $\mathcal{A}_2$ (with elements ordered componentwise). The effect of ρ, informally speaking, is to "bring to the abstract the conjunction of properties we would have in the concrete". Let S_1 and S_2 be elements of $2^{\mathsf{Atom}_{J_1}}$ and $2^{\mathsf{Atom}_{J_2}}$ respectively. Then $\mathcal{A}_\star$ contains a unique element $S_\star$ such that $\gamma_1(S_1) \cap \gamma_2(S_2) = \gamma_\star(S_\star)$. Such an element $S_\star$ exists since the intersection of any two regular types in the original DFTAs is represented in the DFTA of the union. Thus $\mathcal{A}_\star$ is at least as precise as the cartesian product of $\mathcal{A}_1$ and $\mathcal{A}_2$. $S_\star$ is unique (for each S_1 and S_2) due to Property 2. This implies that the reduction operator [1] is the identity function when applied to the product domain.

Lemma 1. *Let J_1, J_2 and $J_\star$ be pre-interpretations constructed as above. Q_1 is the set of states in the FTA used to derive J_1. Let $S_\star \in 2^{\mathsf{Atom}_{J_\star}}$. Then the element $S_1 \in 2^{\mathsf{Atom}_{J_1}}$ defined as $S_1 = \{p(\bar{d}_1 \cap Q_1, \ldots, \bar{d}_n \cap Q_1) \mid p(\bar{d}_1, \ldots, \bar{d}_n) \in S_\star\}$ is the best approximation of $S_\star$ in the domain $2^{\mathsf{Atom}_{J_1}}$. That is, $S_1 = \cap\{S_1' \mid \gamma_\star(S_\star) \subseteq \gamma_1(S_1')\}$. (Similarly for $2^{\mathsf{Atom}_{J_2}}$ by symmetry.)*

Proof. The notation $\bar{d}$ means that $\bar{d}$ is a state in a DFTA, i.e. it is a set of states from the original FTA. First show that $\{p(\bar{d}_1 \cap Q_1, \ldots, \bar{d}_n \cap Q_1) \mid p(\bar{d}_1, \ldots, \bar{d}_n) \in S_\star\} \subseteq \cap\{S_1' \mid \gamma_\star(S_\star) \subseteq \gamma_1(S_1')\}$. Let $p(\bar{e}_1, \ldots, \bar{e}_n) \in \{p(\bar{d}_1 \cap Q_1, \ldots, \bar{d}_n \cap Q_1) \mid p(\bar{d}_1, \ldots, \bar{d}_n) \in S_\star\}$. Then there exists $p(\bar{d}_1, \ldots, \bar{d}_n) \in S_\star\}$ such that for $1 \leq i \leq n$, $\bar{d}_i = \bar{e}_i \cup \bar{f}$ where $\bar{f} \cap Q_1 = \emptyset$. Then $\gamma_\star(S_\star)$ contains an element $p(t_1, \ldots, t_n)$ such that for $1 \leq i \leq n$, $t_i \in L(\bar{e}_i \cup \bar{f})$, where $\bar{f} \cap Q_1 = \emptyset$. For any element $S_1' \in 2^{\mathsf{Atom}_{J_1}}$, if $p(t_1, \ldots, t_n) \in \gamma_1(S_1')$ then $p(\bar{e}_1, \ldots, \bar{e}_n) \in S_1'$ since each $t_i \in L(\bar{e})$ for exactly one $\bar{e} \subseteq Q_1$, and that $\bar{e}$ must be $\bar{e}_i$. Hence $p(\bar{e}_1, \ldots, \bar{e}_n) \in \cap\{S_1' \mid \gamma_\star(S_\star) \subseteq \gamma_1(S_1')\}$.

Now show that $\cap\{S_1' \mid \gamma_\star(S_\star) \subseteq \gamma_1(S_1')\} \subseteq \{p(\bar{d}_1 \cap Q_1, \ldots, \bar{d}_n \cap Q_1) \mid p(\bar{d}_1, \ldots, \bar{d}_n) \in S_\star\}$. Let $p(\bar{e}_1, \ldots, \bar{e}_n) \in \cap\{S_1' \mid \gamma_\star(S_\star) \subseteq \gamma_1(S_1')\}$. If for all $S_1' \in 2^{\mathsf{Atom}_{J_1}}$ such that $\gamma_\star(S_\star) \subseteq \gamma_1(S_1')$, $p(\bar{e}_1, \ldots, \bar{e}_n) \in S_1'$, then $S_\star$ contains at least one element $p(\bar{d}_1, \ldots, \bar{d}_n)$ such that for $1 \leq i \leq n$, $\bar{d}_i = \bar{e}_i \cup \bar{f}$ and $\bar{f} \cap Q_1 = \emptyset$. This is because $\gamma_1(\bar{e}_i) \cap \gamma_\star(\bar{d}) = \emptyset$ for all $\bar{d}$ not of the form $\bar{d} = \bar{e} \cup \bar{f}$ and $\bar{f} \cap Q_1 = \emptyset$. Hence $p(\bar{e}_1, \ldots, \bar{e}_n) \in \{p(\bar{d}_1 \cap Q_1, \ldots, \bar{d}_n \cap Q_1) \mid p(\bar{d}_1, \ldots, \bar{d}_n) \in S_\star\}$.

Property 3. A product domain $\mathcal{A}_1 \star \mathcal{A}_2$ can precisely represent elements of its factors $\mathcal{A}_1$ and $\mathcal{A}_2$. That is, if S_1 is an element of the domain of $\mathcal{A}_1$ then there exists an element $S_\star$ in the domain of $\mathcal{A}_\star$ such that $\gamma_1(S_1) = \gamma_\star(S_\star)$. The element is unique by Property 2. Furthermore, $S_1 = \{p(\bar{d}_1 \cap Q_1, \ldots, \bar{d}_n \cap Q_1) \mid p(\bar{d}_1, \ldots, \bar{d}_n) \in S_\star\}$ by Lemma 1.

Example 5. Let $\langle Q_1, \Sigma, \Delta_1 \rangle$ and $\langle Q_2, \Sigma, \Delta_2 \rangle$ be FTAs, where $Q_1 = \{g, nong\}$ and $Q_2 = \{list, dynamic, int\}$, where these elements have their expected meanings. The DFTA states $\mathcal{Q}_1$ obtained from Q_1 are $\{\{g\}, \{nong\}\}$ and the DFTA states $\mathcal{Q}_2$ obtained from Q_2 are $\{\{dynamic, list\}, \{dynamic, int\}, \{dynamic\}\}$. The states $\mathcal{Q}_\star$ of the DFTA obtained from the union $\langle Q_1 \cup Q_2, \Sigma, \Delta_1 \cup \Delta_2 \rangle$ are

$$\{\{dynamic, list, g\}, \{dynamic, list, nong\},$$
$$\{dynamic, int, g\}, \{dynamic, g\}, \{dynamic, nong\}\}.$$

(Note that there are fewer states in $\mathcal{Q}_\star$ than in the cartesian product of $\mathcal{Q}_1$ and $\mathcal{Q}_2$.) Consider $S_1 = \{p(\{g\}, \{g\}) \in 2^{\mathsf{Atom}_{J_1}}$. Then the element $S_\star \in 2^{\mathsf{Atom}_{J_\star}}$ such that $\gamma_1(S_1) = \gamma_\star(S_\star)$ is

$\{p(\{dynamic, list, g\}, \{dynamic, g\}), p(\{dynamic, list, g\}, \{dynamic, int, g\}),$
$p(\{dynamic, list, g\}, \{dynamic, list, g\}), p(\{dynamic, int, g\}, \{dynamic, g\}),$
$p(\{dynamic, int, g\}, \{dynamic, list, g\}), p(\{dynamic, g\}, \{dynamic, list, g\}),$
$p(\{dynamic, int, g\}, \{dynamic, int, g\}), p(\{dynamic, g\}, \{dynamic, int, g\}),$
$p(\{dynamic, g\}, \{dynamic, g\})\}.$

It contains every possible combination of arguments from the product DFTA states that intersect with $\{g\}$.

In this case, any non-empty subset $S'_\star$ of $S_\star$ also satisfies $S_1 = \{p(\bar{d}_1 \cap Q_1, \ldots, \bar{d}_n \cap Q_1) \mid p(\bar{d}_1, \ldots, \bar{d}_n) \in S'_\star\}$.

3.3   Transformation from One Type Domain to Another

Now we can summarise the general method for representing an element of a domain based on regular types in another domain based on different types.

Proposition 1. *Suppose J_1 and J_2 are two DFTAs (i.e. pre-interpretations) obtained from FTAs $\langle Q_1, \Sigma, \Delta_1 \rangle$ and $\langle Q_2, \Sigma, \Delta_2 \rangle$ respectively. Let $J_\star$ be the DFTA of the union $\langle Q_1 \cup Q_2, \Sigma, \Delta_1 \cup \Delta_2 \rangle$.*

Given $S_1 \in 2^{\mathsf{Atom}_{J_1}}$, let $S_\star \in 2^{\mathsf{Atom}_{J_\star}}$ satisfy $\gamma_1(S_1) = \gamma_\star(S_\star)$. Property 3 shows that this exists (though we did not yet show an explicit procedure for computing it). Then let $S_2 = \{p(\bar{d}_1 \cap Q_2, \ldots, \bar{d}_n \cap Q_2) \mid p(\bar{d}_1, \ldots, \bar{d}_n) \in S_\star\}$. Then $S_2 = \alpha_2(\gamma_1(S_1))$, that is, S_2 is the best representative of S_1 in $2^{\mathsf{Atom}_{J_2}}$.

Proof. $S_2 = \cap\{S'_1 \mid \gamma_\star(S_\star) \subseteq \gamma_2(S'_1)\}$ by Lemma 1. But since we know that $\gamma_1(S_1) = \gamma_\star(S_\star)$ we can write $S_2 = \cap\{S'_1 \mid \gamma_1(S_1) \subseteq \gamma_2(S'_1)\}$. This is equivalent to $S_2 = \alpha_2(\gamma_1(S_1))$ (see Section 2).

4   Construction of a Standard Abstract Domain from the CiaoPP Assertion Language

As already mentioned, a set of assertions in the CiaoPP assertion language about success of a predicate p/n can be interpreted as a set of abstract atoms of form

$p(d_1, \ldots, d_n)$ where $d_1, \ldots, d_n$ are the names of regular types defined within the CiaoPP system. Such a description is called an *abstract success set*. Note that the CiaoPP system itself does not present all such values d_i as regular types. There are modes and primitive types as well; however, as shown below, in the context of a particular program and signature we are able to interpret all of these concepts as regular types defined by a finite set of rules. A discussion of the use of regular types to represent modes is contained in previous work [3, 8].

Having expressed all the abstract values d_i as regular types, we will apply the determinization algorithm on the regular types to obtain an abstract domain, as summarised in Section 3. This will be called the *standard domain* for a program.

Example 6. The abstract success sets for some built-in predicates, as contained in the standard assertion database of CiaoPP, is shown in the following table.

$atom\_concat/2$	$\{atom\_concat(atm, atm, atm)\}$
$write/2$	$\{write(stream, term)\}$
$length/2$	$\{length(list, int)\}$
$is/2$	$\{is(num, arithexpression)\}$

Here, *atm*, *int* and *num* are primitive types; *stream*, *list* and *arithexpr* are defined by means of regular type rules, and *term* denotes the set of all terms. The rules defining *stream*, for example, are as follows:

$$user\_input \rightarrow stream \qquad user\_output \rightarrow stream$$
$$user\_error \rightarrow stream \qquad user \rightarrow stream$$
$$'\$stream'(int, int) \rightarrow stream$$

We will now show how all such descriptions, including primitive types and those such as *term* can be defined as regular types, in the context of a given program.

4.1 Construction of the Standard FTA

Given a program P, we construct the standard abstract domain. It is based on a finite tree automaton $\langle Q_{std}, \Sigma_{std}, \Delta_{std} \rangle$. We now show how each of these components is made up.

The standard types Q_{std}. The states Q_{std} consist of the following components: (1) a set of *defined system types* Q_s, defined by rule Δ_s; (2) a set of *primitive types* Q_{prim}; (3) a set of *contextual types* Q_{cntxt}.

The defined system types Q_s comprise types that are defined by regular type rules in the CiaoPP assertion language. Example include *arithexpr* and *list* as shown in Example 6, which are used in many predicates, and also *keylist*, *lock_mode*, *io_mode*, *stream* and *stream_alias* which concern only one or two library predicates. The primitive types Q_{prim} include *num*, *int*, *flt*, *nnegint* and *atm* which implicitly are defined as infinite (or very large) sets of constants, but are in practice defined by means of a characteristic predicate that is true or false for each constant. The descriptors *gnd*, *nonvar*, *var*, *term* and *struct* are called contextual types since their definition depends on the particular signature. In CiaoPP these are also handled by means of a characteristic predicate, but unlike primitive types they may be true for non-constants. We define the set of standard types $Q_{std} = Q_s \cup Q_{prim} \cup Q_{cntxt}$.

The global signature of a program Σ_{std}. We now construct Σ_{std}, the global signature, which consists of the following components: (1) the *program signature* Σ_P; (2) the *system signature* Σ_s; (3) the *primitive signature* Σ_{prim}. Note that, unlike Q_{std}, the global signature is dependent on the program to be analysed as well as the standard system functions and constants.

Given a program P to be analysed let Σ_P be the set of function symbols occurring in P and let Σ_s be the set of function symbols occurring in Δ_s, the rules defining Q_s. The *primitive signature* Σ_{prim} is a set of constant symbols that contains sufficient constants to distinguish each of the primitive types Q_{prim}. More precisely, for each non-empty subset $D = \{d_1, \ldots, d_k\}$ of Q_{prim}, let Σ_D be the set of constants that are of type d_i for all $d_i \in D$, and are not of any other type. Then Σ_{prim} contains at least one constant from each non-empty set Σ_D. We also insist that Σ_{prim} is disjoint from $\Sigma_P \cup \Sigma_s$. A typical set of constants in Σ_{prim} is $\{0, 1, 1.0, -1, '\$CONST'\}$. Thus for instance, we know that the set *nnegint* $\subset$ *int*; therefore Σ_{prim} should contain at least one constant that is in both *int* and *nnegint* (e.g. 1) and one which is in *int* but not in *nnegint* (e.g. -1). However, note that if P happens to contain the constants 1 or -1 we must pick another member of *int* $\cap$ *nnegint* instead of 1 or another member of *int* $\setminus$ *nnegint* to replace -1.

We define the global signature $\Sigma_{std} = \Sigma_P \cup \Sigma_s \cup \Sigma_{prim} \cup \{'\$VAR'\}$ where $'\$VAR'$ is a constant that does not appear in any other component of Σ_{std}. We will discuss the role of $'\$VAR'$ when constructing the contextual type rules.

The global type rules Δ_{std}. The set of type rules defining the types Q_{std} over the signature Σ_{std} consists of the following components: (1) the *system type rules* Δ_s; (2) the *primitive rules* Δ_{prim}; (3) the *contextual type rules* Δ_{cntxt}.

The system type rules Δ_s are simply extracted from the CiaoPP system. For the primitive rules we assume that the Prolog system provides some built-in predicate for testing whether a given constant is of a given primitive type. Hence given the signature Σ_{std} we can enumerate the set of rules Δ_{prim} of the form $c \to d$ where $c \in \Sigma_{std} \setminus \{'\$VAR'\}$ is a constant, $d \in Q_{prim}$ and c is of type d.

The types in Q_{cntxt} are those whose definitions depend on the signature, such as *gnd*. Given the global signature Σ_{std}, then Δ_{cntxt} is a set of rules defining each type in Q_{cntxt} in terms of Σ_{std}. The details of the rules for *gnd*, *nonvar*, *var*, *term* and *struct* are as follows.

- $f(gnd, \ldots, gnd) \to gnd$, for each n-ary function $f \in \Sigma_{std} \setminus \{'\$VAR'\}$;
- $f(term, \ldots, term) \to nonvar$, for each n-ary function $f \in \Sigma_{std} \setminus \{'\$VAR'\}$;
- $f(term, \ldots, term) \to term$, for each n-ary function $f \in \Sigma_{std}$;
- $f(term, \ldots, term) \to struct$, for each n-ary function $(n > 0)$ $f \in \Sigma_{std} \setminus \{'\$VAR'\}$;
- the single rule $'\$VAR' \to var$.

Note the role of $'\$VAR'$; it is a constant that appears in the type *term* and *var* but no other type. The idea is to distinguish the general type *term* from other types (such as *gnd*), by including a constant $'\$VAR'$ that no other type contains, apart from *var*, which only contains $'\$VAR'$. Thus a predicate argument that is specified as *term* can contain any term (since $L(term) \supset L(d)$ for all d) including terms that are of no other type. This technique has been used to model the presence of variables in previous work applying pre-interpretations for program analysis [9–11].

Determinization of the Standard FTA. Having constructed the finite tree automaton $\langle Q_{std}, \Sigma_{std}, \Delta_{std} \rangle$ we can build a pre-interpretation and hence an abstract domain, called the *standard domain*, as described in Section 3. In the DFTA obtained by determinizing $\langle Q_{std}, \Sigma_{std}, \Delta_{std} \rangle$ the states are elements of $2^{Q_{std}}$. In the worst case, the set of states would be $2^{|Q_{std}|} - 1$, but it turns out to be much less. The number of DFTA states is in fact 37, almost the same as the size of Q_{std}. We can produce a compact representation for Δ_{std}. The number of transitions in the DFTA, if represented explicitly, would be very large (24,239) but we use a compact representation as discussed in [12]. The determinization procedure takes approximately 0.6 seconds. In fact the conversion procedure does not use the DFTA rules, but relies only on the set of states of the DFTA, thanks to the use of the representation of states as elements of $2^{Q_{std}}$.

Representation of Abstract Success Sets in the Standard Domain. An abstract success set obtained from the `CiaoPP` assertion database, such as those shown in Example 6, can be represented as an element of the standard domain. Let M^p be the abstract success set of some predicate p. Let Q_{std} be the set of states in the standard DFTA. Then the representation of M^p in the standard domain is

$$M^p_{std} = \{p(d'_1, \ldots, d'_n) \mid p(d_1, \ldots, d_n) \in M^p$$
$$\wedge \ \forall i : 1 \leq i \leq n : d'_i \in \mathsf{dettypes}(d_i, Q_{std})\}.$$

M^p_{std} is an exact representation of M^p as formalised by the following property.

Property 4. Let γ be the concretisation function in the standard domain. Then $\gamma(M^p_{std}) = \{p(t_1, \ldots, t_n) \mid p(d_1, \ldots, d_n) \in M^p, t_i \in L(d_i), 0 \leq i \leq n\}$. Here $L(d_i)$ refers to the set of terms accepted by d_i in the standard FTA. The property follows from the definition of $\mathsf{dettypes}$.

5   The User Domain and the Construction of the Product Domain

Now we turn to the question of converting the descriptions of predicates given with respect to the states of the standard FTA into descriptions in terms of some other, user-supplied FTA. Let $\langle Q_u, \Sigma_u, \Delta_u \rangle$ be an FTA given by the user. We assume that $\Sigma_u \subseteq \Sigma_{std}$. (This is no loss of generality since the program P can always to modified to contain more function symbols without affecting its intended behaviour, e.g. by adding a dummy clause containing the required function symbols.) Therefore we consider the FTA with the full signature $\langle Q_u, \Sigma_{std}, \Delta_u' \rangle$. Q_u also contains the contextually defined type *dynamic* and possibly other contextual types; Δ_u' is obtained from Δ_u by extending the definitions of those contextual types for the full signature Σ_{std}. We also assume that if a type appears both in Q_u and Q_{std} then it has the same meaning in both.

The intention is to analyse the given program P with respect to the pre-interpretation obtained by determinizing the user-supplied FTA. The *user domain* for analysis is based on the DFTA obtained from $\langle Q_u, \Sigma_{std}, \Delta_u' \rangle$ as described in Section 3.

We construct an FTA combining the standard FTA with the user-supplied FTA $\langle Q_u, \Sigma_{std}, \Delta_u' \rangle$. The *union FTA* $\langle Q_{std} \cup Q_u, \Sigma_{std}, \Delta_u' \cup \Delta_{std} \rangle$ is determinized, and the *product abstract domain* is the abstract domain obtained from the resulting DFTA.

5.1   Converting Abstract Success Sets to the User Domain

As already discussed, we are supplied with an abstract success set of each of the external predicates p/n in P, as a set of atoms of form $p(d_1, \ldots, d_n)$ where $d_1, \ldots, d_n \in Q_{std}$. (We can safely assume a default abstraction where all arguments are of type *term*, if no abstraction is defined).

Representing an abstract success set in the product domain. Let p/n be a predicate and let its abstraction over Q_{std} be M^p. Let Q be the set of states in the product DFTA that is obtained from the standard FTA and some user FTA. Then the corresponding abstract success set, defined over the set of determinized types $Q_\star$, is defined as

$$M_\star^p = \{p(d_1', \ldots, d_n') \mid p(d_1, \ldots, d_n) \in M^p \\ \wedge \forall i : 1 \leq i \leq n : d_i' \in \mathsf{dettypes}(d_i, Q_\star)\}.$$

Property 5. Let γ be the concretisation function in the product domain. Then $\gamma(M_\star^p) = \{p(t_1, \ldots, t_n) \mid p(d_1, \ldots, d_n) \in M^p, t_i \in L(d_i), 0 \leq i \leq n\}$. Here $L(d_i)$ refers to the set of terms accepted by d_i in the standard FTA. As for Property 4 this shows that an abstract model has an exact representation in the product domain.

Example 7. Let the given abstract success set of $length/2$ be $\{length(list, int)\}$. Let the user FTA be the following definitions of the types *matrix* and *row* along with the rules $f(dynamic, \ldots, dynamic) \to dynamic$ for each $f/n \in \Sigma_{std}$.

$$[] \to row \qquad [] \to matrix$$
$$[dynamic|row] \to row \qquad [row|matrix] \to matrix$$

Then the abstract success set in the product domain includes 32 abstract atoms. An example of an atom in the set is

$length(\ \{callable, list, struct, term, dynamic, row, sourcename, struct, term\},$
$\qquad \{arithexpression, callable, character\_code, constant, gnd, int, nnegint,$
$\qquad num, struct, term, dynamic, sourcename, atom\_or\_number\})$

The first argument represents one of the disjoint types that make up the type *list* in the product DFTA, and similarly the second argument is a part of the *int* type.

Projecting a model onto user types. The final stage is to project the model from the product domain onto the user domain. Let $p \in E_P$ be an external predicate and let $M_\star^p$ be the model of p over the determinized types T'. Then the projection of $M_\star^p$ onto the user types Q_u is defined as $M_u^p = \{p(d_1' \cap Q_u, \ldots, d_n' \cap Q_u) \mid p(d_1', \ldots, d_n') \in M_\star^p\}$, Note that we can ensure that each argument $d_1' \cap Q_u$ is non-empty by including *dynamic* in Q_u.

Example 8. Let $M_\star^{length}$ be the model of *length* in the product domain as in the previous example. Let $Q_u = \{matrix, row, dynamic\}$. Then the projection of $M_\star^{length}$ onto Q_u is

$$\{length(\{row, dynamic\}, \{dynamic\}),$$
$$length(\{matrix, row, dynamic\}, \{dynamic\})\}$$

The projected model is not expressed directly in the set of user types Q_u but rather in the disjoint types resulting from determinizing Q_u. The model expressed in this form is exactly what is required for computing a model of the program P over the user types, using the approach in [3].

The projected models are safe approximations of the models over the standard types, and are the best available approximations in the user domain.

Proposition 2. *Let P be a program and let p be an externally defined predicate occurring in P. Let M^p be an abstraction of the success set of p over the standard types Q_{std} and let M_{std}^p be the exact representation of M^p in the standard domain. Let M_u^p be the projection onto the user types Q_u. Then $M_u^p = \alpha_u(\gamma_{std}(M_{std}^p))$, which is the best available safe approximation of M_{std}^p in the user domain.*

Proof. This is a direct consequence of Proposition 1 and Property 5.

6   Implementation and Experiments

We have implemented the procedure in Ciao-Prolog and used it to compute built-in tables for a range of built-ins over simple domains, such as the POS domain and the default domain used with the binding time analysis tool for the LOGEN system [8].

Note that the results obtained are not always the best possible for a given domain. This is due to two main causes. Firstly, the assertion database of CiaoPP is not yet complete. Secondly, even where values have been entered they do not always capture dependencies between arguments. For example, for the list append

Table 1. Standard Abstract Models

Predicate	Standard model
is/2	is(num,arithexpression)
number/1	number(num)
member/2	member(term,struct)
length/2	length(list,int),
=../2	=..(term,list)
write/1	write(stream,term)
atom_concat/3	atom_concat(atm,atm,atm)

predicate $app/3$ the given abstraction might be $\{app(list, list, list)\}$. Since a *list* can be either ground or non-ground, we cannot derive an accurate description of *app* over the Pos domain from the given information. The optimal result would be $\{app(g, g, g), app(g, nong, nong), app(nong, g, nong), app(nong, nong, nong)\}$, but our procedure will return the most general model having all eight possible combinations of g, *nong* arguments.

We show in Table 1 the abstract models of certain predicates extracted from the CiaoPP database. Table 2 shows the derived models over the FTA defining the types *dynamic* and *static* (which denote the same as *gnd* and *term* in the standard models, but are the names used in the binding time analysis of LOGEN). The DFTA has two states $\{\{dynamic, static\}, \{dynamic\}\}$ denoting ground and non-ground terms respectively. An underscore stands for either state. This domain is equivalent to Pos [13] but the models derived in Table 2 are not the best possible within the domain, though they are optimal with respect to the given standard models. Table 3 shows the derived models over the FTA defining the types *dynamic* and *var*. The corresponding DFTA contains states $\{\{dynamic, var\}, \{dynamic\}\}$ denoting variable and non-variable terms respectively.

Regarding performance and scalability, we remark that so far we handle the full set of types from the CiaoPP database without problems, using a Prolog implementation. The conversion is performed off-line, not during analysis, so

Table 2. Models over {dynamic,static} (*ground*) and {dynamic} (*non-ground*)

Predicate	Abstract model for types $\{dynamic, static\}$
is/2	is({dynamic,static},{dynamic,static})
number/1	number({dynamic,static})
member/2	member(_,_)
length/2	length({dynamic},{dynamic,static}) length({dynamic,static},{dynamic,static})
=../2	=..(_,_)
write/1	write({dynamic,static},{dynamic}) write({dynamic,static},{dynamic,static})
atom_concat/3	atom_concat({dynamic,static},{dynamic,static},{dynamic,static})

Table 3. Models over {dynamic,var} (*var*) and {dynamic} (*non-var*)

Predicate	Abstract model for types {*dynamic, var*}
is/2	is({dynamic},{dynamic})
number/1	number({dynamic})
member/2	member(_,{dynamic}),
length/2	length({dynamic},{dynamic})
=../2	=..(_,{dynamic})
write/1	write({dynamic},{dynamic,var})
	write({dynamic},{dynamic})
atom_concat/3	atom_concat({dynamic},{dynamic},{dynamic})

absolute time is not critical. However, so far the target user domains have been small. The efficient determinization algorithm described in [12] performs well and we do not anticipate problems moving to larger domains. Scalability issues do arise in representing the models themselves, in domains based on DFTAs with a large number of states. Compact representations of relations using techniques such as BDDs [14, 15] seem to be promising approaches to this problem, and we have already made use of BDDs in handling DFTAs [12].

7   Conclusions and Future Work

We have described a method for translating abstract descriptions of success sets of predicates from a general purpose assertion language, the CiaoPP assertion language, into any regular type-based abstract domain. Current work is directed towards automatic translation of the assertions for all standard library predicates into commonly used domains. Effort also needs to be put into completing and making more precise the existing assertions on predicates. We have described the method applied to success set descriptions, but the method applies to call patterns, or backwards analyses, provided that the abstract domain is based on regular types.

We believe that this work also underlines the generality and versatility of regular types for constructing analysis domains. The fact that special purpose, program specific domains can be constructed easily makes it all the more relevant to be able to render information about imported code in such domains, as this work does. Future work will continue to explore the potential of regular type domains and combine them with other domains such as numeric domains.

Acknowledgements. We thank Patrick Cousot for some enlightening remarks, and the LOPSTR referees for useful comments on the extended abstract. This work was funded in part by the Information Society Technologies programme of the European Commission, Future and Emerging Technologies under the FP5 IST-2001-38059 *ASAP* and FP6 IST-15905 *MOBIUS* projects and by the Spanish Ministry of Science and Education under the TIC 2002-0055 *CUBICO* project. J. Gallagher's research is supported in part by the IT-University of Copenhagen.

References

1. Cousot, P., Cousot, R.: Systematic design of program analysis frameworks. In: ACM SIGPLAN-SIGACT Symposium on Principles of Programming Languages, San Antonio,Texas, ACM Press, New York, U.S.A. (1979) 269–282
2. Hermenegildo, M.V., Puebla, G., Bueno, F., López-García, P.: Integrated Program Debugging, Verification, and Optimization Using Abstract Interpretation (and The Ciao System Preprocessor). Science of Computer Programming 58(1–2) (2005)
3. Gallagher, J.P., Henriksen, K.S.: Abstract domains based on regular types. In Lifschitz, V., Demoen, B., eds.: Proceedings of the International Conference on Logic Programming (ICLP'2004). LNCS 3132. (2004) 27–42
4. Filè, G., Giacobazzi, R., Ranzato, F.: A unifying view on abstract domain design. ACM Computing Surveys 28(2) (1996) 333–336
5. Cousot, P., Cousot, R., Feret, J., Mauborgne, L., Miné, A., Monniaux, D., Rival, X.: The ASTREÉ analyzer. In Sagiv, S., ed.: ESOP. LNCS 3444. (2005) 21–30
6. Comon, H., Dauchet, M., Gilleron, R., Jacquemard, F., Lugiez, D., Tison, S., Tommasi, M.: Tree Automata Techniques and Applications. http://www.grappa.univ-lille3.fr/tata (1999)
7. Lloyd, J.: Foundations of Logic Programming: 2nd Edition. Springer-Verlag (1987)
8. Craig, S., Gallagher, J.P., Leuschel, M., Henriksen, K.S.: Fully automatic binding time analysis for Prolog. In Etalle, S., ed.: Pre-Proceedings, 14th International Workshop on Logic-Based Program Synthesis and Transformation, LOPSTR 2004, Verona, August 2004. (2004) 61–70
9. Boulanger, D., Bruynooghe, M., Denecker, M.: Abstracting s-semantics using a model-theoretic approach. In Hermenegildo, M., Penjam, J., eds.: Proc. 6th International Symposium on Programming Language Implementation and Logic Programming, PLILP'94. LNCS 844 (1994) 432–446
10. Boulanger, D., Bruynooghe, M.: A systematic construction of abstract domains. In Le Charlier, B., ed.: Proc. First International Static Analysis Symposium, SAS'94. LNCS 864 (1994) 61–77
11. Gallagher, J.P., Boulanger, D., Sağlam, H.: Practical model-based static analysis for definite logic programs. In Lloyd, J.W., ed.: Proc. of International Logic Programming Symposium, MIT Press (1995) 351–365
12. Gallagher, J.P., Henriksen, K.S., Banda, G.: Techniques for scaling up analyses based on pre-interpretations. In Gabbrielli, M., Gupta, G., eds.: Proceedings of the 21st International Conference on Logic Programming, ICLP'2005. LNCS 3668 (2005). 280–296
13. Marriott, K., Søndergaard, H.: Precise and efficient groundness analysis for logic programs. LOPLAS 2(1-4) (1993) 181–196
14. Iwaihara, M., Inoue, Y.: Bottom-up evaluation of logic programs using binary decision diagrams. In Yu, P.S., Chen, A.L.P., eds.: ICDE, IEEE Computer Society (1995) 467–474
15. Whaley, J., Lam, M.S.: Cloning-based context-sensitive pointer alias analysis using binary decision diagrams. In Pugh, W., Chambers, C., eds.: PLDI, ACM (2004) 131–144

Experiments in Context-Sensitive Analysis of Modular Programs

Jesús Correas[1], Germán Puebla[2],
Manuel V. Hermenegildo[2,3], and Francisco Bueno[2]

[1] School of Computer Science,
Complutense University of Madrid (UCM)
[2] School of Computer Science,
Technical University of Madrid (UPM)
[3] Depts. of Computer Science and Electrical and Computer Engineering,
University of New Mexico (UNM)
jcorreas@fdi.ucm.es
{german, herme, bueno}@fi.upm.es

Abstract. Several models for context-sensitive analysis of modular programs have been proposed, each with different characteristics and representing different trade-offs. The advantage of these context-sensitive analyses is that they provide information which is potentially more accurate than that provided by context-free analyses. Such information can then be applied to validating/debugging the program and/or to specializing the program in order to obtain important performance improvements. Some very preliminary experimental results have also been reported for some of these models, providing some initial evidence on their potential. However, further experimentation, needed in order to understand the many issues left open and to show that the proposed modes scale and are usable in the context of large, real-life modular programs, was left as future work. The aim of this paper is twofold. On one hand we provide an empirical comparison of the different models proposed in previous work, as well as experimental data on the different choices left open in those designs. On the other hand we explore the scalability of these models by using larger modular programs as benchmarks. The results have been obtained from a realistic implementation of the models, integrated in a production-quality compiler (CiaoPP/Ciao). Our experimental results shed light on the practical implications of the different design choices and of the models themselves. We also show that context-sensitive analysis of modular programs is indeed feasible in practice, and that in certain critical cases it provides better performance results than those achievable by analyzing the whole program at once. This is specially the case regarding memory consumption and when reanalyzing after making changes to a program, as is often the case during program development.

1   Introduction and Motivation

Global analysis of logic programs has received considerable theoretical and practical attention, and as a result it is now possible to infer a wide range of program

P.M. Hill (Ed.): LOPSTR 2005, LNCS 3901, pp. 163–178, 2006.
© Springer-Verlag Berlin Heidelberg 2006

properties with a considerable degree of accuracy and for a significant number of programs. Also, tools have been developed which in addition to inferring these properties, allow debugging, validating, and specializing programs, achieving important improvements in both correctness and efficiency. However, most of these techniques were originally designed to be applied to a complete, monolithic program. In contrast, real programs invariably have a more complex structure combining a number of user modules with other modules from system libraries. This is one of the reasons why most global analysis tools are still prototypes and, though numerous experiments demonstrate their effectiveness, they have not yet made their way into existing real-life programming systems.

Performing global analysis on modular programs differs from doing so in a monolithic setting in several interesting ways and poses non-trivial problems which must be solved (see, for example, [6] and its references where the main approaches to separate modular static analysis by abstract interpretation are described). Regarding the analysis of modular logic programs, a preliminary study of the extension of context-sensitive analysis and specialization to the case of modular logic programs was presented in [14]. A full practical proposal for context-sensitive analysis of modular logic programs was presented in [4]. In fact, in [4] a collection of models was proposed, each of them with different characteristics and representing different trade-offs. Some very preliminary experimental data was also reported for an implementation of some of these models in the context of the Ciao system. Also, another implementation of [4] in the context of the HAL system [8] was reported in [11]. These early experimental results provided initial evidence on the overall potential of the approach, but were limited in that they studied only a partial implementation. It was left as future work to perform further experimentation in order to understand the many issues and trade-offs left open in the design, and to study whether the proposed models scale and are usable in the context of large, real-life modular programs.

The aim of this paper is twofold. On one hand we provide an empirical comparison of the different models proposed in [4], as well as experimental data on the different choices left open in those designs. To this end we have completed a full implementation in CiaoPP [9] (the preprocessor of the Ciao system [2]) of the framework for context-sensitive analysis described in [13] and its different instances, and we have studied experimentally the behavior of the resulting system. These results have been compared with traditional, non modular analyses in terms of time and memory consumption.

Our second aim is to explore the scalability of these models and of the implementation. To this end we have used some larger modular programs as benchmarks, including some real-life examples such as a working partial evaluator and parts of the Ciao compiler.

In the following section we present an overview of the general problems in analyzing large modular programs, and the solutions proposed in previous work, including the major design trade-offs. Section 3 then describes the tests performed and analyzes the results obtained. Finally, Section 4 presents our conclusions.

2   Analysis of Modular Programs

As mentioned in the previous section, the framework used herein is based on [13, 14], where a detailed description of the issues related to the analysis of modular programs and the different approaches to it can be found. The following subsections present an overall summary of [13], with special emphasis on the issues that are most relevant to our experimental study.

2.1   Modular Programs

A program is said to be modular when its source code is distributed in several source units named modules, and they contain language constructs to clearly define the interface of every module with the rest of the modules in the program. This interface is composed of two sets of predicates: the set of exported predicates (those accessible from other modules), and the set of imported predicates. For concreteness, and because of its appropriateness for global analysis, in our implementation we will use the module system of [5]. This module system is *strict* in the sense that procedures external to a module are visible to it only if they are part of its *interface*. A predicate defined in a given module can be called from another module only if it appears in the exported list of its module and in the imported list of the caller module, i.e., procedures which are not exported are not visible outside the module in which they are defined.

We note the distinction between *global* tasks and *local* tasks. In global tasks the results of processing a part of the program (say, a procedure or a module) may be needed in order to process other parts of the program. In contrast, a local task processes only one procedure or module at a time and, most importantly, all the information required for performing the task can be obtained by inspecting that procedure or module. The fundamental issue is that global processing often requires iterating on the whole program until a fixed point is reached.

Context-sensitive program analysis is an example of a *global* task: in a modular setting, it may well be the case that part of the information needed to perform the analysis on (a procedure in) module m has to be computed in modules other than m. We will refer to the information originated in modules different from m as *inter-modular* information in contrast to the information originated in m itself, which we will call *intra-modular*.

2.2   Flattening a Program Unit vs. Modular Processing

Applying a framework for non-modular programs to a module m which belongs to a modular program has the difficulty that m may not be self-contained. However, there should be no problem in applying the framework if m is a leaf module. Furthermore, given a global process such as program analysis it is not obvious that it makes sense to apply the process to a module m alone. In fact, it could make more sense, at least in principle, to apply analysis to the complete program instead, which would be then self-contained.

Given a modular program P it is always possible to build a single module m_{flat} which is equivalent to P and which is a leaf. The process of constructing such a module m_{flat} usually only amounts to renaming apart identifiers in the different modules in P so as to avoid name clashes. We will use $flatten(P) = m_{flat}$ to denote that the module m_{flat} is the result of renaming apart the code in each module in P and concatenating its code into a monolithic module m_{flat}. This points to a simple solution to the problem of processing modular programs (at least for the case in which all the code is available): to transform P into the equivalent monolithic program m_{flat}. It is then straightforward to apply any tool for non-modular programs to the leaf module m_{flat}. In the rest of this work, we will refer to this approach as the *flattened* or *monolithic* approach.

Assuming the existence of an implementation for non-modular analysis, this approach to analyzing modular programs is often simple to apply. Also, the flattening approach has theoretical interest: in our case it will be used as a base case in order to compare to it the efficiency of the different approaches to modular handling of programs that will be studied. However, as a practical way of actually performing analysis of large programs the flattening approach also has important potential drawbacks. The most obvious one is that the complete program must be loaded into the analyzer, and thus large programs may make the analyzer run out of memory. Moreover, as the internal analysis data structures include information for all the program source code, in the monolithic case analysis of a given procedure may take more time than when keeping in memory only the module in which such procedure resides. Another, perhaps more important drawback is that the program must be self-contained: this can be a problem if the analyzer is used while developing the program, when some modules are not yet implemented, or if there are calls to external procedures, i.e., procedures for which the source code is not available, or which are implemented in other languages.[1]

2.3 Analyzing One Module at a Time

The approach taken in [13] and implemented in CiaoPP is based on the separate analysis of the modules in a modular program. The analyzer is invoked (possibly several times) for each module in the program, in order to obtain the analysis results needed by the analysis of other program modules. We denote the process of obtaining the answer value AP of any predicate P for a call CP as: $P : CP \mapsto AP$. The analysis results obtained for the exported predicates of every module are stored in a *Global Answer Table* (GAT).

Analyzing a module separately presents the difficulty that, from the point of view of analysis, the code to be analyzed is *incomplete* in the sense that the code for procedures imported from other modules is not available to analysis. More precisely, during the analysis of a module m there may be calls $P : CP$ such that the procedure P is not defined in m but instead it is imported from another module m'. We refer to determining the answer value of P, AP ($P : CP \mapsto AP$) as the *imported success problem*. In addition, in order to obtain analysis information

---

[1] However, several approaches have been proposed for the analysis of incomplete programs (*open programs*), for example [1, 3].

for m' which is as accurate as possible we need to somehow propagate the call $P : CP$ from m to m' so that the next time m' is analyzed such a call pattern is taken into account. We refer to this as the *imported calls problem*.

Solving the Imported Success Problem. The imported success problem is solved by means of a *success policy*, or SP for short. The behavior of the analyzer for predicates defined in m remains exactly as before. SP is needed because given a call pattern $P : CP$ it will often be the case that no entry of exactly the form $P : CP \mapsto AP$ exists in the analysis results stored in the GAT for m'. In such case, the information already present may be of value in order to obtain a (temporary) answer pattern AP, and continue the analysis of module m.

In contrast, in many formalizations of non-modular analysis there is no explicit success policy. This is because if the call pattern $P : CP$ has not been analyzed yet, the analysis algorithm forces its computation. Thus, the results of analysis do not depend on any particular success policy: when the analyzer reaches a fixed-point there is always an entry of the form $P : CP \mapsto AP$ for any call pattern $P : CP$ which appears in the analysis graph. However, in a modular setting it is often convenient to delay the analysis of predicates defined in other modules until those modules are revisited. In general, those modules may have already been analyzed or they may be analyzed in the future. We will simply do the best possible given the information available in the GAT.

Several success policies can be defined which provide over- or under-approximations of the exact answer pattern $AP^=$ with different degree of accuracy. Note that this exact value $AP^=$ is the one which the flattening approach (that we will thus denote $SP^=$) would compute. In this work we consider two kinds of success policies, those which are guaranteed to always provide over-approximations, i.e. $AP^= \sqsubseteq SP(P : CP, GAT)$, and those which provide under-approximations, i.e., $SP(P : CP, GAT) \sqsubseteq AP^=$. We will use the superscript $^+$ (resp. $^-$) to indicate that a success policy over-approximates (resp. under-approximates).

In the experiments shown in this work, a quite precise over-approximating success policy has been used, already proposed in [14] and defined as:

$$SP^+_{All}(P : CP, GAT) = topmost(CP) \sqcap_{AP' \in app} AP' \text{ where}$$
$$app = \{AP' \mid (P : CP' \mapsto AP') \in GAT \text{ and } CP \sqsubseteq CP'\}$$

The function *topmost* obtains the topmost answer pattern for a call pattern. The notion of *topmost description* was already introduced in [3]. Informally, a topmost description preserves the information on properties which are *downwards closed* whereas it loses information for those which are not. Note that taking $\top$ as answer pattern is also a correct over-approximation, but often less accurate than using topmost substitutions. For example, if a variable is known to be ground in the call pattern, it will continue being ground in the answer pattern and taking $\top$ as the answer pattern would lose this information. However, the fact that a variable is free on call does not guarantee that it will keep on being free on success.

We refer to this success policy as SP_{all}^+ because it uses *all* entries in GAT which are *applicable* to the call pattern in the sense that the call pattern already computed is more general than the call being analyzed.

The counter-part of SP_{all}^+ is the function SP_{all}^- which is defined as:

$$SP_{All}^-(P : CP, GAT) = \sqcup_{AP' \in app} AP' \text{ where}$$
$$app = \{AP' \mid (P : CP' \mapsto AP') \in GAT \text{ and } CP' \sqsubseteq CP\}$$

Note the change in the direction of the applicability relation (the call pattern in the GAT has to be more particular than the one being analyzed) and the use of the lub operator instead of the glb. Also, note that taking, for example, $\bot$ as an under-approximation is correct but SP_{all}^- is more precise.

As shown in [13] using SP^+ policies has the advantage that at any point during the modular analysis, even when a fixpoint has not been reached yet, the information obtained for each module is always a correct over-approximation. The drawback is that when the fixpoint is reached it may not be minimal, i.e., information is not as precise as it could be. In contrast, SP^- policies obtain the least fixpoint (most precise information) but only produce correct results when the fixpoint it reached. SP^+ policies can be useful during program development.

Solving the Imported Calls Problem. As the analysis is context-sensitive, the call patterns for imported predicates are only known after the calling module is analyzed, but they cannot be processed until the imported module is selected for (re)analysis. These call patterns are therefore stored in another global data structure, the *temporary answer table* (TAT for short).[2] When the imported module is scheduled for (re)analysis, all call patterns in the TAT are used as input for the analyzer.

2.4 Computing an Intermodular Fixed Point

The intermodular fixed-point algorithm of CiaoPP takes one module of the program that needs (re)analysis, analyzes it storing the relevant information in GAT and TAT tables, and looks for another module which needs reanalysis. When a module is analyzed, it updates the entries in the global tables, and marks the modules which import it if the analysis results may improve the results of those modules. An intermodular fixed point has been reached when there are no modules which need reanalysis.

Determining the optimal order in which the different modules in the program unit should be analyzed in order to get to a fixed-point as efficiently as possible is not trivial. Finding good scheduling strategies for intra-modular analysis is a topic which has received considerable attention and highly optimized algorithms exist which converge to a fixed-point quickly. Unfortunately, it is not possible to

---

[2] In fact, GAT and TAT are implemented using the same table, and TAT entries are marked as needing reanalysis, in order to provide more precise results than those obtained applying the success policy, as soon as the module is scheduled for (re)analysis. There are more details in Section 2.4 and [13].

directly translate the same heuristics used in the intra-modular case to the inter-modular case. In the inter-modular case we have to take into account the time required to change from analysis of one module to another since this typically means reading a new module from disk. Thus, requests to process call patterns have to be grouped by modules in order to reduce the number of times we change context.

In the current implementation two simple strategies have been used which allow studying the behavior of the analysis of modular programs in two clearly different situations. Both strategies take the list of modules in a given order (a top-down and a bottom-up traversal of the intermodule dependency graph, respectively),[3] and traverse the list analyzing the modules which have pending call patterns, updating the corresponding global tables with the analysis results. This process is repeated until there are no pending call patterns for any module in the program.

We will refer to this intermodular fixed-point algorithm, which schedules one module at a time for analysis as the *modular approach*.

3   Empirical Results

As mentioned in Section 1, the framework has been fully implemented in CiaoPP. This implementation allows performing both monolithic and modular analysis, and the modular analysis is parametric in several ways. This makes it possible to study the overall behavior of the system for different strategies and policies and thus performing several experiments and comparisons:

Flattened vs. modular. First, the flattened approach of Section 2.2 has been compared to the intermodular fixpoint of Section 2.4. Although it is predictable that the analysis of a program for the first time in a modular, separate analysis fashion will be slower than the flattened approach (due to the overhead in loading/unloading modules, etc.), it is interesting to study by how much. On the other hand, in some cases the analysis of a whole program may be unfeasible due to hardware (memory) limitations, but in the intermodular fixpoint approach this limitation can be overcome.

Intermodular scheduling policies. Another aspect to study is related to the influence of the module selection policy in the efficiency of the analysis. The scheduling policies used have been already described in Section 2.4. We will refer to them as *naive_top_down* and *naive_bottom_up*, respectively.

Success policies. Two success policies have been compared in both scheduling policies: an over-approximating policy, SP_{all}^+, and an under-approximating one, SP_{all}^-, as described in Section 2.3. Although there may be other success policies, we estimate that these ones are the most effective policies, as they bring the closest results to $SP^=$.

Incremental analysis of modular programs. Finally, the analysis of a modular program from scratch using the monolithic approach has been

---

[3] All modules which belong to the same cycle in the graph have been considered at the same depth, and therefore those modules will be selected in any order.

compared to the reanalysis of that program after making specific modifications in the source code. This comparison illustrates the advantages of
analyzing only the module which has changed (and the modules affected by
that change) instead of reanalyzing the whole program from scratch.

Three different kinds of source code modifications have been studied: 1) a
simple change that keeps the same analysis results, 2) a change that results
in the exported predicates producing a more precise answer pattern, and
3) a modification in the source code such that after the change exported
predicates produce more general analysis results.

Note that when there are changes in the source code which do not improve or invalidate previous analysis results, nor generate new call patterns
for imported modules (i.e., case 1 above), using the modular approach is
clearly advantageous (at least theoretically), since it is more incremental
and only one module needs to be analyzed after each change. In contrast,
in the monolithic (non-modular) analysis the whole program must be (re-)
analyzed.

The second kind of change studied represents a change that makes the
analysis results for exported predicates be more precise than the ones obtained before. This is done by removing all clauses of exported predicates of a
module except the first non recursive one.[4] This will bring in general analysis
results which are more specific than the results previously obtained, making them invalid in most cases, and producing the reanalysis of the calling
modules.

The third type of source change corresponds to performing a modification in an exported predicate which results in this predicate providing more
general analysis results. The change consists in the addition of a clause to
all the exported predicates of a module in which all arguments are pairwise
distinct and free variables.[5] This approach generally forces the reanalysis of
the modules which use the changed module. In turn, this may transitively
require reanalysis of other modules until analysis information stabilizes.

In the following subsections the selected benchmark programs are described,
and the results of the tests are studied in detail. Two "modes" domains have been
considered: Def [7], which keeps track of properties (in particular, groundness)
through definite propositional implications and $Sharing$-$freeness$ [10], which
keeps track of information on variable sharing and freeness in a combined way.

3.1   Brief Description of the Benchmarks Used

The central focus of this paper is to study how the intermodular analysis framework of CiaoPP will behave with real-life programs. Therefore, we have striven in

---

[4] Mutually recursive predicates are also considered. If the exported predicate has only
recursive clauses, they are replaced by a fact with all arguments ground.

[5] In the $Sharing - Freeness$ domain this addition might not provide a more general
analysis result, as this kind of clause does not provide a top success substitution.
However, the tests have been performed using the same change also in the case of
$Sharing - Freeness$ to make the tests homogeneous across the different domains.

the selection of benchmark programs to include not only characteristic examples used in the LP analysis literature, but also other programs which are specially difficult to analyze in a modular setting (for example, because there are several mutually recursive predicates which conform intermodular cycles), and real-life programs. A brief description of the selected benchmarks follows:

ann This is the &-Prolog implementation of the MEL annotator (by K. Muthukumar, F. Bueno, M. García de la Banda, and M. Hermenegildo). In this case the code is distributed in 3 modules with no cycles in the intermodular dependency graph.

bid This program computes an opening bid for a bridge hand (by J. Conery). It is composed of 7 modules, with no cycles in the intermodular dependency graph.

boyer The boyer benchmark is a reduced version of the Boyer/Moore theorem prover (by E. Tick). The program has been separated in four modules with a cycle between two modules.

peephole This program is the SB-Prolog peephole optimizer. In this case, the program is split in three modules, but there are two cycles in the intermodular dependency graph, and there are several intermodular cycles at the predicate call level.

prolog_read corresponds to a simplified version of the code used by the Ciao compiler for reading terms. It is composed by three modules, having a cycle between two of them.

unfold_ is a fragment of the CiaoPP preprocessor which contains the partial evaluator. It is distributed in 7 modules with no cycles between them, although many other modules of CiaoPP source code, while not analyzed, are consulted in order to get assertion information.

managing_project is a program used by the authors for EU project management. It is distributed in 8 modules with no intermodular cycles.

check_links is an example program for the *Pillow* HTML/XML/HTTP connectivity package (by D. Cabeza and M. Hermenegildo) that checks that links contained in a given URL address are reachable. The whole Pillow package is analyzed together with the sample program, and it is composed of 6 modules without intermodular cycles.

It should be noted that for all these programs the number of modules indicated above correspond to the user modules of the benchmark. However, they are not the only ones processed: any benchmark is likely to use quite a large number of modules from the system libraries. In particular, in Ciao all builtins are in system libraries. For efficiency, library modules are pre-analyzed for a representative set of call patterns and the analysis results are expressed using the assertion language described in [12]. Instead of analysing library modules over and over again, the analysis algorithm computes success information from such assertions using a SP^+ policy.

The benchmarks have been run on a Dell PowerEdge 4600 with two Pentium processors at 2 Ghz and 4 Gb of memory, and normal workload. Each test has been run twice, reporting the arithmetic mean of these runs.

3.2   Analysis of a Modular Program from Scratch

Table 1 shows the absolute times in milliseconds spent in analyzing the programs using the flattening approach. **Mod** reflects the number of modules comprising each benchmark (excluding system modules). For every benchmark, the total analysis time is divided into several categories, represented by the following columns:

Load This column corresponds to the time spent loading modules into CiaoPP. This time includes the time used for reading the module to be analyzed and the time spent in reading the assertions of the imported modules.

Ana. This is the time spent analyzing the program and applying the success policy for imported predicates together with some preprocessing of the code.

Gen. Corresponds to the task of generating the global information (referred to before as the GAT and TAT tables). The information generated is related to the analysis results of all exported and multifile predicates, new call patterns of imported predicates generated during the analysis of each module, and the modules that import the module and can improve their analysis results by reanalysis.

Total Time elapsed since the analyzer is called until it finishes completely. It is the sum of the previous columns, plus some extra time spent in other tasks, such as the generation of the intermodular dependency graph, handling the list of modules to get the next module to be analyzed, etc.

Table 1. Time spent (in milliseconds) by the monolithic analysis of different benchmark programs

Def					
Bench	**Mod**	**Load**	**Ana.**	**Gen.**	**Total**
ann	3	387	343	170	1151
bid	8	631	35	182	1177
boyer	4	385	161	100	871
peephole	3	350	205	175	907
prolog_read	3	343	279	370	1179
unfold_	7	1622	540	117	2744
managing_project	8	1154	6128	302	8025
check_links	6	1492	3720	365	6002

Sharing-freeness					
Bench	**Mod**	**Load**	**Ana.**	**Gen.**	**Total**
ann	3	387	480	217	1513
bid	8	631	50	192	1400
boyer	4	385	181	102	1098
peephole	3	350	542	305	1643
prolog_read	3	343	3112	633	4490
unfold_	7	1622	521069	286	523692
managing_project	8	1154	781	256	2911
check_links	6	1492	4044	484	6706

Table 2. Geometric overall results for analysis of modular programs from scratch using different global scheduling algorithms and success policies. Numbers relative to the monolithic approach.

Type of test		automatic SP_{all}^{+}				automatic SP_{all}^{-}			
		Load	Ana.	Gen.	Total	Load	Ana.	Gen.	Total
Def	top_down	2.25	1.30	1.44	1.47	3.64	1.60	2.39	2.08
	bot_up	2.26	1.25	1.44	1.45	3.80	1.66	2.47	2.16
Shfr	top_down	2.23	20.51	1.83	11.60	3.85	3.13	2.65	3.51
	bot_up	2.23	20.02	1.68	11.43	3.96	3.14	2.75	3.53

Table 2 gives the summary of the weighted geometric means of the comparative times for all benchmarks for the Def and $Sharing\text{-}freeness$ analysis domains. The numbers in this table are relative to the monolithic case (shown in Table 1), and the number of clauses of each program is used as weight for each benchmark when computing the weighted geometric mean. The $naive\_bottom\_up$ and $naive\_top\_down$ global scheduling policies are compared, as well as the SP_{all}^{-} and SP_{all}^{+} success policies. Table columns have the same meaning as before.

This table shows the overall time spent in the analysis of the different benchmarks without previous analysis information. It is clear that the modular analysis from scratch, in general, is slower than monolithic analysis, as expected. Using Def the intermodular analysis from scratch is only somewhat slower compared to the monolithic analysis, and in particular the analysis time is not much larger than the monolithic time in most cases. However, in simple domains like Def, the analysis time is not the most important fraction of the total time, and therefore other tasks such as module loading or results generation can in fact be more relevant than the analysis itself. On the other hand, more complex domains as $Sharing - freeness$ increase the difference with respect to the monolithic case. It is important to note that using SP_{all}^{+} is clearly not recommended for performing modular analysis from scratch in the $Sharing - freeness$ domain. The result in this case is biased a great deal by the results of the analysis of `managing_project`, in which most predicates have many arguments, resulting in large sharing sets that tend to approximate to $\top$ (which is the powerset of the variables in the clause). However, SP_{all}^{-} produces reasonable results.

On the other hand, when comparing the global scheduling policies, only a slight difference in the time taken using the $naive\_top\_down$ or the $naive\_bottom\_up$ strategies can be observed. This result seems to reflect that the order of the modules is not so relevant when analyzing a modular program as was initially expected.

Memory Consumption when analyzing from scratch. We have also compared the maximum memory required for the analysis in the flattened and the modular approaches to the analysis of modular programs from scratch. Table 3 shows the maximum memory consumption during the analysis of the flattened approach (column **Monolithic**), and the use of memory of the modular approach (using both global scheduling policies described before) relative to the monolithic case (columns SP_{all}^{+} and SP_{all}^{-} for the corresponding success policies). The

Table 3. Overall memory consumption of Non-modular vs. SP^+ and SP^- policies

| | | Global scheduling policy: naive_top_down | | | | | |
| | | Def | | | Sharing-Freeness | | |
Bench	Mod	Monolithic	SP^+	SP^-	Monolithic	SP^+	SP^-
ann	3	2825160	0.69	0.49	4070806	0.54	0.39
bid	8	2201134	0.54	0.54	3241842	0.36	0.36
boyer	4	2405980	0.42	0.42	3495038	0.61	0.35
peephole	3	2390936	0.68	0.68	3761442	0.42	0.43
prolog_read	3	2766260	0.53	0.51	5429194	0.84	0.84
unfold_	7	5775798	0.54	0.54	16168722	0.31	0.37
managing_project	8	5555454	0.32	0.32	6565038	3.65	0.26
check_links	6	10431662	0.70	0.65	18643226	0.83	0.77
Weighted Geom. mean			0.48	0.46		1.12	0.40
		Global scheduling policy: naive_bottom_up					
		Def			Sharing-Freeness		
Bench	Mod	Monolithic	SP^+	SP^-	Monolithic	SP^+	SP^-
ann	3	2825160	0.52	0.49	4070806	0.54	0.39
bid	8	2201134	0.57	0.54	3241842	0.36	0.36
boyer	4	2405980	0.42	0.42	3495038	0.61	0.40
peephole	3	2390936	0.68	0.68	3761442	0.42	0.43
prolog_read	3	2766260	0.53	0.51	5429194	0.84	0.84
unfold_	7	5775798	0.54	0.54	16168722	0.31	0.37
managing_project	8	5555454	0.33	0.33	6565038	3.65	0.28
check_links	6	10431662	0.69	0.66	18643226	0.81	0.78
Weighted Geom. mean			0.47	0.47		1.11	0.41

results show that the modular approach is clearly better in terms of maximum memory consumption than the monolithic approach, except for the outlying result of managing_project for the particular case of the combination SP^+_{all} and $Sharing - freeness$, as mentioned above. However, given a program split into N modules, the memory used for analyzing it in a modular way might be expected to be M/N, where M is the memory required for the monolithic analysis. This is not true because the complexity of the program is in general not evenly distributed among its modules. Since Table 3 shows maximum memory consumption, figures are strongly influenced by the most complex modules.

3.3   Reanalysis of a Modular Program After a Change in the Code

As explained at the beginning of Section 3, we have also studied the incremental cost of reanalysis of a modular program after a change, for different typical changes, as explained above.

In the first case, shown in Table 4, a simple change in a module with no implications in the analysis results of that module has been tested. It has been implemented by "touching" a module, i.e., changing the modification time without actually modifying its contents, in order to force CiaoPP to reanalyze it. As

Table 4. Geometric overall results for reanalysis of modular programs after touching a module, using different global scheduling algorithms and success policies. Numbers relative to the monolithic approach.

Type of test		automatic SP^+_{all}				automatic SP^-_{all}			
		Load	Ana.	Gen.	Total	Load	Ana.	Gen.	Total
Def	top_down	0.68	0.39	0.19	0.44	0.63	0.38	0.19	0.43
	bot_up	0.66	0.41	0.20	0.45	0.65	0.38	0.19	0.43
Shfr	top_down	0.67	0.53	0.26	0.44	0.65	0.40	0.25	0.40
	bot_up	0.65	0.52	0.28	0.43	0.67	0.41	0.26	0.40

Table 5. Geometric overall results for reanalysis of modular programs after removing all clauses of exported predicates of a module except the first non-recursive one, using different global scheduling algorithms and success policies. Numbers relative to the monolithic approach.

Type of test		automatic SP^+_{all}				automatic SP^-_{all}			
		Load	Ana.	Gen.	Total	Load	Ana.	Gen.	Total
Def	top_down	0.97	0.18	0.33	0.45	0.99	0.20	0.33	0.46
	bot_up	0.97	0.18	0.32	0.45	1.00	0.20	0.34	0.46
Shfr	top_down	1.00	0.36	0.41	0.49	0.94	0.26	0.33	0.44
	bot_up	0.97	0.33	0.39	0.47	0.98	0.27	0.33	0.46

before, numbers refer to the geometric overall results, relative to those obtained with the monolithic approach (Table 1). As it is suggested in the results shown in Table 4, the modular analysis is clearly better than the monolithic approach for this kind of change. Obviously, global scheduling and success policies are not relevant, since only the module which has been modified is reanalyzed.

The second case (summarized in Table 5) corresponds to a source code modification in which, as already mentioned, all the clauses of the exported predicates of a given module have been replaced by the first non-recursive clause of the predicate. As in the previous case, different policies do not seem to be very relevant for this change. It is interesting to note that this kind of change is even more efficient than just touching a module: since some part of the code is being removed, the analysis tends to be simplified (specially the recursive clauses, which cause more iterations of the fixed-point computation algorithm).

And, finally, the third case shown in Table 6 is implemented by adding a most general fact to all exported predicates of a given module. Like in the previous case, this kind of change is an extreme situation in which all exported predicates are affected. Even in this case modular analysis is more efficient than the monolithic approach. With respect to the differences between the success policies, the SP^- policy is slightly more efficient in complex domains such as $Sharing - freeness$, although both policies and domains behave incrementally. On the other hand, the bottom-up global scheduling policy produces better results than top-down scheduling.

Table 6. Geometric overall results for reanalysis of modular programs after adding a most general fact to all exported predicates of a module, using different global scheduling algorithms and success policies. Numbers relative to the monolithic approach.

Type of test		automatic SP_{all}^+				automatic SP_{all}^-			
		Load	Ana.	Gen.	Total	Load	Ana.	Gen.	Total
Def	top_down	1.09	0.63	0.43	0.70	1.05	0.59	0.42	0.66
	bot_up	1.02	0.58	0.40	0.64	1.04	0.60	0.43	0.66
Shfr	top_down	1.18	1.00	0.69	0.80	1.27	1.00	0.69	0.86
	bot_up	1.14	0.97	0.67	0.77	1.21	0.98	0.70	0.83

The overall results in Tables 4,5, and 6 indicate that in many cases the reanalysis time is much better than in the monolithic case. It is important to note that the analysis domain used is very relevant to the efficiency of the modular approach: the analysis of a complete program in complex domains such as $Sharing - freeness$ is much more expensive than the reanalysis of a module, while the difference is smaller (although still significant) in the case of Def. This suggests that modular analysis can make it practical to use domains which are precise but rather costly. On the other hand, the results in Table 6 for reanalysing after a more general change using $Sharing - freeness$ are very close to monolithic analysis from scratch, although still below it. That means that even in the presence of the most agressive change in a module, modular analysis is not more time-consuming than analyzing from scratch. Simpler changes provide better results of the modular analysis with respect to the flattened approach, as is shown in Tables 4 and 5 for other kinds of changes.

4   Conclusions

We have presented an empirical study of several proposed models for context-sensitive analysis of modular programs, with the objective of providing experimental evidence on the scalability of these models and, specially, on the impact on performance of the different choices left open in those models.

Our results shed some light on the different choices available. In the case of analyzing a modular program from scratch, the modular analysis approach has been shown, as expected, to be slower than the flattening approach (i.e., having the complete program in memory, and analyzing it as a whole), due to the cost in time of loading and unloading code and related analysis information, and the restriction of not being able to analyze predicates in modules other than the one being processed. However, the modular analysis times from scratch are still reasonable, excluding the case of the $Sharing - freeness$ domain with SP_{all}^+ success policy. In addition, our results also provide evidence that modular analysis does imply a lower maximum memory consumption which in some cases may be of advantage since it may allow analyzing programs of a certain critical size that would not fit in memory using the flattening approach.

Across the domains we can see that in simple domains SP_{all}^+ and a naive bottom up scheduling policy appear to be the best. These strategies appear substantially better for some experiments (in particular, for more general changes) and not much worse than others on most experiments. Another conclusion which can be derived from our experiments is that, as already mentioned, no really significant difference has been observed between the top-down and bottom-up strategies.

We have also considered the case of reanalyzing a previously analyzed program, after making changes to it. This is relevant because it represents the standard situation during program development in which some modules change while others (and the libraries) remain unchanged. While in this phase the analysis results may not be needed in order to obtain highly optimized programs, they are indeed required for other important steps during development, such as static program debugging and validation. In this context our results show that modular analysis, because of its more incremental nature, can offer clear advantages in both time and memory consumption over the monolithic approach.

Acknowledgements

The authors would like to thank María García de la Banda, Kim Marriott, and Peter Stuckey for many interesting discussions on analysis of modular programs. This work was funded in part by the Information Society Technologies programme of the European Commission, Future and Emerging Technologies under projects FP5 IST-2001-38059 *ASAP* and FP6 IST-15905 *MOBIUS*, the Spanish Ministry of Science and Education under project TIC 2002-0055 *CUBICO*, and FEDER infrastructure UNPM03-33-2. M. Hermenegildo is also supported in part by the Prince of Asturias Chair in Information Science and Technology at the University of New Mexico. Part of this work was performed during a research stay of Germán Puebla at Roskilde University supported by a grant from the Secretaría de Estado de Educación y Universidades.

References

1. F. Besson and T. Jensen. Modular class analysis with datalog. In *10th International Symposium on Static Analysis, SAS 2003*, number 2694 in LNCS. Springer, 2003.
2. F. Bueno, D. Cabeza, M. Carro, M. Hermenegildo, P. López-García, and G. Puebla (Eds.). The Ciao System. Reference Manual (v1.10). The ciao system documentation series–TR, School of Computer Science, Technical University of Madrid (UPM), June 2004. System and on-line version of the manual available at http://clip.dia.fi.upm.es/Software/Ciao/.
3. F. Bueno, D. Cabeza, M. Hermenegildo, and G. Puebla. Global Analysis of Standard Prolog Programs. In *European Symposium on Programming*, number 1058 in LNCS, pages 108–124, Sweden, April 1996. Springer-Verlag.
4. F. Bueno, M. García de la Banda, M. Hermenegildo, K. Marriott, G. Puebla, and P. Stuckey. A Model for Inter-module Analysis and Optimizing Compilation. In *Logic-based Program Synthesis and Transformation*, number 2042 in LNCS, pages 86–102. Springer-Verlag, March 2001.

5. D. Cabeza and M. Hermenegildo. A New Module System for Prolog. In *International Conference on Computational Logic, CL2000*, number 1861 in LNAI, pages 131–148. Springer-Verlag, July 2000.

6. P. Cousot and R. Cousot. Modular Static Program Analysis, invited paper. In *Eleventh International Conference on Compiler Construction, CC 2002*, number 2304 in LNCS, pages 159–178. Springer, 2002.

7. M. García de la Banda and M. Hermenegildo. A Practical Approach to the Global Analysis of Constraint Logic Programs. In *1993 International Logic Programming Symposium*, pages 437–455. MIT Press, October 1993.

8. María J. García de la Banda, Bart Demoen, Kim Marriott, and Peter J. Stuckey. To the Gates of HAL: A HAL Tutorial. In *International Symposium on Functional and Logic Programming*, pages 47–66, 2002.

9. Manuel V. Hermenegildo, Germán Puebla, Francisco Bueno, and Pedro López-García. Integrated Program Debugging, Verification, and Optimization Using Abstract Interpretation (and The Ciao System Preprocessor). *Science of Computer Programming*, 58(1–2):115–140, October 2005.

10. K. Muthukumar and M. Hermenegildo. Combined Determination of Sharing and Freeness of Program Variables Through Abstract Interpretation. In *1991 International Conference on Logic Programming*, pages 49–63. MIT Press, June 1991.

11. Nicholas Nethercote. The Analysis System of HAL. Master's thesis, Monash University, 2002.

12. G. Puebla, F. Bueno, and M. Hermenegildo. An Assertion Language for Constraint Logic Programs. In P. Deransart, M. Hermenegildo, and J. Maluszynski, editors, *Analysis and Visualization Tools for Constraint Programming*, number 1870 in LNCS, pages 23–61. Springer-Verlag, September 2000.

13. G. Puebla, J. Correas, M. Hermenegildo, F. Bueno, M. García de la Banda, K. Marriott, and P. J. Stuckey. A Generic Framework for Context-Sensitive Analysis of Modular Programs. In M. Bruynooghe and K. Lau, editors, *Program Development in Computational Logic, A Decade of Research Advances in Logic-Based Program Development*, number 3049 in LNCS, pages 234–261. Springer-Verlag, Heidelberg, Germany, August 2004.

14. G. Puebla and M. Hermenegildo. Some Issues in Analysis and Specialization of Modular Ciao-Prolog Programs. In *Special Issue on Optimization and Implementation of Declarative Programming Languages*, volume 30 of *Electronic Notes in Theoretical Computer Science*. Elsevier - North Holland, March 2000.

Author Index

Lecture Notes in Computer Science

For information about Vols. 1–3789

please contact your bookseller or Springer

Vol. 3836: J.-M. Pierson (Ed.), Data Management in Grids. X, 143 pages. 2006.

Vol. 3835: G. Sutcliffe, A. Voronkov (Eds.), Logic for Programming, Artificial Intelligence, and Reasoning. XIV, 744 pages. 2005. (Sublibrary LNAI).

Vol. 3834: D.G. Feitelson, E. Frachtenberg, L. Rudolph, U. Schwiegelshohn (Eds.), Job Scheduling Strategies for Parallel Processing. VIII, 283 pages. 2005.

Vol. 3833: K.-J. Li, C. Vangenot (Eds.), Web and Wireless Geographical Information Systems. XI, 309 pages. 2005.

Vol. 3832: D. Zhang, A.K. Jain (Eds.), Advances in Biometrics. XX, 796 pages. 2005.

Vol. 3831: J. Wiedermann, G. Tel, J. Pokorný, M. Bieliková, J. Štuller (Eds.), SOFSEM 2006: Theory and Practice of Computer Science. XV, 576 pages. 2006.

Vol. 3829: P. Pettersson, W. Yi (Eds.), Formal Modeling and Analysis of Timed Systems. IX, 305 pages. 2005.

Vol. 3828: X. Deng, Y. Ye (Eds.), Internet and Network Economics. XVII, 1106 pages. 2005.

Vol. 3827: X. Deng, D.-Z. Du (Eds.), Algorithms and Computation. XX, 1190 pages. 2005.

Vol. 3826: B. Benatallah, F. Casati, P. Traverso (Eds.), Service-Oriented Computing - ICSOC 2005. XVIII, 597 pages. 2005.

Vol. 3824: L.T. Yang, M. Amamiya, Z. Liu, M. Guo, F.J. Rammig (Eds.), Embedded and Ubiquitous Computing – EUC 2005. XXIII, 1204 pages. 2005.

Vol. 3823: T. Enokido, L. Yan, B. Xiao, D. Kim, Y. Dai, L.T. Yang (Eds.), Embedded and Ubiquitous Computing – EUC 2005 Workshops. XXXII, 1317 pages. 2005.

Vol. 3822: D. Feng, D. Lin, M. Yung (Eds.), Information Security and Cryptology. XII, 420 pages. 2005.

Vol. 3821: R. Ramanujam, S. Sen (Eds.), FSTTCS 2005: Foundations of Software Technology and Theoretical Computer Science. XIV, 566 pages. 2005.

Vol. 3820: L.T. Yang, X.-s. Zhou, W. Zhao, Z. Wu, Y. Zhu, M. Lin (Eds.), Embedded Software and Systems. XXVIII, 779 pages. 2005.

Vol. 3819: P. Van Hentenryck (Ed.), Practical Aspects of Declarative Languages. X, 231 pages. 2005.

Vol. 3818: S. Grumbach, L. Sui, V. Vianu (Eds.), Advances in Computer Science – ASIAN 2005. XIII, 294 pages. 2005.

Vol. 3817: M. Faundez-Zanuy, L. Janer, A. Esposito, A. Satue-Villar, J. Roure, V. Espinosa-Duro (Eds.), Nonlinear Analyses and Algorithms for Speech Processing. XII, 380 pages. 2006. (Sublibrary LNAI).

Vol. 3816: G. Chakraborty (Ed.), Distributed Computing and Internet Technology. XXI, 606 pages. 2005.

Vol. 3815: E.A. Fox, E.J. Neuhold, P. Premsmit, V. Wuwongse (Eds.), Digital Libraries: Implementing Strategies and Sharing Experiences. XVII, 529 pages. 2005.

Vol. 3814: M. Maybury, O. Stock, W. Wahlster (Eds.), Intelligent Technologies for Interactive Entertainment. XV, 342 pages. 2005. (Sublibrary LNAI).

Vol. 3813: R. Molva, G. Tsudik, D. Westhoff (Eds.), Security and Privacy in Ad-hoc and Sensor Networks. VIII, 219 pages. 2005.

Vol. 3812: C. Bussler, A. Haller (Eds.), Business Process Management Workshops. XIII, 520 pages. 2006.

Vol. 3811: C. Bussler, M.-C. Shan (Eds.), Technologies for E-Services. VIII, 127 pages. 2006.

Vol. 3810: Y.G. Desmedt, H. Wang, Y. Mu, Y. Li (Eds.), Cryptology and Network Security. XI, 349 pages. 2005.

Vol. 3809: S. Zhang, R. Jarvis (Eds.), AI 2005: Advances in Artificial Intelligence. XXVII, 1344 pages. 2005. (Sublibrary LNAI).

Vol. 3808: C. Bento, A. Cardoso, G. Dias (Eds.), Progress in Artificial Intelligence. XVIII, 704 pages. 2005. (Sublibrary LNAI).

Vol. 3807: M. Dean, Y. Guo, W. Jun, R. Kaschek, S. Krishnaswamy, Z. Pan, Q.Z. Sheng (Eds.), Web Information Systems Engineering – WISE 2005 Workshops. XV, 275 pages. 2005.

Vol. 3806: A.H. H. Ngu, M. Kitsuregawa, E.J. Neuhold, J.-Y. Chung, Q.Z. Sheng (Eds.), Web Information Systems Engineering – WISE 2005. XXI, 771 pages. 2005.

Vol. 3805: G. Subsol (Ed.), Virtual Storytelling. XII, 289 pages. 2005.

Vol. 3804: G. Bebis, R. Boyle, D. Koracin, B. Parvin (Eds.), Advances in Visual Computing. XX, 755 pages. 2005.

Vol. 3803: S. Jajodia, C. Mazumdar (Eds.), Information Systems Security. XI, 342 pages. 2005.

Vol. 3802: Y. Hao, J. Liu, Y.-P. Wang, Y.-m. Cheung, H. Yin, L. Jiao, J. Ma, Y.-C. Jiao (Eds.), Computational Intelligence and Security, Part II. XLII, 1166 pages. 2005. (Sublibrary LNAI).

Vol. 3801: Y. Hao, J. Liu, Y.-P. Wang, Y.-m. Cheung, H. Yin, L. Jiao, J. Ma, Y.-C. Jiao (Eds.), Computational Intelligence and Security, Part I. XLI, 1122 pages. 2005. (Sublibrary LNAI).

Vol. 3799: M. A. Rodríguez, I.F. Cruz, S. Levashkin, M.J. Egenhofer (Eds.), GeoSpatial Semantics. X, 259 pages. 2005.

Vol. 3798: A. Dearle, S. Eisenbach (Eds.), Component Deployment. X, 197 pages. 2005.

Vol. 3797: S. Maitra, C. E. V. Madhavan, R. Venkatesan (Eds.), Progress in Cryptology - INDOCRYPT 2005. XIV, 417 pages. 2005.

Vol. 3796: N.P. Smart (Ed.), Cryptography and Coding. XI, 461 pages. 2005.

Vol. 3795: H. Zhuge, G.C. Fox (Eds.), Grid and Cooperative Computing - GCC 2005. XXI, 1203 pages. 2005.

Vol. 3794: X. Jia, J. Wu, Y. He (Eds.), Mobile Ad-hoc and Sensor Networks. XX, 1136 pages. 2005.

Vol. 3793: T. Conte, N. Navarro, W.-m.W. Hwu, M. Valero, T. Ungerer (Eds.), High Performance Embedded Architectures and Compilers. XIII, 317 pages. 2005.

Vol. 3792: I. Richardson, P. Abrahamsson, R. Messnarz (Eds.), Software Process Improvement. VIII, 215 pages. 2005.

Vol. 3791: A. Adi, S. Stoutenburg, S. Tabet (Eds.), Rules and Rule Markup Languages for the Semantic Web. X, 225 pages. 2005.

Vol. 3790: G. Alonso (Ed.), Middleware 2005. XIII, 443 pages. 2005.